MEDIEVAL FRENCH LITERATURE

Medieval French Literature

BY

JESSIE CROSLAND
Author of 'The Old French Epic'

GREENWOOD PRESS, PUBLISHERS
WESTPORT, CONNECTICUT

Library of Congress Cataloging in Publication Data

Crosland, Jessie Raven.
  Medieval French literature.

    Reprint of the 1956 ed. published by Blackwell, Ox-
ford.
    Includes index.
    1. French literature--To 1500--History and criticism.
I. Title.
PQ156.C7 1976   840'.9'02   76-17313
ISBN 0-8371-8971-3

Originally published in 1956 by Basil Blackwell, Oxford

Reprinted with the permission of Basil Blackwell Publisher

Reprinted in 1976 by Greenwood Press,
a division of Williamhouse-Regency Inc.

Library of Congress Catalog Card Number 76-17313

ISBN 0-8371-8971-3

Printed in the United States of America

FOREWORD

In any account of Medieval French literature it is inevitable that attention should be mainly directed to the works produced during the second half of the twelfth and the first half of the thirteenth centuries—a period marked by an outburst of literary activity in France which had its repercussions over almost the whole of Europe. In the course of these hundred or so years many works of real literary value made their appearance, and the language in which they were clothed was a fit medium for their contents. But although the output in the vulgar tongue before this period of flowering was relatively small, yet the seeds were there and it would be impossible to consider this remarkable *floraison* without reference to what preceded it. There was, in fact, much promise of what was to come —indeed, there are many signs that a considerable work of preparation had been going on of which but a scanty record has survived. This I have tried to indicate in the introductory chapter. Later my chief aim has been to emphasize certain outstanding features which emerge from a careful study of the more important texts and trace their development during the period mentioned. In types already existing, such as the drama or the animal fables, I have tried to indicate the specifically medieval stamp which was affixed to already existing themes. Origins, always so elusive, whether epic or lyric in character, have been less studied than development, especially where this synchronizes with the fast-moving social changes of an unsettled age. The disorders of the twelfth century which affected England and much of France so profoundly under the Angevin kings cannot be too much stressed, whether in considering the gloomy character of the Anglo-Norman religious poetry, or the romantic nature of what clearly constituted a kind of escape literature produced in the artificial atmosphere of the courts.

Many omissions will doubtless be noted in the following pages as mainly representative works and authors have been chosen for somewhat detailed study. The most notable omission, however, springs from a different cause. The three main epic cycles have deliberately been left aside as so many reliable works on this subject are easily available. It seemed of greater importance to show the subsequent development of this outstanding genre when the heroic

v

ideal was extended to a different stratum of society. Another un-
avoidable feature of the present work is a certain amount of overlapping—fact and fiction rub shoulders together in the chronicles
and histories; story-telling invades every form of literature—even
that of a serious, didactic nature, so that the types are very difficult
to treat apart.

Other technical difficulties are bound to arise when dealing with
a period in which the language is not yet completely fixed, and
especially when dialectal forms differ as widely as they do between
the language employed in England (even by writers of French
birth) and that spoken in the *Ile de France*. The question as to the
translation of extracts is also a difficult one. These have been mainly
left in the original as the book is intended primarily for those who
have some knowledge of Old French. A few obscure expressions
have, however, been supplied with an English equivalent. The
number of line is not invariably given where the passage occurs in
a short text or when the quotation is taken from a not very well
authenticated or hitherto unpublished text. Some inconsistencies in
such technical matters are almost impossible to avoid in a work of
this kind. There would have been many more had it not been for
the invaluable assistance of Miss Moore (the Librarian of Westfield
College) in reading the proofs and compiling the Index. I owe
grateful thanks, too, to Miss Dickinson (Reader in French at Westfield College) who read many of the chapters in manuscript, and
acknowledgements to Dr. Robson of Oxford who made some
suggestions in the early stages which caused a salutary reconstruction
of certain sections of the work. The subject is such a vast one that
the selective method is imposed from the outset unless a mere
catalogue of texts is envisaged. I would like to think that, besides
being a guide to students of this fascinating period, some suggestions
may have been thrown out which may lead more advanced students
to further investigations. Most of the texts are now available in
trustworthy editions and the possibilities for comparative studies
and works of synthesis are greater than ever before.

JESSIE CROSLAND

ABBREVIATIONS

Anc. poètes. Anciens poètes de la France publiés sous la direction de M. F. Guessard. Paris 1858–70.

Ausg. u. Abh. Ausgaben und Abhandlungen aus dem Gebiet der romanischen Philologie. Herausg. E. Stengel. 1881ff.

Bibl. Norm. Bibliotheca Normannica. Herausg. von H. Suchier. Halle 1879ff.

CFMA. Les Classiques français du moyen âge, publiés sous la direction de Mario Roques. 1910ff.

Cl. de l'Hist. de France. Classiques de l'Histoire de France au moyen âge, publ. sous la direction de Louis Halphen. Paris 1923 etc.

Paul Meyer, Recueil. Recueil d'anciens textes bas-latins, provencaux et français. 2 vols. Paris 1874, 1877.

Rom. des XII Pairs. Romans des douze pairs de France. Paris 1833–1843.

SATF. Société des anciens textes français. Paris, Firmin-Didot, 1875ff.

CONTENTS

MEDIEVAL FRENCH LITERATURE

CHAPTER I

INTRODUCTORY. LITERATURE BEFORE 1100

ALTHOUGH the period covered by these *Studies* will be mainly the second half of the twelfth and the first half of the thirteenth centuries—that period of splendour during which the French way of thinking and of giving expression to its thoughts was paramount in Europe—yet it would be impossible to assess the value of much of the literature of that period without going back for a century or so to see what lay behind it. The seeds of that great 'éclosion littéraire' which reached its height during the period roughly from 1150 to 1250 must obviously have been in the soil for a considerable time before even the earliest shoots began to appear. And herein lies that mysterious nature of medieval French literature which has baffled the most penetrating scholars for many decades and caused so many theories to be put forward that they have almost buried the texts themselves. For the fact is French literature seems to spring into being as it were ready-made, like Minerva fully armed from the head of Zeus. The first epic poem known to us in the vulgar tongue, the first drama that has come down to us, the first lyric poem that greets us from the soil of France—each of these first-fruits of French literature, if not the best of its kind, shows signs of either a creative skill or a technique which would indicate some previous attempts in its own kind. But, though the origins of any particular form of literature may be buried in obscurity, we must at least cast a glimpse at what preceded the outburst and see if it throws any light on later developments. The earliest document that comes to the mind in this respect is that of the well-known *Serments de Strasbourg*, drawn up in 842 between two of the sons of Charlemagne. But these need not detain us here as, in spite of their linguistic and historical value, they cannot be included under the head of literature either as regards form or contents.

The first actual composition in Old French that has come down to us is a short poem contained in a manuscript from the extreme north-east of France and dating from about the year 900—a time when the descendants of Charlemagne were still quarrelling over their adjacent territories and, to add to the confusion, the Normans were already spreading themselves over Gaul. It is of interest to note that in the same manuscript which contains the *Cantilène de Ste. Eulalie*—the poem of which we are speaking—is to be found a German poem (known as the *Ludwigslied*) written to commemorate the victory of the 'Francs' under Louis III in 882, over those very Northmen (those 'heidinc man' whom God had sent from overseas to punish them for their ungodly ways) who later played such a part in laying the foundations of serious French literature. But the rapid conversion of the Northmen to Christianity was remarkable. Guillaume de Poitiers tells us in his history of William the Conqueror that by the first half of the eleventh century Normandy rivalled Egypt in its number of monastic communities.[1] The 'Franki' in the 'rythmus teutonicus' are portrayed as singing their warlike songs as they fought—whilst on another page of the same manuscript the saintly Eulalie is engaged in resisting the world (*argent et paramenz*), the flesh (the loss of her virginity), and the devil (*diaule servir*). Eulalie desired nothing but a martyr's death: 'Volt lo seule (= siècle) lazsier, si ruouet Krist' (*sic rogat Christum*). Fire would not touch her, but her head was severed by a sword whereupon her soul flew to heaven in the form of a dove. In this same fruitful manuscript is a short Latin poem of a lyrical character in honour of the same saint. The Latin poem is an example of a branch of activity in the monasteries which originated in the ninth century. It consisted in fitting words to music and forming a tail-piece or 'sequentia' to certain portions of the liturgy. The importance of this development will be studied in another chapter. The French poem is not a translation, or even an adaptation of the Latin one. It is lyrico-epic in character and not unskilful in form. The language is primitive and interspersed with Latin words:

> Buona pulcella fuit Eulalia,
> Bel auret corps, bellezour (= encore plus belle) l'anima (ll. 1-2).

but the antitheses and short, clipped sentences have a certain charm:

> Enz enl fou la getterent cum arde tost,
> Elle colpes non auret, poro nos coist (ll. 10-11).

Quite a lot of narrative is contained in the twenty-nine lines which conclude with a short prayer just as does the *Ludwigslied* on another page.

---

[1] 'Aemulabatur ejus tempore beatam Aegyptum regularium coenobiorum collegiis.' See *Hist. de Guill. le C.* CL. DE L'HISTOIRE DE FRANCE AU M.A. 1952. Para. 51, p. 124.

Fortunately *Sainte Eulalie* is not quite the only example we have of attempts to instruct the ignorant. Not far removed in date or place of origin from the *Sainte Eulalie* is a valuable example of that other form of popular instruction—the sermon. The *Jonas-fragment*, as it is generally called, has come down to us in a manuscript from Valenciennes. The parchment on which it was written was used as binding to another tenth-century manuscript. The mutilated state in which the manuscript now exists can be seen from any facsimile, but the difficulty of deciphering does not end there. It is partly in Latin, partly in French, and partly in a kind of shorthand ('notes tyrrhoniennes', which seem to have gone out of fashion in France shortly after this time)[1]—each obviously the work of a hasty writer jotting down notes of a Latin sermon. The passages translated into the vulgar tongue are introduced by 'dunc co dixit' or 'dunc co dicit'—which we may take roughly to mean 'now this is what he says', or more concisely 'now that is to say...' The language is unformed and the vocabulary limited, and it was obviously easier for the writer to make his notes in Latin than in French. It cannot be said to have any literary value, but a sentence such as 'si (rogat) deus ad un verme que percussist cel edre sost que cil (sedebat)' is rather a gift for the student of language. The real importance of the fragment is that, like the *Vie de Sainte Eulalie*, it is the forerunner of a long line of literature, first in Latin, then in the vulgar tongue. The preacher has based his sermon on the Vulgate story of Jonas and on the commentary of St. Jerome on this subject. We can detect in this French fragment the tripartite form which became almost obligatory for later sermons. First, there is the 'literal', i.e. the historical narrative based on the text; then the 'allegorical', giving the interpretation ('postea per mersionem Jone profete si debetis intelligere', or 'si debetis intelligere per Judaeos...'), and finally the 'moral' or practical application: 'aiet cherté (= charité) inter vos'; 'seiez unanimes...'; 'faites vos almones' and suchlike admonitions. Here we have already in crude form the style of homily brought to perfection some two centuries later. The Jonas homily cannot have been the first of its kind for it was ordained at the Council of Tours in 812 that the sermons should be preached 'in lingua romanica' for the benefit of the unlearned. So that from that date we may begin to speak of French prose, however crude and

---

[1] See Koschwitz: *Commentar zu den ältesten französischen Sprachdenkmälern*, p. 121.

uncouth it may have been and however unreadily it came to the lips or pen of those trained in ecclesiastical circles where Latin was both spoken and written.

Straightforward translation of the Bible (except of the *Psalter*) was not encouraged in the tenth century, but no exception could be taken to a poem narrating some of the episodes of Christ's condemnation and death. To make these known to the uninstructed must have been the object of the composer of *La Passion du Christ* which is contained in a tenth-century manuscript at Clermont— entered into the empty spaces between the words of a Latin glossary. Both the *Passion* and another poem in the same manuscript on the life of St. Leodogarius (*La Vie de Saint Léger*) are composed in a curious mixed language, containing characteristics of both the north (east) and the south of France. Undoubtedly many of the inconsistencies in the language are due to scribal lack of reverence for the original or to an endeavour to be intelligible to a local audience. Both poems are composed in the octosyllabic metre which later became so popular for narrative poems in France. The *Passion* consists of 560 lines grouped in quatrains of couplets joined by rhyme or assonance. It is based on the gospel story with some additions from the apocryphal gospel of Nicodemus. The author occasionally throws in a remark of his own or interpolates a little prayer. A few words spoken by the Virgin at the foot of the cross seem like a hint at the prophetic role she will play one day. Although she sees her son dying on the cross 'el resurdra cho sab per uer' (l. 336). Her virginity was exemplified by the purity of the new grave, and Christ's undivided garment signifies the unity of Christians in love ('*zo fu granz signa tot per uer*', l. 272). The author closes with an admonition to his hearers to stand fast. After enumerating the tortures to which martyrs for the faith had formerly been subjected, he adds that *our* fight is not against these dangers but against ourselves and our own will, especially in view of the end of the world which is approaching: 'Quar finimenz non es mult lon . . .' (l. 501 ff.). Was he thinking of the dreaded year 1,000?

There was clearly something of the sermon about the *Passion* with its emphasis on *one* faith and *one* truth (l. 273) and its exhortation to 'faire le bien' and leave the world. In *La Vie de Saint Léger* there is less of admonition and more of the miraculous, as we should expect from that cult of the saints which had by now spread to the West and added many new local saints to those already venerated in the East. The French poem is a translation of the Latin 'Life' of Ursinus, whose *Vita Scti. Leodogarii* goes back to the ninth century and tells of the saint's persecution and martyrdom. It is a considerably abbreviated version of the Latin prose work and the sequence of events is not always very clear. The southern overlay of language is slightly more pronounced than in the *Passion*, but it is in the same octosyllabic metre which always seems to give a certain lightness to a poem. It is in three sections, each of which was destined to be recited or read aloud to an audience—(1) 'Primos didrai vos dels honors'; (2) 'Quandius visquet ciel reis lothiers/bien honorez fud sancz lethgiers . . . ' (3) 'Or en aurez las poenas granz que cil en fisdra li tiranz . . .,' and it ends with a prayer to the saint to help us. In spite of the rather lyrical form of the strophes, each consisting of six assonancing lines, we can almost feel the effort that was required to substitute French forms for the Latin original:

> Rex chielperings il se fud mors,
> por lo regnet lo sourent toit.
> vindrent parent e lor amic
> li sanct .l. li evruin.
> cio confortent ad ambes duos
> que s'ent ralgent in lor honors. (ll. 115–20).

At any rate the scribe was conscious of an effort if we may judge by the 'cri de joie' he appends to the poem—'Finit, finit, ludendo dicit'. But, in spite of the difficulty of writing in a language which had as yet barely evolved as a vehicle of thought, we have by the end of the tenth century two examples of saints' lives in metrical form, one fragment of a prose sermon, and a narrative poem with definite dramatic possibilities. We can already foresee great developments.

After a gap of about half a century the first work of real literary value comes into view. *La Vie de Saint Alexis*, which can be roughly dated as about 1050, shows what a remarkable development had taken place as regards language and emotional content. We cannot go into the early biography of Saint Alexis which has been excellently done by Gaston Paris and Canon J. M.-Meunier in their respective editions of the French poem.[1] Suffice it to say that the version of his life that we find in the Old French poem and its Latin original, with its duplicated period of seventeen years and the twice

---

[1] See Bibliography.

repeated miraculous voice, is really based on two separate legends fused into one. The original Syriac story goes back to the fifth century—in this the saint is not named but is always spoken of as 'the man of God', and he ended his life in poverty at Edessa. He was buried in a pauper's grave, but when his identity was discovered and a search was made for his body, it had disappeared. The second half of the Alexis story really concerns another young saint, Jean le Calybite, who also left his home to embrace a life of poverty. Warned, however, by a miraculous voice to return to his place of birth, he actually asked for shelter in his father's house and was granted a tiny hut (καλύβη) close by in which he lived and died. These two lives, telescoped into one, are the origin of the 'Life' as we know it in both Latin and French. The gradual development of this legend from the first crude, unadorned tale to the tendentious, romantic account which we find in the later French versions, is one of the most interesting examples we have of the change in taste which can be exemplified in successive forms of a work of art.

The popularity of the legend of Saint Alexis was great through all its different stages. And yet there is little action; there are no heathen tyrants, no malignant devils, no tortures or miraculous deliverances—it is the simple story of the almost superhuman self-immolation and fanaticism of a young man who renounced all human affections, all worldly ambitions, wealth, military glory and power for his one fixed object—to be a servant of God—a 'Dieu serf' as the French version puts it. His parents, though themselves Christians; his betrothed, though herself devout, reproached him bitterly after his death for his unpitying inflexibility; but the common people (*la menue gent*) knew better. They refused to be deflected by gifts of money from paying tribute to his corpse, and God honoured the saint by a profusion of posthumous miracles. Such is the story told by this first French poem of literary value. Here we have a narrative of epic dimensions, told in a flexible language in almost impeccable decasyllabic metre (each strophe of five lines being bound together by assonance), without rhetorical devices, without pomposity or exaggerated epithets although it is charged with human emotions. The bereaved mother is not like a 'lioness escaped from the net' (as in the Latin *Vita*); she is merely a poor distraught woman (*feme forcenede*); she does not cry: 'Who will give to my eyes a fountain of tears to weep day and night for my grief?'; she merely shows all the usual symptoms of grief and calls on others to weep with her. She speaks pathetically of her son's hardness:

> 'Fils Alexis, molt eüs dur curage,
> cum avilas tut tun gentil linage.
> Set a mei sole vels une feiz parlasse,
> ta lasse mere si la reconfortasses,
> Ki sist dolente, chier fiz, buer i alasses.' (str. xc)

The lament of the 'pucelle que il out espusede' is more lyrical in character:

> 'O bele buce, bel vis, bele faiture,
> Cum est mudede vostre bela figure ...' (xcvii)

a forerunner of many a 'regret funèbre' in poems of a later date, as is also that of the father who feels bitterly the loss of a son who would have attained high honours and carried on the family tradition:

> 'Tei convenist helme e bronie a porter
> espede ceindre cume tui altre per;
> a grant maisnede doüses governer,
> le gunfanun l'emperedur porter
> cum fist tes pedre e li tons parentez.' (str. lxxxiii)

There is a pleasing touch in the fact that the father is not speaking only from his own personal point of view but refers to the mother's grief in a rather moving way:

> 'Filz Alexis, de ta dolente medre.
> tantes dolurs ad pur tei andurede
> ... cist dols l'aurat enquor par acorede.' (str. lxxx)

Further light is thrown on the father's character by the reply of his servant, who, when offered a reward for looking after the pilgrim, replies quite simply: 'pur tue amur an soferai l'ahan' (l. 230): It is no exaggeration to say that each one speaks entirely in character and is portrayed with considerable psychological skill. In the narrative part of the poem, too, there is something simple and direct. We can immediately visualize the two emperors and the pope as they 'sedent es bans e pensif e plurs' and then introduce themselves, much in the same way as the characters do in the primitive drama: 'Ci deuant tei estunt dui pechethur / par la Deu grace vocet amperedur ...', and in the next strophe: 'Cist apostoile deit les anemes baillir / ço est ses mesters dunt il a a servir' (str. lxxiii, lxxiv). The Latin *Vita* describes the same events but in far more pompous style. The devil is described as 'antiquus humani generis inimicus'. Alexis' face after death is 'velut lampadem lucentem vel sicut vultum angeli Dei', and the 'sposa' cries rhetorically: 'Nunc ruptum est speculum meum et periit spes mea'. The French version throughout is less rhetorical but more poetic and better suited to a less learned but none the less appreciative audience.

The *Vie de Saint Alexis* is, strictly speaking, anonymous. Nothing is known of its author either as regards status or place of origin. It has been suggested, and with considerable plausibility, that the author was a canon of Rouen—Tedbalt de Vernon by name. Rouen was a centre of ecclesiastical activity in the middle of the eleventh century. Guillaume de Poitiers in his *Gesta Guillelmi ducis Normannorum et regis Anglorum* tells us of two young men who rivalled Maurilius—Archbishop of Rouen from 1055 to 1067—in their struggle for holiness. Both of them, in the flower of their age, had renounced the vain 'impedimenta' of temporal things, despising the schools of worldly philosophy to which they had been so much addicted, and the sweet beckoning of their native soil. Even the attractions of wealth and noble birth, of attaining positions of the highest honour had not deflected them from embracing the cenobite's life of exile and devoting themselves to whatever this entailed, in order to acquire an eternal and blessed repose.[1] These facts recounted by Guillaume of Poitiers would add some support to the suggestion of Gaston Paris that the author was that Tedbalt de Vernon, Canon of Rouen, who is cited in a monkish record as a translator of 'Lives of Saints' from their *Latinity* into pleasant songs with a 'rythme tintant'.[2] One of these was a 'Life' of St. Wandrille to whose shrine certain health-giving relics were brought in 1053. It is tempting to think that the 'amiable cançun esperitel', as our poem is called in the prologue preceding the text in the best manuscript, was another of these—and not one of the worst by any means. However that may be, the straightforward, simple and yet dramatic story of St. Alexis and his *noces virginales* must have impressed his hearers greatly, for the legend was one of the most popular in France and elsewhere for several centuries. We are fortunate in possessing some later French versions which illustrate certain changes in taste and feeling.

The eleventh-century poem deals with a difficult subject in a purely narrative way without comment from the author. The Latin version reflects only the familiar idea of consecrated virginity.

---

[1] See Guillaume de Poitiers: loc. cit. pp. 134–5.
[2] 'Ad quamdam tinnuli rythmi similitudinem urbanas ex illis cantilenas edidit.' See Preface to Gaston Paris' edition, p. 44.

Alexis departs with a brief farewell to his spouse telling her to keep the ring and the buckle of his sword-belt as long as God permits— 'et Dominus sit inter nos'. It is in the French version that we find those touching laments of the relatives and the insistence on the hardness and unfeelingness of Alexis' behaviour, particularly in the second half of the story when he is in his father's house. In fact we are up against a difficult psychological, even moral, problem. Need Alexis have waited until the actual wedding night to have made up his mind to depart for good and qualify for *parfite amor*? It was as he looked at the bed that he cried out in anguish: 'E Deus (dit il), cum fort pecet m'appresset' (l. 59). It was not spoken of as a sin in the Latin version. Yet the maiden echoes his words:

> Ço dist la spuse: 'Pechiét le m'a tolut;
> e chers amis, si poi uus ai oüt:
> or sui si graime que ne puis estre plus'. (ll. 108 f.)

After seventeen years of exile he still feels that, if his parents recognize him, they will drag him to his ruin (l. 905). It has been suggested[1] that we have here a reflexion of the Cathar doctrine which condemned all intercourse between the sexes and decreed that no salvation was possible without previous renunciation of marriage. But the cruelty to those left behind so suddenly and without warning is obvious, especially if his one fixed idea was to save his own soul. It would look as though at one point he had a tinge of conscience:

> Mais ne purhuec mun pedre me desire,
> si fait ma medre plus q(ue) feme qui vivet
> avoc ma spuse que io lur ai guerpide . . . (ll. 206–9).

and the next line ('or ne lairai nem mete an lur baillie') gives the impression that he risks recognition as a kind of penance. It certainly must have been a test of his resolution when he constantly saw them (during his second period of seventeen years) 'grant duel mener / e de lur oilz si tendrement plurer'—and all for him, not for any other reason. But he has his gaze so fixed on God that he cares not for what he sees (l. 245). If that second period of seventeen years was the greatest test for St. Alexis it was also the cause of the deepest feelings in his relatives. It is not till they learn after his death that he has actually been seventeen years in their own house suffering all sorts of indignities without letting them know of his presence that their really bitter feelings burst forth, and the *dur corage* of Alexis,

[1] See Meunier: *La Vie de Saint Alexis*, p. 24. Note to Strophe xii, l. 59. Cf. also H. Sckommodau: *Zst. für rom. Phil.*, Bd. 70, 1954.

in never speaking a word to his sorrowing mother and leaving his spouse in constant 'hope deferred', produces some of the most heartfelt plaints in French literature. How far was St. Alexis to blame? This was the problem which faced the *remanieurs* of the twelfth and thirteenth centuries when church doctrines and rules of conduct had become more explicit and universal. God might hate a *vieux luxurieux* but lawful marriage was fully sanctioned by the Church (except in the case of priests). It was not a sin—even though, as St. Jerome had said, the married man obviously could not 'pray without ceasing'. Hence the effort to reconcile Alexis' self-immolation with his social duties and consideration of his parents and (above all) his young wife could not be very successful. A version of the story in which the actual lines of the original are preserved, but interspersed (*farcis*) with considerable addition to the text can be dated as belonging to the twelfth century, at a period when much was expected from a lover. The author was in a very real quandary and he makes clumsy efforts to be just to both sides. After the lines of the original in which he recommends the maiden to accept a heavenly spouse ('celui tien a espous' ...), he cuts the wedding ring in halves, telling her to keep her half till his return, and then he launches forth into a warning as to what will happen to the body if the soul is lost. To her very natural question as to when that return will be ('com ert del repairier'?) he answers deceitfully, or at least non-committally:

> Certes, pucele, del terme ne sai nient;
> L'en set quant va, mais l'en ne sait quant vient (ll. 254–5).

leaving her with the strong impression that he is merely going to Jerusalem to pray for both their souls. The author knows well what the public of his day will like. The young spouse is more in evidence than the mother in this version. She gets into touch with the poor pilgrim under the stairs in a way the mother cannot. She washes his garments, receives his confidences and actually comforts him on his death-bed when he fears the devils will snatch away his soul, by telling him she can hear the angelic bells ringing to announce that all is well. Many little dramatic touches are added. When Alexis, on his arrival in Rome, brought back their loss to the parents' memory, the father wrung his hands so vigorously that he dropped his gloves. Alexis stooped and picked them up, remarking to himself: 'Quele amistié entre pere et enfant.' He then prayed to God to pardon him for his *felonie* in causing them such grief, and

resigned himself to another period of penance to atone for this
felonie, for the punishment must balance the wrong, as in the legend
of St. Gregory.[1] The author realizes that the chief *felonie* of which
Alexis was guilty concerned his young wife. Hence, after his death,
when he relaxed his grip on the document he had written and
which the pope had taken from his hand, to the amazement of all,
it flew from the pope's hand into the bosom of the maiden:

> A le pucele s'en ala a la place,
> Ens en son sain en son bliaut de paile'... (ll. 1088–9).

and immediately the author uses this as the text of an admonition
to his hearers on the sanctity of marriage:

> Oies, signour, con grande loiauté
> Tout home doivent a lor moiller porter,
> Car tel monstrance fist le jour Damedés
> Que a sa mere ne vuet la cartre aler
> Ne a son pere qui l'avoit engenré,
> Mais a l'espouse ki bien avoit gardé
> La compaignie de son ami carnel... (ll. 1106–14).

The faithful spouse then brings out the half of the ring which she
had kept faithfully in her bosom and it fits perfectly into the other
half enclosed in St. Alexis' letter. The rest of the poem is practically
in the words of the original except for the addition of two rather
unnecessary lines at the end:

> Or sont en glore sans nule repentance:
> Iluec conversent et si lisent lor salmes.

There is no need to point out the difference in tone between the
eleventh- and twelfth-century poems—the one sincere and deeply
religious in spite of its poetic form, the other didactic and superficial
(in its added parts) and clearly adapted to meet a popular demand.
But it must be remembered that a spirit of revival and asceticism
was abroad in the second half of the eleventh century. We have
already mentioned the two young men at Rouen, and there were
hermits in the forests of Normandy as well as in other parts of
France. There were men like Robert d'Arbrissel and Vital de
Mortain who gave up family and country to adopt a life of
renunciation and who founded abbeys and worked for the reforma-
tion of the Church.[2] The original story of St. Alexis might easily
have been an incentive to go and do likewise, but by the end of the
twelfth century the wave of intense reforming fervour was past.

---

[1] Cf. Ch. II.
[2] See J. Buhot: *L'Abbaye Normande de Savigny*. Le Moyen-Age. 8e. série XLVI, 1936–7.

Of a rhymed thirteenth-century version of the *Vie de Saint Alexis* little need be said as it is based on the interpolated version we have just been examining. Like most poems as they became popular, it was written in rhyme and not in assonance. Further picturesque details were added to the original poem: devils rush about to drag a wicked soul to hell where worms and biting adders await it; the bells of Rome do not ring till after the saint's death in this version, but then they ring *si douchement* that no one had ever heard the like before (ll. 1049–50). St. Alexis is strangely conscious of what he will have to answer for 'au grant juise' in causing such grief to his parents, and the passage on marriage following the flight of the charter into the spouse's breast is amplified in such a way that one trembles for Alexis' soul:

> Chi puet on bien aprendre et escouter
> Ke esposailles sont forment a amer:
> . . . Ke cascuns hon doit sa femme honorer,
> Aussi les dames lor signor bien warder,
> Et ki nel fait tres bien se puet fier
> Dedans infier l'en estovra aler
> Od les diables tot de fi convierser. (str. xciii)

The preservation of the eleventh-century *Vie de Saint Alexis* is probably due to its edifying character which would make it a suitable work to be copied in a monastery. As regards its form—the decasyllabic line, the conventional opening, the vocabulary, the apostrophes and lamentations—it is (except for the five-line strophe) typical of many an epic of later date. The *plaintes* or 'regrets' have often been remarked on. The outward expressions of grief are almost stereotyped. We may compare *Alexis* 'ad ambes mains derompt sa barbe blanche' and *Roland*: 'se barbe blanche comencet a detraire'; or *Alexis*: 'Trait ses chevels et debat sa poitrine' and *Roland*: 'Trait ses crignels pleine ses mains ansdous'; or the apprehensive cry of the emperor at the thought of his nephew's death: 'Ki guierat mes oz a tel poeste?' and the words of Alexis' father: 'O filz cui ierent mes granz hereditez?' There must have existed by the middle of the eleventh century an established poetic form and a stock of epic formulae which make it probable that other poems of a similar character have been lost to us in those seventy years or so which separate the *Alexis* from the *Roland*. They may not have been considered of sufficient moral import to occupy the time and the materials of the inmates of a monastery. And yet how much they can teach us, when we remember the summing up of the contents of the *Roland* in the line: 'Mult ad apris qui bien conuist ahan', or the equally pregnant line in *Raoul de Cambrai*: 'Hom desreez a molt grant peine dure.' Subject-matter was not lacking: feats of battle between the Franks and the Normans (as in the *Ludwigslied* and the later *Gormont et Isembart*); contests between the powerful barons and crusades against the Saracens in Spain; legends of King Borrel and his twelve sons, of Ogier the Dane, of Pippin the Short, of Roland washing the bloodstained fields with water to hide the stains, of the *Pers de Vermandois*, of the enchantress Orable (wife of Thibaut) who later became the faithful spouse of Guillaume d'Orange. Were the records of all these more secular stories lost or did they only exist 'in patriensium memoria' in the words of Hariulf the chronicler when relating briefly the victory of King Louis over King Guaramundus and Esumbardus the traitor? And yet the problem of the young saint was not so different from that of the young warrior. There was surely a streak of egoism and *démesure* in Alexis who sacrificed all his relations and dependents for his own soul's salvation, just as there was in the young Roland who sacrificed his friends and his men for his ideal of personal honour. Each was justified by divine approval in the end—a voice out of heaven testified to Alexis' holiness and angels descended to carry Roland's soul to heaven. But the lives of both saint and warrior exhibited that moral conflict which consists in being torn between two loyalties—a conflict which so often occurs in medieval French literature and which unfortunately degenerated (in the later literature of romance) into the frivolous form of the *question dilemmatique*.

The interval between the composition of the *Vie de Saint Alexis* and the sudden flowering of French literature in the twelfth century may be regretted by the student of the period. Much must have been going on underground, however (and possibly overground, but not destined to survive) which was preparing the way for what was soon to come to fruition. Not only the older epics show signs of earlier growth; the first lyric poems in the vulgar tongue bear signs of a technique and a vocabulary already in existence; the seeds of the drama were clearly ready to put forth shoots and even the rather uncouth bestiaries and chronicles must have had forerunners in the vulgar tongue. As regards the 'Lives' of the saints which became so immensely popular in the following two centuries, no more need be said than to refer to the *Vie de Saint Alexis*.

BIBLIOGRAPHY

Cantilène (Séquence, Prose) de Sainte Eulalie. In all good 'chrestomathies', e.g. Bartsch, Constans, Paul Meyer (*Recueil d'anciens textes*, Pt. II), Koschwitz und Förster (*Altfr. Uebungsbuch*), Studer and Waters (Historical French Reader) etc. See also: Koschwitz: *Commentar zu den ältesten franz. Denkmälern.* 1886.

Le Fragment de Jonas. Koschwitz: Les plus anciens monuments de la langue française, I. Textes diplomatiques, II. Textes critiques, glossaire, etc. 3rd ed. 1913. Koschwitz und Förster, loc. cit.

Das Ludwigslied. Wilhelm Braune: *Altdeutsches Lesebuch*, No. xxxvi.

La Passion du Christ. Koschwitz und Förster: loc. cit.; Koschwitz: loc. cit.

La Vie de Saint Léger. Gaston Paris: Romania, t. I, 1872.

Koschwitz u. Förster: loc. cit.

Koschwitz: loc. cit.

La Vie de Saint Alexis. G. Paris et L. Pannier: *La Vie de Saint Alexis*, poème du XIe siècle et renouvellements des XIIe et XIIIe siècles. Ed. 1903.

G. Paris: *La Vie de Saint Alexis*, texte critique. Paris 1933. (CFMA).

Meunier (Chanoine J.-M.): texte du ms. L. Paris 1933.

C. Storey: *Saint Alexis: étude de la langue du MS.* L. suivié d'une édition critique du texte, etc. Paris 1934.

Articles, emendations, etc., too numerous to quote. For influence of the Cathar heresy, cf. Sckommodau, *Zeitschr. für rom. Phil. Bd.* 70. 1954.

Guillaume de Poitiers: *La Vie de Guillaume le Conquérant*, éditeé et traduite par Raymonde Foreville. Cl. de l'hist de France au m.-â. Paris 1952.

CHAPTER II

DIDACTIC LITERATURE

(a) SERMONS

THE earliest types of literature in the French language, which as we have seen were of a religious nature, did not fail to thrive and produce a growth which continued to flourish all through the twelfth and thirteenth centuries. Much work of preparation may have been going on in the field of epic poetry, or popular song, but, until well after the year 1100, all evidence of this is unfortunately lacking. This may be due to the fact that works composed for recitation, if of a secular nature, were less likely to be committed to writing than those composed with a view to edification. Formal prose sermons in the vulgar tongue do not make their appearance before the middle of the twelfth century, but there is proof in early bestiaries, in translations of the Bible and in other works, that the sermon was not neglected and that biblical teaching was fairly widespread, even though sometimes in a rather legendary form. 'Lives of Saints', too, must have enjoyed a more or less continuous popularity and multiplied, first in Latin then in French, to an extraordinary degree—but this, as we shall see later, may be attributed to various causes.

From whatever sources it may have sprung a good deal of teaching and exhortation in the vulgar tongue must have been available during the twelfth century for the unlearned and the lay-folk in general. Besides partial translations of the Bible (particularly of the *Psalter*) we meet with short poems on moral subjects or sermons in verse—'petits sermons' as the authors sometimes modestly call them. These increase in number, if not always in quality, as we pass from the twelfth to the thirteenth century, by which time the use of allegory had tended to become excessive. The early ones, however, which mostly sprang from territory overrun by Normans (whether in France or England) were of a simple and eminently pious nature. For the Normans, despite their energy in action, seem to have been inclined to gloomy reflections. One or two of special interest will suffice to give some idea of this branch of religious instruction. It is as teaching for the lay population that they must be judged.

15

A short poem in an interesting metre, which the author tells us is meant for the 'simple gent' and not for the *lettrés*, begins with the words '*Grant mal fist Adam*' and is generally known by that name. It was written at the beginning of the twelfth century, probably by a Norman living in England—though at this time it is increasingly difficult to determine who was of English and who of Norman birth. The light and graceful form of the metre rather gives the lie to the somewhat depressing nature of the subject which is a variation on the theme that 'Time like an ever-rolling stream bears all its sons away'. Into a brief survey of the generations from Adam to Christ the author introduces a tirade against pride and envy and all the misery caused by Adam and his apple:

> O deus! quel dolor
> e cum grant tristor
> lor vint a soffrir
> par icele pome
> qui a un sul ome
> vint si a plaisir (str. 9).

He gives a depressing picture of one generation succeeding another, of the futility of trusting in wealth or high birth, for all are descended from Noah, both wise and foolish, rich and poor. How dare the rich man tell him he is not a 'frans huem'? God loves the poor, and the rich man's death-bed repentance has no value in God's sight. Only true repentance with confession can save a soul. A contrasting description of heaven and hell is less realistic and therefore more convincing than most of the stereotyped descriptions in the Middle Ages and the author reverts once more to the theme of the perpetual motion of human existence caused by the regular succession of births and deaths:

> Tot tens vont naissant
> Et tot tens morant,
> Or vait l'en, or vient;
> Cil les fait torner
> Venir et aler
> Qui la röe tient (str. 112).

It is God who controls the wheel in this pious poem, not Fortune— nor does it turn of itself.

Much the same subject is treated in a poem entitled *Les Vers de la Mort* which enjoyed great popularity in the Middle Ages and later —as indeed did the subject of death generally in both the philoso- phical and religious treatises of the period. In Hélinand's poem it is

Death who performs the function of Fortune 'Mort . . . qui ne seras lasse / De muer haute chose en basse'. For death is the great leveller and it is as inevitable as it is inexorable for it is the 'arc qui ne faut'. Most of the poem is a variation on this one theme, though *Richesce* replaces *Mort* in a few of the later stanzas. Hélinand, who also indulges in the same freedom of speech and democratic outlook as his predecessor has a hit at Rome ('li mauz qui tot assomme') as well as at the old pagan philosophy which does not believe in an after-life. He is a genuine poet and we have here a veritable 'Hymne de la Mort' (as Pasquier called it in his *Recherches de la France*), not a mere sermon in rhyme. In many of the strophes—particularly in the one beginning 'Morz, douce as bons, as maus amere', he is in fact a worthy precursor of Ronsard. The skilful form of versification again gives a touch of lightness to a gloomy subject, towards which his attitude throughout reflects the orthodox Church doctrine that the only 'confort' against death and the ensuing judgment is:

> (C'est) le repenter isnelement
> Et purgier soi parfaitement
> De quanque li cuers se remort.

Hélinand himself is known to us from his correspondence. He was a convert to the religious life after a youth spent in frivolity (cf. his *Liber de reparatione lapsi*) and wrote his celebrated poem probably in the last quarter of the twelfth century. The form of the poem which is composed of twelve octosyllabic lines grouped by the rhyme-scheme *aabaab, bbabba* seems to have been his own invention.

Another sermon in verse which can be dated as belonging to the first decade of the thirteenth century is the *Besant Deu* of Guillaume 'uns clers qui fu Normanz'. It is hardly necessary for Guillaume to tell us of his place of origin for his poem, with all its heavy gloom and solemn warnings, betrays him. Not that he had always been such a dismal prophet—he had written 'fablels e contes . . . en fole e en vaine matire' (*Besant* 81–2). But in a solemn moment, in his bed one Saturday evening, he was reflecting on 'cest siecle qui si passa' and realized he had not made use of the talent (*besant*) God had given him. Moreover, he had a wife and children to keep and must earn something 'por ses diz' to keep them. So he set to work. The *Besant Deu* is not a very inspiring poem. The author gives vent to the usual laments for what Adam did 'por une pome'. He gloats over the repulsive details of old age, death and decay, the process of digestion, the depressing aspect of childbirth and the pain it entails and all for no good in most cases. He fulminates in the familiar style against rich prelates, grasping 'clercs', tyrannous kings and courts, and it is all very depressing:

> Allas, allas! as fiz Evain!
> Allas au monde, qui ui est
> A tute vilainie prest!
> Allas as membres e au chief!
> Allas, tant es la dolor grief
> Quant l'enemi del chief descent
> Qui par tuz les membres s'estent (ll. 2192–8).

In England, in France, in Ireland and Germany, wherever the pope sends his cardinals, his legates and his priests, it is just the same—they only serve for reward (*por loier*) and to obtain bishoprics 'a lor nevoz, a lor parenz', and to amass wealth. Guillaume prays earnestly, however, for the safety of the Church—'la nef saint Pere'—that it may not make shipwreck in the tumultuous seas, which it is in danger of doing when Christians fight amongst themselves. What will our Lord say to the great nobles who have taken the cross (*croizer se font*) against the Albigeois? They are just as much to blame as those they are trying to crush. Far better would it be if they turned their arms against the heathen to avenge the Holy Sepulchre:

> Crestiens qui entre els font guerre
> E ont laissié la sainte terre
> Si longement desconfortee
> Ont bien lor proesce avortee (ll. 2835–39).

This was what put the Church in danger:

> E por ceo semble que la nef
> N'a mie biau tens ne suef (ll. 2425–26).

These were brave words and atone somewhat for the dreary allegorical passages about the 'chastel as puceles' and its inhabitants, or the sower of the seed and his soil. 'Guillaume le clerc' was well acquainted with the religious instruction of his time. He makes full use of the *De miseria humanae conditionis* of Pope Innocent. He knows the Bible well and quotes Maurice de Sully ('li bons evesques de Paris') under whose influence, perhaps, he falls into the regular sermon-style towards the end of his poem when expounding the parable of the vineyard in the orthodox manner: 'Li prosdom ... Segnifie le rei de gloire ...' and ending with a personal exhortation to his hearers: 'Bone gent, ausi deus m'aït', etc.

A work on an altogether larger scale—for it consists of 4,000 lines, although the author designates it as 'nostre petit sermon', is the treatise known as *Poème moral*. There is a great deal that is of interest in this poem of the early thirteenth century for, besides the warnings against the dangers of worldliness and riches and avarice, for which the author blames the evil time in which he lives, we have very valuable *tableaux de moeurs* of the period. We learn, for instance, something about feminine make-up in those days—how the ladies pluck their eyebrows (*le sobrecil plomeir*, l. 512), how they tight-lace and bind themselves so much (*si forment lace et loie*, l. 515) that they can hardly bend; we learn how the pilgrims, when they returned from a pilgrimage, often behaved much worse than they had done before they went, and how people would hurry out of church to hear a 'jongleur' recite a favourite story. The 'jongleur' (*li jugleires*) with his antics and his stories excites the special wrath of our moralist, but he is severe on other vanities also, for he condemns dancing, and even the games of chess and *tric-trac* wherewith folk while away the dreary winter evenings. The author is well-read in the moral literature in vogue at the time. He is penetrated by the writings of St. Gregory, particularly the *Moralia in Job*—the Bible, the Fathers, the *Vies des Pères* are largely drawn upon and he obviously knows the current literature of his day. The only classical author who, though not named, has contributed something to his sermon is Horace, who has, however, had no influence in matters of morality. A good part of his poem is devoted to the conversion of Ste. Thaïs by the monk Paphnutius, who entered the apartment of this beautiful Egyptian courtesan disguised as a gallant. Thaïs underwent a sudden conversion, burned all her possessions and submitted to being shut up in a little cell as a penance for her former life. Even then she fears to die 'desconfesseiz' but St. Paphnutius reassures her 'merci avras, ce cui'. It was for another hermit in the same poem to learn the salutary lesson that there are other modes of life just as pure as his own—even that of a *jongleur* or a rich merchant; that one may get to heaven 'sor son cheval' just as well as on foot and that 'Nul ne cognoist les homes, se Deus non'. Some of this he may have found in his Latin original, but his reflections are a good index to the mind of our author who is an earnest preacher burning to save souls, of a severe but not a bitter spirit.

The mention of Maurice de Sully takes us back to the more exclusively biblical teaching of the twelfth century—an important matter, for French prose begins with translations from the Bible.

Orthodox religious instruction in the vulgar tongue was not abundant as prose sermons were mostly in Latin. There were inter-linear translations of the *Psalter*—the two earliest of which (the Oxford and Cambridge) were executed in England in the first half of the century. Translations of the Bible were not encouraged by the Church and the translators had to proceed with great caution. The author of the Metz psalter version in the fourteenth century insists on the 'peril de translateir la saincte escripture en romans', but he insists on the profit 'pour les gens laye'. To avoid the danger of mistranslation he makes great use of synonyms . . . e.g., 'en prise et en caption', 'delivree et garantie', 'uns passerez ou uns moixons'— and we have that irritating habit of *dédoublement* which reached its height in the sixteenth century. Prose was the normal form for translations from the Bible, though the author of the most con-siderable Bible-translation of the twelfth century often lapses into a kind of rhythm in rhyme-pairs into which perhaps he fell im-perceptibly. The *Quatre Livres des Reis* is of either Norman or English origin. It is not a slavish translation, either as regards the text or the numerous glosses added by the author. The earlier part is more inclined to be decorative and rhetorical than the latter. Anna's prayer (I. Sam. 1.) falls almost entirely into verse and is followed by an appeal to the hearers in best sermon style: 'Fedeil Deu, entend l'estoire—l'estoire est paille, le sen est grains, le sen est fruit, l'estoire vains. . . .' Obviously he has the regulation interpreta-tion of scripture in mind which was the vogue when sermons conformed to St. Gregory's tripartite treatment of biblical subjects, viz. (1) the literal or historical, (2) the theoretical and (3) the moral— a method which finds its way into the bestiaries and such-like sym-bolical works in which everything has a 'significance'. It was about the year 1170, when there was so much literary activity in France that the earliest collection of sermons in French prose took form. These were the homilies of the above-mentioned Maurice de Sully, in the time of Louis VII and Philip Augustus. Little is known of Maurice's youth. He first became archdeacon of Paris and even-tually archbishop in 1160. He must surely have come under the influence of Abelard in his early days and his sermons conform strictly to the type above-mentioned. The homilies, not all of which are translations from Latin, are in the literary language as it was then evolving in central France. They are impeccable in form, impersonal in treatment and sound in application. The audience might be pardoned if a slight sigh of relief escaped them when the

'segnor orez que ces coses signifient' (Part II) fell upon their ears,
and the relief perhaps became a little more audible when it was
followed by 'Segnor, esgardez vers vos-meismes' (Part III). One
wishes there were more 'exempla' of the type of the story of the
monk who was visited by an angel 'en semblance d'oisel' and
'oblia totes les coses terriennes' for 300 years whilst he listened
enchanted by the bird's sweet song. When, like the Seven Sleepers
of Ephesus, he returned whence he had come, to his amazement he
recognized no old friends and was recognized by none. How great
must be the beauty and sweetness of heaven if 300 years pass like
an afternoon, remarks the preacher. The homilies were based on
traditional Church teaching, but Maurice's disciplined oratory and
lucid prose left their mark on both the religious literature and the
prose of succeeding years.

(b) HAGIOGRAPHY

St. Augustine in the *City of God* tells us that it would be the work
of volumes to relate all the miracles of St. Stephen, for within two
years seventy accounts had been written at the shrine of Hippo
alone. His only regret is that saints' 'Lives' were not more widely
known so as to benefit a larger proportion of mankind. Two
centuries later, Gregory of Tours, when hesitating about undertaking his *Vita Scti. Martini* on account of his lack of literary skill,
was told by his mother in a dream that it would be wicked ('crimen
tibi erit') to desist on that account. And so he persisted, though
conscious of being 'stultus et idiota', and thus gave us a work
valuable as an example both of the language and literary taste of
his time. After the recognition of Christianity martyrs for the Faith
were naturally less numerous, but there were still holy men (especially in the East) and the finding of the true cross by Helena, mother
of the Emperor Constantine, caused an increase in the number of
pilgrims to the holy places and a trade in relics. Iron filings from
the nails and splinters of wood were spread over many lands.
During the eighth and ninth centuries this trade flourished and
became very lucrative. It also brought about a certain competition
for the possession of the bodies and relics of departed saints who
might add lustre to a religious foundation situated in a remote spot.
From the tenth century date many of the Latin 'Saints' Lives' which
were disseminated in the West and which rapidly achieved great
popularity: 'une activité hagiographique plus zelée que vraiment

louable' as Gaston Paris has called it. It must not be assumed, however, that the reason for writing these legends was exclusively mercantile. Since the time of Gregory's vision it was an established principle that to know a good thing and to keep it to oneself was a crime and most displeasing to God.

Some two hundred 'Vies de Saints et de Saintes' in the French tongue are known to us which have come down from the Middle Ages. They gradually lost something of the simplicity and dignity of former days when, by replacing legends of pagan heroes they helped to smooth the transition from the old to the new religion. But in the Middle Ages the Persons of the Trinity were matters of erudite discussion and often obscured by theological argument. Hence the need for something less removed from human life was generally felt, especially by the uneducated. It is impossible in a limited space to do more than refer to one or two outstanding examples of this branch of literature—which, it has to be admitted, is largely a literature of translation as we have already seen in the case of St. Alexis and St. Léger (Ch. i). Leaving aside for the moment collections such as the *Vitas Patrum* or 'Lives of the desert fathers' which were translated *en masse*, we will confine ourselves to the lives of three characteristic Western saints who enjoyed widespread popularity and who represent three different types of devotion, each appealing to a different side of human nature.

La Vie de St. Brendan, which dates from the first or second decade of the twelfth century, was composed by an Anglo-Norman writer for an English queen. Pleading for indulgence because he is doing his best and relating truthfully what he knows, the author adds:

> Mais cil que peot e ne voile
> Drei est que cil mult s'en doile. (ll. 17-18)

The *Vie*, or, as it is often called, the *Voyage* of St. Brendan is a free translation of a prose Latin work—the *Navigatio Sancti Brendani* and, as its name indicates, it is a romance of the sea. A work treating of a somewhat similar subject which also had a considerable vogue both in Latin and French versions was the *Espurgatoire de Saint Patrice*, another Irish saint. The best-known version of this, based on a Latin original, is that of Marie de France. This was probably not composed till after 1189. We shall therefore concentrate on the earlier poem as depicting the adventures of a characteristically adventurous Irish saint. The *Navigatio* describes the adventures of the saint and his companions in their voyage to the confines of heaven and hell. The translator, who rather mysteriously describes himself as 'li apostoiles danz Benedeiz', was commissioned to write his poem by 'Donna Aeliz la Reïne', the wife of Henry I of England.[1] Thus the poem must have been written between 1100 and 1118 and is one of the earliest Anglo-Norman poems we possess. The Latin original had an immense vogue in the Middle Ages, as is attested by the existence to-day of not less than eighty manuscripts scattered over Europe. The translation is by no means slavish. The author occasionally omits tedious passages and embellishes interesting ones. The pains of hell, for instance, are amplified in accordance with medieval taste for horrors. The legend of Judas and his 'days off' for acts of kindness he had performed was well known, so also was the story (culled from the bestiaries) of the big fish on which the ship's crew anchored thinking it was an island, only to be disillusioned when the whale was stung into movement by a fire they lighted on its back. All these medieval legends, including the description of the Island of Sheep (as big as stags), the Paradise of Birds, etc., were contained in the Latin version. But the legend of Judas is greatly expanded. His round of torments is enlarged and the kindly St. Brendan is moved to pity. Before he learned the identity of Judas he experienced such grief that 'Unches dolor nen out graindre' (l. 1256) and even after discovering that it was the arch-traitor with whom he was talking he 'pluroit a larges plors' (l. 1445). This is in accordance with the saint's character all through. Although he is capable of being severe, he is easily moved to pity. The birds in the 'Paradise of Birds' are the angels who fell 'de si halt si bas' with Satan when he rebelled 'par superba' against God. But because they had merely obeyed and followed a very clever master God had taken pity on them and they had not shared the full punishment of Satan, though deprived of the joy and glory of God's presence. The author makes out a good case for the birds, going further, perhaps, than theologians would have permitted. He is sharply taken to task for this in a satirical poem contained in a Latin manuscript of Lincoln College, Oxford,[2] which, not content with pouring scorn on some of the fantastic stories contained in the legend, severely censures the author for allowing these fallen angels any amelioration of their fate and giving them permission to praise God: 'quod est nimis inimicum fidei catholice: / Recta quippe fides

---

[1] See note on p. 196.
[2] Cf. Romania xxxi—Mélanges: *Satire en vers rythmiques sur la légende de Seint Brendan*, publ. by Paul Meyer.

C

habet quod, ruente principe, / Nullus nisi periturus secum posset
ruere.' At all events the author has provided us with a pleasantly
told series of adventures at sea, including visions of heaven and hell,
under the leadership of a firm yet kindly saint, adventures which
are expressly meant to test and confirm the faith of the pilgrims:

> Sainz hoen cum ad plusurs travailz
> De faim, de seif, de freiz, de calz,
> Ainze, tristur e granz poürs—
> De tant vers Deu creist ses oürs (= by so much increases his
>   merit towards God) (ll. 1177–80).

He has no axe to grind other than to edify and this gives a certain
charm to a rather crude poem. Yet it is not without its dramatic
moments. The description of the waves as they hurl Judas back and
forth is vivid:

> L'une le fert, pur poi ne funt;
> L'altre detriers jetet l'amunt.
> Peril devant, peril desus,
> Peril detriers, peril dejus.
> Turmente grant ad a destre,
> Ne l'a menur a senestre (ll. 1235–40).

It is interesting and not without significance, perhaps, that the hero
of this adventurous voyage was an Irish saint. He was, of course,
of noble birth (*de regal lin*)—this was claimed for most of the saints—
but he left all the honours and fine clothes to become a monk and,
eventually, like St. Gilles, an abbot, though he, too, was elected to
this honour 'par force' and not of his own desire. Being of an
adventurous or curious turn of mind, although fully occupied with
pious duties, one idea obsessed him—a great longing to see paradise:

> Mais de une ren li prist talent,
> Dunt Deu prier prent plus suvent,
> Que lui mustrast cel paraïs
> U Adam fud primes asis. . . .

Hell, too, he longed to see and the punishments which felons suffered
there for having neither 'amur ne fei'. This very natural curiosity,
combined with a true desire to help his fellow men, has given us a
pleasing picture of a saint of natural proportions without undue
ambition and not invested with a too brilliant aura of sanctity.

The cult of St. Aegidius (St. Gilles) seems to have originated
in the tenth century. The first known Latin *Vita* was probably
composed with the tendentious object of adding lustre and authority
to a religious foundation and vindicating its rights against a neigh-

bouring bishop.[1] This mercantile and somewhat questionable proceeding, however, an exemplary legend which became one of the most famous in literary history. St. Aegidius who, in the legend, was contemporary with Charlemagne, became an almost ideal saint. A Greek by birth and of noble lineage, his vocation was clear from the beginning. As a mere child he gave his cloak to a beggar and when questioned by his parents about its disappearance, stated that it had been taken from him by an unknown person. A lie in a good cause was evidently no stumbling-block to the author of the legend of those days. A desire for solitude and complete dedication drove him to foreign parts. Miracles accompanied him wherever he went. Sickness was cured, sterile land became fertile, storms abated, mariners were saved. His reputation would have been even greater were it not for his eagerness to avoid publicity. His visit to a hermit ended when he realized that some of the resulting miracles were being laid at his door, thus rendering further retirement necessary. His wanderings came to an end at last, when he found a grotto with a stream running close by in the depths of the forest. From this time he became the typical hermit living on herbs and the milk of a beautiful hind which joined itself to him in his exile. One day the huntsmen of a local king pursued the magnificent beast. At first the dogs held back when the hind took refuge in the hermit's grotto, but a stray arrow intended to arouse the hind struck the hermit and wounded him grievously. He refused remedies, however, and his fame spread more and more until it reached the ears of Charlemagne, who immediately conceived a desire to see such a holy man. The king had committed a heinous sin which he had never confessed to anyone. He now summoned the saint to come and join him, and one Sunday, shortly after their meeting, Aegidius was celebrating Mass when an angel descended and placed a document on the altar. The saint perused it and found that it contained the account of Charlemagne's sin and an assurance of pardon if he would repent and never act in the same way again. Moreover, the *charte* stated that if anyone else committed a sin, he, too, would be pardoned if he called upon St. Aegidius and gave up his sinful ways. This unusual power of granting pardon without confession doubtless added to the saint's fame. After a visit to Rome to establish his right to his church (for which he received the gift of two beautiful sculptured doors) he returned to France, where he shortly afterwards received

[1] See E. C. Jones: *Saint Gilles, Essai d'histoire littéraire.* Champion, Paris 1914.

notice of his approaching death. Listening monks heard the angels singing as they carried the saint's soul to heaven.

The cult of St. Gilles originated at an obscure spot 'in Galliae finibus . . . juxta Massiliam, ubi Rodanus intrat mare, circa Provinciam'. His *Vita* was written, as we have seen, for local and tendentious reasons. In spite of that fact St. Gilles rapidly became a European celebrity—venerated not only in France and England, but in Italy, Germany, Poland and Hungary. Doubtless this was partly due to the fact that his foundation was placed on one of the arterial routes which took pilgrims from the North to the great shrines of Rome and Compostella. Indeed, the route was actually known as the *Via Aegidiana*. His fame spread rapidly northwards. His role of historiographer is well known from the curious passage in the *Chanson de Roland*.[1] His personality was interwoven with the stories which grew up around the legends of Aiol and Raoul de Cambrai and other romantic heroes and heroines. The story of Charlemagne's secret sin appears in legendary chronicles.[2] The devoted hind and the two sculptured doors which swam miraculously to the door of his hermitage proved worthy of imitation and became popular 'motifs'. Indeed, St. Gilles was almost the ideal, gentle, beneficent saint, performing miracles wherever he went, making sterile land fertile, patron of the shipwrecked and the unfortunate—especially of the cripples because of the wound in his own thigh. But his reputation was highest in districts far away from his own home. How can we account for this fact? In a way this legend is a double one. There is a story of the rich man giving up everything, retiring to the wilderness, being fed by a hind and becoming a beneficent local saint, and there is the legend of Charles' secret sin, the way in which it is revealed to St. Gilles and the pardon granted without confession. How did these two stories become welded together? It must have happened at an early date for it was a widespread element in the popularity of St. Gilles. Was it originally introduced to enhance the saint's fame in the North? If so, it certainly succeeded. A notable translation, or rather adaptation of the story, the only French verse version which has come down to us, is the composition of the poet, Guillaume de Berneville. Guillaume was probably

---

[1] *Chanson de Roland*, 2095:

> Ço dit la geste et cil ki el camp fu:
> Li ber Gilie, por qui Deus fait vertuz,
> E fist la chartre el muster de Loüm.

[2] E.g. Chronicle of Turpin; Philippe Mousket; etc.

a Norman living in England.[1] He writes excellent French, though
with certain Anglo-Norman characteristics. He is familiar with
English marine terminology, he uses an occasional English word
(e.g. welcome), and he is evidently unfamiliar with the localities in
Southern France which he describes. But he is French at heart. He
talks of 'dulce France',[2] of French money (a *romasin*) of 'la franceise
nurreture' which renders the king 'mult curteis'. His description of
the boy (St. Gilles) is the stylized description so common in French
court literature. His quick style of conversation, of question and
answer, is almost reminiscent of Chrétien de Troyes, and he com-
pares the rough English manner of dress with the elegant French
attire:

> N'unt pas vestu burels engleis
> Mes peliçuns veirs e hermins
> E ciclatuns e osterins (ll. 1548–50).

He does not let Gilles tell an untruth when his father asks him where
is the *cote* that he has given to a beggar, for that would have been
against the rules of French 'courtoisie'. On the other hand, he is,
as we have said, familiar with seafaring terms, with hunting terms
common to other Anglo-Norman texts, and has the almost sentimental love of animals so often found in the English:

> Vus, sire rei, voill jo preier,
> Ne venez meis ici chascer:
> Leissez *ma nurice* aver peis.' (= the hind)
> Li reis rit e dit ke ja meis
> Ne serrat par lui adesée . . . (l. 2065 f.).

Although the author allows St. Gilles to laugh slyly at Charlemagne
and ask him 'cum longement / Avez vus esté sermoner?' (l. 2721),
yet he himself with true Norman piety strews his poem with sermons
and long prayers. St. Gilles, as a small boy, preaches to his father.
Perhaps he did so to his young companions who teased him for
wanting to be 'sainterel' and quoted the proverb (which later
Philippe of Novare so indignantly refuted): Young saint, old devil:

> Li vileins dit en repruver
> De josne seint veil adverser.

It is with the King of France that St. Gilles becomes most animated.
In thirty lines of quick question and answer Guillaume reminds us
of the battle of wits between Adam and the devil in the *Mystère*

---

[1] See Introduction to edition of *Vie de St. Gilles*. Ed. Paris & Bos. SATF.
[2] Ça sumes venuz par la guerre
De dulce France nostre terre (ll. 2375–6).

d'Adam. Of the South of France, the actual home of the saint, the author is singularly ignorant. He does not know the French equivalents of the towns of *Nesmaus* (Nîmes) and of *Arrelais* (Arles); he tells us that between the Rhône and Montpelier the country abounds in bears, lions, elephants, tigers, vipers and tortoises besides the other more ordinary inhabitants of 'deserz' and 'boscages'. Strangely enough, the one important miracle in the Latin *Vita* that he omits is that of rendering the sterile land fertile. Perhaps that would not have appealed so much to northern hearers less accustomed to parched soil. In spite of all his digressions he keeps the main object of the saint's *Life* in view. He describes St. Gilles' visit to Rome in detail and the saint is eloquent in his plea for the 'privilege' and the 'confermement' to be granted to his abbey and for 'la frarie de la meison' to be maintained after his death. The arrival of the undamaged sculptured doors bore testimony to the fact:

> K'il est de Roume confermé
> E tenu en auctorité (ll. 3485–6).

On his death-bed he tells his monks to keep careful guard over his body for pilgrims will come from far and near. That this was a necessary injunction a short digression into provençal literature may be here permitted.

If a saint belonged to the South of France the body ought to be allowed to remain there. It was obviously out of the question for the time-honoured kings of France to be ignored, but 'la France du Nord' must not be allowed to get possession of more than its fair share of relics. Where southern shrines were concerned the personalities even of kings must be kept in their proper place. This was very skilfully managed in the *Vie de Seinte Enemie*, which in some ways forms a counterpart to that of St. Gilles. Ste. Enemie's foundation with its attendant chapels was, like that of St. Gilles, situated in the extreme south of France. Her grotto was beside the river Tarn (a tributary of the Garonne) and in the diocese of Mende —a territory not far removed from that of St. Gilles. The first known Latin 'Life' of Ste. Enemie dates from the first half of the twelfth century when that of St. Gilles was already well known. A provençal *Vie de Seinte Enemie* dates from a few decades later. Ste. Enemie was a beautiful maiden of royal descent, being a direct descendant of the first king of France, daughter of the present king, and sister of the future King Dagobert. But the scene of all her activities was the south, and even royal demands were not going to be allowed to rob the south of the honour it deserved. She had many suitors while still quite young. One of these having been selected by her parents, she prayed earnestly that her virginity might be preserved, for she felt that irresistible vocation to serve God that we have seen in St. Alexis (see Ch. i) and in St. Gilles. Her prayer was answered in a terrible way. To the dismay of her relatives and friends, she became leprous, lost all her beauty, and was no longer desired in marriage 'per baro ne per chavalier'. For some years she remained in this state, humbly thankful to God for her preservation. Nevertheless, she received with joy a message sent from God by an angel that she would recover her health if she went and bathed in the clear water of a holy well, Burla by name. For this a journey to Gavalda (Gevaudon) was necessary, and twice she journeyed thither, accompanied by an imposing cortège of noble folk. Each time, however, that she quitted the banks of the tarn, her leprosy returned, so that at last she determined to stay there and live in a grotto beside the stream. Here in her solitude she undertook the construction of an abbey. The work was much hindered by the devil in the form of a dragon, and Ste. Enemie had to appeal for help to St. Hilarius, bishop of Gevaudan, who, after strenuous efforts, managed to dispose of the evil creature. Then the work of construction proceeded, and eventually Ste. Enemie became abbess of the foundation. After a few years of beneficent rule she died, and her death was almost immediately followed by that of her maid who also rejoiced in the name of Enemie. The latter's death was inevitable, for the saint declared that she could not do without a maid in heaven. This was not so selfish as it seemed. Ste. Enemie knew that, as soon as she was dead, her rich relations would want to get possession of her body, so she took her precautions. She left directions that the coffin containing her maid's body should be placed above her own with the name Enemie clearly inscribed upon it. As she foresaw, her brother Dagobert, now king of 'la terra reyale', hastened to the south to claim his sister's body. He was completely taken in by the ruse. The maid's body was removed and that of Ste. Enemie remained in its place. After many days the nuns' foundation was replaced by a monastery of 'monges neirs'. Not till then did the Holy Spirit feel it was time that the truth should be known, for all believed that the body of the saint was at St. Denis in France and had been added to the already numerous relics which the king had gathered from far and near:

> Car dels santz de quela proensa
> e de las altras loinh e pres
> en qualque loc los atrobes
> prendia lo cors e la ossa
> so que trobava en la fossa
> e portava n'o tot en Fransa (ll. 1490 f.).

It would, indeed, have been a great loss to the south if the saint's body had been removed, for her actual presence ('sa persona') had, as in the case of St. Gilles, rendered the sterile land so fertile that vines and fruit and corn now flourished in abundance. An angel appeared to an old monk (Jehan by name) in a vision by night on three distinct occasions. Twice Jehan ignored the vision, but the third time, though he tried to hide under the bed-clothes, he could not ignore the light and the voice. Greatly alarmed, he addressed the apparition:

> 'Nomine Patris, qui es tu?
> Si mala causa es, vay t'en;
> Si bona, digas belamen
> qui es, que vols ni que mi quiers' (ll. 1888 f.).

The angel reproved his incredulity but revealed the welcome news that St. Enemie's body was still amongst them. Great was the joy in the monastery, and the bishop of Mende and all his retinue arrived to share in the rejoicing. When the coffin was opened such a sweet odour issued from it that miracles were multiplied:

> cobreron salut aquel dia
> malaute, cec, contrech e clop
> sorz e lebros e d'altres trop.

It was a wonderful victory for the south.

Historical, rather than legendary, and of real literary value is the 'Life' of the Archbishop Thomas of Canterbury whose murder in the cathedral in 1170 had repercussions all over Europe. Guernes de Pont-Ste-Maxence was a Frenchman by birth: 'Mis langages est bons, car en France fui nez'—but he tells us in his *Vie de Saint Thomas* that he had learnt his facts from those on the spot who had witnessed the crime and that he is relating the truth and nothing but the truth: 'ci n'a mis un sul mot si la verité nun' (l. 6159). Guernes has, in fact, drawn much from other accounts, but this does not detract from the merit of his own. For though historically he does not add much to our information, the poem abounds in interesting features.

The author speaks his mind freely and is outspoken in his criticism even, on occasion, of the archbishop whom he so much admires. He shows the sudden change in the behaviour of St. Thomas when he ceased to be Chancellor and became Archbishop, the obstinacy of his nature which even his friends recognized, his courage in face of danger, his capacity to bear the most repulsive forms of penance. For we learn that St. Thomas had not only a hair-shirt but hair pants next his skin which made it torture to sit astride a horse and—what plagued him more even than the self-inflicted nightly beatings—troops of vermin all over him which gave him no rest day or night. No wonder his miracles were so numerous both before and after his death, for he only removed his hair shirt once in six weeks. The vindictive character of Henry II is criticized, the cruelty of the forestry laws, the ignorance of monks and the atrocious Latin they spoke; the greed of cardinals and their love of *Angot* (= the ingot, Fr. *lingot*). His freedom of speech at times surprises us. A democratic spirit peeps through as it so often does in Old French literature:

> Mielz valt fiz a vilain qui est prouz et senez
> Que ne fait gentilz hom failliz et debutez (ll. 2544-5).

Besides his biblical references and examples taken from history, he has a predilection for well-known proverbs: 'Veir se dit li vilains que "de si haut si bas"' (l. 2594), and others less known than this favourite reflection on Fortune. His skill in composition and versification is considerable. He has managed to compress all his reflections and translations of legal documents into stanzas of five alexandrines bound by the rhyme. Guernes himself describes his metre as follows: 'Li vers est d'une rime en cinq clauses cuplez'—the last line being often supernumerary and adding little to the sense. His descriptive power is noteworthy. The four murderers of Becket are 'la maisnie al Satan' (5496), 'li fil a l'aversier' (5446), 'li serf d'iniquité' (5641); death is 'le non repairant port' (775); when St. Thomas falls, anyone who saw the blood and brain on the pavement 'De roses et de lilies li peüst sovenir' (5638). He opens the poem in the approved fashion by a proverb and the customary maxim that a good thing should be made known for the edification of others. Unfortunately towards the end of the poem he indulges, when his story is really finished, in rather trivial references to coincidences of times and days (cf. str. 1175 *Par un marsdi fu nez*, etc.). References to the prophecies of Merlin are introduced to enforce his antipathetic view of the English king and his troublesome sons (*si enfant ki sunt de sens poi esforcie*, l. 6128). But he ends with a prayer for peace and a hope that he will be honoured for his work (str. 1231). One might conclude from these last lines that Guernes, instead of doing a little propaganda for his monastery or religious foundation, was composing for his own ends and with a view to reward. This would undoubtedly be partly true. In a short *epilogue* to his poem he tells us how generously he had been treated—by the sister of St. Thomas, by other ladies ('*les dames m'ont fait tut gras*', Ep. l. 7), the good prior of the cathedral and his monks. Indeed, he was well rewarded for his long and wearisome task even by St. Thomas himself, so that he set off loaded with gifts on his wanderings: 'tuz li munz est miens envirun'. This, however, does not detract from the value of the work, viewed not so much from the historical aspect as from the human and literary standpoint. The author does not disguise his own feelings which probably represented those of his educated French contemporaries and these, combined with the urge to improve the minds of his hearers and to give a true account of events, are expressed in well-sustained metrical form which must indeed have entailed considerable effort.

The three 'Lives' of saints we have been considering cannot be taken as entirely characteristic of the *genre*. As time went on the number of *Vies* in verse and prose increased and the characters tended to become stylized. They were rendered familiar to the unlearned in many ways other than pictorial. Some were dramatized at an early date (e.g. St. Alexis and St. Nicholas); they were introduced into epic poems—there were the warrior saints who might be seen on the field of battle, where their presence was always duly attested by those who actually saw them: 'Moult furent bien et veü et choisi';[1] others were introduced into sermons and more exclusively didactic literature, as we have seen in the case of Ste. Thaïs. It is unnecessary to give a mere list of all the saints (both male and female) whose lives were composed or translated during the twelfth, and more particularly the thirteenth centuries, as they can be found in any good bibliography of this period. They form but one branch of the stock of didactic literature which flourished from an early date particularly in the North and West, and which was perhaps cultivated partly with a desire to prove that the Latin saints were as potent in action as the desert fathers. It is, however, interesting to note a certain change in tendency which creeps in as time

---

[1] Cf. Garin le Lorrain: *Et Saint Denise, sor un bon cheval siet*
Et Saint Maurisse et Saint Jorge autressi. Ed. P. Paris, p. 108.

goes on. St. Alexis adopted a life of poverty and self-abnegation out of pure asceticism and a desire to devote himself wholly to God's service—'De tut an tut ad a Deu son talent' (l. 50). He has committed no crime; the devil is hardly mentioned; no wicked heathen tries to cross his will. It is the almost unattainable height of self-sacrifice: 'Sell all that thou hast and give to the poor and thou shalt have treasure in heaven.' In the *Vie de St. Grégoire*, composed a century later but showing definite affinities with the *Vie de St. Alexis*, the emphasis is a different one. The saint, who is the son of an incestuous marriage and who, after many wanderings, comes back and unknowingly marries his own mother, has an appalling sin to expiate. The author is imbued with church doctrine. He insists again and again that the punishment must match the crime (inadvertent though it is) and the penitence must be 'selon la colpe et le pechié'. The balance is emphasized throughout. St. Gregory is chained to an island rock and subsists on water only for seventeen years; not till a celestial voice, as in the case of Alexis, is heard at Rome commanding the cardinals to find the saint and make him pope, is Gregory released from his rock. The devil is a designing agent throughout: 'Haï Diables, fel tiranz / cum es crueus e sorduianz', laments the saint's mother when she realizes what she has done. But the devil rejoices: 'Bon porchaz fera, ce li samble.'

The gifted author of the *Vie de St. Grégoire* gives us a picture of contemporary life, of the glamour of knighthood, of the greed of the peasant redeemed by the episode of the fisherman's kindly wife. But he never forgets his central theme: 'Selon le fait le gueredon.'

(c) THE WISDOM OF THE AGES

Less religious in tone, though equally ethical, is another stream of didactic literature which flows steadily through the Middle Ages and does not lose itself in the sand until well on into the sixteenth century. We shall not find the Church doctrines here, although there is a strong Old Testament flavour about it and it is not undeserving of the name of 'The Wisdom Literature of the Middle Ages'. The Proverbs of Solomon and the wisdom book of Jesus Sirach were, of course, a mine of wealth from the beginning of the Christian era. But the collection of sayings and proverbs known as the *Disticha Catonis* ran them very close for they were translated and quoted in almost every treatise on morals which was not specifically concerned with Church doctrine, and in many other works of diverse kind which have come down to us. Cato, or the Pseudo-Cato, or Dionysius Cato as he was often called, cannot be traced back with certainty further than the fourth century A.D., although there is some evidence of his aphorisms having been utilized on grave inscriptions at an earlier date.[1] In any case his popularity from that time onwards is attested by the number of manuscripts of his aphorisms which are still in existence. It was a clever stroke of the author to call himself Cato—assuming this to be merely a *nom de plume*—for the Utican Cato, as portrayed by Lucan in the *Pharsalia*, had assured a good reception for the wise sayings of anyone bearing such an honoured name. Indeed, the confusion between the two sages was pretty general up to the time of Caxton, for in the preface to his edition of Cato's *Disticha* (one of the first books to be printed) Caxton calls him 'the noble Catho' and classes him with the Scipios and others who 'put theyr bodyes and lyves in jeopardy and to the deth as we may see in th'actes of Romains'.[2]

The *Disticha Catonis* are of a utilitarian character—often reminiscent of Horace, often of the Wisdom of Jesus Sirach, the preacher. Ethical rather than pious in character, they appealed to those who were not attracted by the self-immolation of the saints and martyrs. The instructions are addressed by a father to his son and after a few disconnected exhortations to revere God and honour one's parents the 'sententiae' proper begin with the rather curious one:

> Si Deus est animus, nobis ut carmina dicunt,
> Hic tibi praecipue sit puramente colendus.[3]

In a way this first couplet gives a clue to the eclectic nature of the document, for it is the strangest collection of wise sayings, reminiscent of Solomon, Ecclesiasticus, the Greek philosophers and Horace. Cato may be described by a writer treating of more romantic subjects as 'the father of copy-book headlines',[4] but he is much more than that. He is a late exponent of the wisdom-literature of the ages. He is imbued with stoic ideas and terminology, and steeped in Horace whom he rivals in opportunism. The instructions as to silence (I, 3; I, 12, etc.), as to the value of a 'fidum amicum', of a good physician and the care of one's health; the warning against trying to penetrate God's secrets (*archana Dei*) or blaming God for

---

[1] Cf. Rheinisches Museum LXXXI, 2—1932. M. Boas: *Cato und die Grabschrift der Alia Potestas.*

[2] A reference to *Li Fait des Romains*, based largely on Lucan.

[3] Quotations from Ms. 371, Lambeth Palace Library.

[4] See Helen Waddell: *The Wandering Scholars*. Pagan learning, Section II.

one's misfortunes, or undertaking what is beyond one's strength and neglecting good teaching (*doctrina*)—all take us straight back to Ben Sirach the preacher. But Horace's practical instructions to avoid deep waters, to enjoy the 'commoda vitae', to avoid exciting envy, to beware of despising a little man, etc., give character to this exaltation of 'la sagesse humaine' in an unmistakable way. The popularity of Cato as a 'wise man' in the Middle Ages was very great. He was translated into most European languages; words of wisdom were attributed to him indiscriminately by French writers. Béroul quotes him; Chrétien de Troyes is imbued with his precepts, though, with pleasant irony, he makes the old philosopher contradict himself. The 'ugly damsel' blames Perceval for obeying Cato and the 'preudom' and holding his tongue. He should have obeyed Cato's other maxim and taken time by the forelock and spoken when he had the chance:

> 'Ha, Percevaus, Fortune est chauve
> Derriers et devant chevelue...
> Ce es tu le maleüreus
> Qui veïs qu'il fu tans et leus
> De parler et si te teüs.
> Assez grant leisir an eüs.
> Au mal eür tant te teüsses,' etc. (ll. 4646 f.).

Alas, it takes much wisdom to know when to 'compescere linguam' and when to speak. It was not 'un bon teisir' Perceval had lost this time, but 'si bel tens et leus' (i.e. *occasio*) which would never occur again. Chrétien tells us that it was sin that prevented his hero from speaking and this must be expiated by repentance and penance. Cato was a 'sage homme', but not a Christian. Nevertheless, he was too good to lose on this account. There is nothing in his writings 'qui se descorde a seinte escriture' as one of his translators tells us when apologizing for the fact that 'Catun esteit paien'. Indeed, his 'sayings' rivalled the *Psalter* in popularity as instructions for youth. The author of the Franco-Italian epic *L'Entrée d'Espagne* mentions the fact that something happened before Roland had learnt either his 'Psalter' or his 'Cato', as a proof of his extreme youth. Several translations of the distichs into French and Anglo-Norman are extant—those of Élie de Winchester and 'Everard le moine', both composed in England in the twelfth century; that of Adam de Suel in France in the thirteenth, of which no less than twelve copies have been located; slightly later in date were those of Jean de Paris and Jean Lefievre and other anonymous ones. The translation of

'Everard le moine' is interesting. It shows a certain amount of skill in versification, but also the difficulty of translating these short aphorisms into rather elaborate verse. 'Datum serva, foro te para' becomes

> Mult seit ben gardé
> Chose ke te est duné, par Deu hu par gent.
> Al marché kaunt alez
> Ben vos aturnez, et acesméement.

The same lengthiness is noticeable in the above-quoted description of *occasio* which Cato expresses so neatly in the line:

> Fronte capillata, post est occasio calva.

In this case the Anglo-Norman monk feels obliged to add an explanatory postscript:

> Fortune est chanchable, ne seit de tei lassé,
> le front od peil est bel,
> Quant le haterel chauf est et pele,
> Par le front pelu, de vos seit entendu
> le riche commencail:
> Et par le chef detres, ki tut est kauf e res,
> le povre definail.

But Everard's intention was good. He knows that one should not keep a good thing to oneself, 'Sun sen et sun savir, pur bien multiplier / Deit chascun despendre' and so he plods through with his rather diffuse translation.

Of a similar utilitarian character is another work which was translated and retranslated from one language to another in the twelfth century and after. This collection of tales, proverbs and wise sayings is the work of a converted Jew, Petrus Alfonsus (or, more correctly, Alfonsi), a native of Spain. The importance of his treatise, commonly known as the *Disciplina Clericalis*, cannot be overstressed in the field of medieval didactic literature. His stories and prudent counsels became common property even where their source was not known, and before the end of the twelfth century the *Disciplina* was translated into French under the title of the *Chastoiement d'un pere a son fils*. Petrus Alfonsi claims to have collected his fables and aphorisms from maxims of philosophers, from Arab wisdom (contained in fables and verses) and from animal similes. Many of them are well known in medieval lore. Arab philosophers are frequently quoted and some of the stories may come from the East, but it is notoriously difficult to check up on sources of stories which have come down through the ages. In any case much of his wisdom, like that of Cato, can be traced back to Ecclesiasticus the Preacher, and, while not representing Christian teaching, bears a strongly-marked Old Testament character. Here we find a fund of familiar proverbial wisdom which crops up incessantly in Old French literature: the value of a true friend (*au besoin connaist on l'ami*), with stories to illustrate it; the wisdom of silence, or at all events of 'mesure' in speech; the uselessness of immoderate grief (*en duel faire n'a nul profit*); the necessity of consorting with good people and the danger of an unknown travelling companion (if he carries a sword, walk on his right side, if a spear on his left); the wisdom of following the beaten track and not taking a short cut—such are the sane counsels which we find again and again in warnings given by parents and wise friends—to the young Perceval by his mother and the 'prud'ome'; to Aiol as he sets out by his father; by the Chevalier de la Tour Landry to his three daughters. Here again, as in the case of Cato's 'distichs', we are dealing with a branch of European rather than purely French literature. But it has special importance in the case of the French and Anglo-French productions because it coincided with, and may have been partly responsible for a code of manners largely comprehended under the term *courtoisie* which held sway amongst educated French people for many years. During the following centuries (Petrus Alfonsi flourished in the first half of the eleventh) instructions for young men, for clerics, for princes and rulers flooded the market. They were soon extended to cover both sexes and even children. The *Disciplina Clericalis* ('reddit enim clericum disciplinatum') is one of the first of these. Its collection of stories and fables each inculcating some moral precept includes proverbs and *dicta* culled from many sources but all concerned with the philosophy of life—the danger of avarice, of pride and lust; the wiles of evil women and how to avoid them—indeed, instructions how to behave in all circumstances and how to make the best of one's life. They are materialistic and utilitarian in tone—indeed, the practical wisdom of Ecclesiasticus, of Cato and of Boethius, which we find so often scattered about in later French literature, abounds in this one short text. There is no castigation of the Church—just a general, commonsense attitude towards life. The disciple (sometimes the son) listens with all his ears (*arrectis auribus*) and sometimes almost exhausts his preceptor by his requests for more. The French verse-translation has slightly adapted the original to his audience. It is a little more religious in character and the son has completely taken over the role of the disciple. The translator thoroughly enjoys the practical nature of the instructions and sometimes caps them with a neat proverb. When encouraging a young man to work and thus avoid poverty he adds:

> Tant as, tant valz, tex est li sens,
> En tenue mantel tenue sens.

and he endorses the advice to attach oneself 'rei crescenti' and by no means 'rei deficienti':

> Beax filz, ne pren pas compaignie
> se tu crois chose que ge die,
> A la rien qui vait descroissant,
> mais a cil qui vait amendant.

One may judge of the opportunist nature of the work from these short quotations. But both author and translator agree on the subject of birth. Nobility derived from one's ancestors has but little value if not accompanied by personal nobility (*sua nobilitas*). Just as Boethus' instructress insists that 'foreine gentilesse ne maketh thee not gentil' but 'gentilesse of thyself',[1] so Petrus insists that the man 'in quo sua desinit nobilitas, avorum nobilitatem haut congrue reservat'. The French translator waxes even more eloquent than his source on this theme which runs through all medieval French literature (even through the 'court-literature' if one looks for it)— so much so that 'gentillece de cuer' almost becomes a cliché. He insists that 'Tel qui est de basse gent né' ought to be all the more honoured if he produce something good:

> Ne li doit on savoir bon gré
> Se il est de bas parenté
> Quant il vos passe par proece
> Et vos et vostre gentillece?

On the subject of the 'mala femina', the disciple is quite insatiable, and in Petrus Alfonsi we find stories which are familiar to us in the 'Seven Sages' (*De puteo*), amongst the *fabliaux* (*De canicula lacrimante*), and in later collections. There is as yet no trace of 'courtoisie' towards women in spite of the fact that some of the instructions clearly have a well-born youth in view. The utilitarian outlook is marked even when mere outward behaviour and good manners are in question. How to obtain favour with the great, how to eat in

---

[1] See Chaucer's pleasant translation.

the king's presence so as not to offend, how to reply to an invitation according to the rank of the inviter, these are delicate questions and are discussed in detail. Indeed, this consideration of manners produced an important sideline in French literature. For the first time the father makes a distinction between what is 'prava rusticitas' and what is suited to life at court. A special section is devoted to rules for table manners (*De modo comedendi*). This was not altogether new. Ovid, in his *Ars Amatoria*, had instructed the lover who wished to be 'urbanus' and not 'rusticus', how to behave when dining out. The ladies especially, besides being clean, were to be restrained and dainty in their habits, for 'Priamides Helenen avide si spectet edentem / Oderit et dicat "stulta rapina mea est" '. At a later date, when manners were rough, monks had to be warned not to be greedy, snatching their food and putting their hands before others in the dish. But Petrus Alfonsi is far more explicit. Such fundamental rules as: Don't swallow too big a morsel lest you choke; don't drink while you have food in your mouth; don't let the crumbs fall all over the place (*hinc et inde*)—indeed, all the instructions reminiscent of the nursery are here. They must have supplied a felt need for, during the twelfth and thirteenth centuries a crop of Latin rules sprang up on the same subject and obviously inspired by the examples of Petrus Alfonsi. They appear under various titles: *Modus cenandi*, *Liber Faceti*, or (after their first lines) *Ut te geras ad mensam*, or *Stans puer ad mensam*. These treatises were translated into nearly all the European languages. Under the title of *Contenances de Tables* and beginning 'Enfant qui vuet estre courtoys' a number of adaptations appeared in France. *Tischzuchten* became very popular in Germany and, judging from some of the details, were much needed. In England the *Boke of Nurture* or *Babees' Boke* and similar works abounded. Even as late as the fifteenth century the Italian poet Bonvicino did not think it beneath him to compose *Cinquante Cortesie da Tavola*. The later ones were destined for a less general public than the earlier ones, but the influence of the *Disciplina Clericalis* is unmistakable. Thus many streams met and mingled in these instructive books of rules—the urbane instructions of Ovid to lovers, the utilitarian recommendations of the father to his son, the more general rules for young men serving in their patron's families (for whom the *Stans Puer* and others were meant)—all combined to form a code of behaviour which undoubtedly had its effect on the external manners of good

D

society. The French version of the *Facetus* (*Facet en franceys*) is frankly a treatise on 'courtoisie':

> ... un livre moult petitet
> Lequel nous appellons *facet*,
> Qui parle bien de courtoisie
> de noblesce et de seignourie
> coment on se doibt maintenir
> Pour saige et courtois devenir
> Et de pluseurs enseignemens
> De quoy Chaton fut negligent.

Obviously Cato, wise man though he was, could not 'de tout traicter'. The subject of behaviour in polite society did not arise much among those fundamental wisdom-maxims collected by Cato although the pupil is warned that if he wishes to be considered 'urbanus' and not merely 'loquax' he must be modest in his conversation when he is 'inter convivas'. It was left for the medieval writers to develop this idea.

A conglomeration of such instructions as we have been considering, culled from those of Cato, Boethius, and other Latin writers, is to be found in another collection of *enseignements* which goes back to the twelfth century. Robert de Ho, or *Trebor*, as he likes to call himself in an anagram, was probably a Norman living in England. He makes no pretence of being original. He tells us that his 'treitié' recounts the 'diz qu'il a allors oïz' of 'danz Chatun', 'Salemun', and other ancient writers. He was probably a 'clericus vagans' for he tells us that all the world is the good man's country just as the fish is at home in all waters (ll. 35-39). He does not actually mention Petrus Alfonsi, but it is impossible not to see the influence of the Spanish Jew in his work. Here again we find the opportunist outlook on life, though slightly coloured by more pious considerations. Wealth is a snare, but it must be amassed because of the friends and advantages it brings:

> Tant as, tant vaux, tant t'amerai
> Por ce te ai je dit issi
> Ke tu entendes bien de fi
> Ke riche home a assez d'amis (ll. 1026 ff.).

But he, too, waxes warm on the subject of 'gentillece' which comes from the heart and has nothing to do with wealth or birth. This sentiment goes back to Boethius, as we have seen. But Robert comes down from the heights a little when he recommends anyone who is obliged to tell a lie to do it skilfully and boldly—in fact 'si

cointement / Et si tres acesmeement / K'il resemble bien verité'
(l. 119 f.). Even lying, however, should be indulged in sparingly
lest 'us' should become 'secunde nature'. Yet it is hardly enough to
assign to Robert merely 'lieux communs d'une moralité banale'.
His maxims may be 'bourgeois' and opportunist in character, but
a strong streak of this tendency runs all through the literature of the
period. After all, courtesy does not cost much—'estre doulz et
courtois, la chose est peu coustable'. Robert de Ho, in addition to
his utilitarian advice, includes a section on *courtoisie* as well as his
long tirade on *gentillece* in which he regrets that 'manantise
(= wealth) a abatue / Gentillece e del tot veincue'. The 'exemplum'
of the two fellow-travellers, one an '*envieux*' and the other a '*con-
veitous*', is well told: Jupiter, meeting them in the way, offered them
each a gift—the only condition being that the one who did not
choose it should receive a double portion. This was a real dilemma
for neither could bear to see the other have a double portion of
anything good. At last the envious man, out of pure spite, chose
to lose an eye so that his companion should be worse off than
himself and lose both. There is quite a lot of good in Robert de Ho
though he loses himself too often in trivialities.

Amongst other works, written either by educated Englishmen or
Frenchmen living in England in the first half of the thirteenth
century, is the *Petit Plet* in which the common-sense maxims of Cato
('si cum Catun enseigne e dit') are much more in evidence than any
Christian morality. It is in the form of a dialogue between a disillusioned old man and an optimistic youth. It has been called the
Candide of the middle ages. The trite advice given to his senior
by the young man recurs several times:

> Pur mun conseil fetes le ben
> E ne vus esmaiez de ren (ll. 1767–8).

The author admires the English but is critical of their love of beer
and their women. He does not name himself, but the poem is
generally attributed to Chardri, whose *Vie des Set Dormans* might
almost be included amongst the lives of saints. It was written partly
for the time-honoured reason that 'vertu . . . ne deit pas trop estre
celee' (ll. 1–3) and partly in support of the truth of resurrection.
Chardri's poem is a translation of a well-known Latin legend so
need not detain us here, but he introduces a diatribe against the
prelates who are the most covetous and the most dishonest of men.
Another poem of a didactic nature in which Chardri names himself,

is a verse version of the story of the young prince Josaphat who, brought up like the youthful Buddha, in a garden of delights, is horrified when he realizes what the world is really like. He is converted by the ancient hermit Barlaam and ends by renouncing all his honours and retiring to the desert to live. Josaphat does not have to suffer tortures or martyrdom, but he incurs the wrath of his father and is subject to fearful temptations, after one of which he is granted visions of heaven and hell similar to those vouchsafed to St. Brendan. He has the joy of witnessing his father's conversion, but is a little shocked to learn from a vision that the crowns laid up for his father and himself are identical. He has to learn the hard lesson (similar to the one recounted of the hermit in the *Poème moral*) that the father's humble repentance was as efficacious as his own sufferings. The poem ends with the pious wish that we may not prefer the tales about Roland and Oliver and the battles of the twelve peers to the story of the Passion of Jesus Christ. Chardri was evidently well-versed in the secular literature which he affects to disdain.

Less moralizing in tone and more concerned with the practical virtues are the rules for behaviour composed in the first half of the thirteenth century by a writer of undoubted French origin, Robert de Blois. Excluding a tedious romance entitled *Beaudoux*, this author's work is grouped under two heads, entitled *Enseignements as Princes* and *L'onor des Dames*. The former, beginning with the stock lament of the 'laudator temporis acti', proceeds to impress on his hearer the necessity of 'mesure' in all things, with special reference to the difficulty of striking a mean between 'trop parlier' and 'trop teisir'. He then goes on to the usual warnings against envy, pride, flattery, and taking counsel of a 'serf', but he only waxes really eloquent on the subject of avarice. He repeats the adage (drawn from *Ecclesiasticus*) that God hates three kinds of people: 'riche home avar, povre orgoilleux et vieil home luxurieux'. He only deals in detail with the first of these—comparing the fate of ambitious Porus at the hands of Alexander with that of King Arthur's lasting renown which was due to the fact that he was such a generous giver (*ainz tel donerres ne fu*). He even goes so far as to say that generosity (*largesce*) can save a soul—'Deu conquerre'. The *enseignements* for ladies are of a purely practical nature—how to walk to church (*gardez vos du trot et du cors*), how to behave when you get there, how to eat in polite society, and how to reply to an offer of marriage.

It would take us beyond the limits of the present study to follow up these efforts to produce a well-polished, well-informed member of society. They become more diffuse as time goes on and verse is superseded by prose. Philippe de Navarre, writing in the second half of the thirteenth century, has some wise things to say in his *Quatre Ages de l'Homme,* based on the experience of seventy years of active life. He insists on the necessity of discipline and chastisement for children ('il sont si ort et si anuieus en petitesce'). A boy should apply himself to some 'mestier', preferably *clergie* or *chevalerie* as being the most honourable. Girls should be taught to spin and sew, but neither to read nor write (unless with a view to taking the veil), for they might be tempted to correspond with a lover and 'au serpent ne puet on doner venin car trop i en a'. The section on youth, which he considers the most dangerous age, is full of sensible advice with examples from all the well-known sources. Training should begin young for he does not agree with the foolish saying 'De jone saint, vieil diable', but counters it with another one: 'lons usages torne presque a nature'. He is full of all the old saws of his predecessors, but his work is pious in tone: 'li soverains des sens si est de Dieu servir', and he warns in a little poem against the many paths that lead to Hell with its wide-open doors ('granz et larges overtes sont les portes d'anfer'). The section on old age revolves largely round the saying that God hates three kinds of sinners— 'vieil luxurieus, povre orgueilleus et riche convoiteus'. Like Robert de Blois, he chiefly inveighs against the last of the three but *his* model of 'largesce' is King Alexander. There is something rather winning about Philippe de Navarre. His hopeful nature can turn a warning into its opposite. For Robert de Ho, the gloomy Anglo-Norman, the proverb: 'us est secunde nature' is a warning against lying too much; for Philippe the Italian (the *Navarre* of the edition quoted[1] is strictly *Novare* in Italy) it is a comforting thought because even a hypocrite who goes on long enough giving so as to appear generous, may himself become generous in the end out of habit.

Another Italian, who composed a medley of lore in which Cato and Petrus Alfonsi rub shoulders with Solomon, Jesus Sidrac and Seneca, is Brunetto Latini, author of an encyclopaedic work in French which he called *Le Trésor.* He wrote in French partly because he was in France at the time, partly because 'la parleüre franceise est plus delitable et plus commune a toutes gens'—an interesting tribute to the spread of French language and culture during the

---

[1] See Philippe de Navarre: *Les Quatre Ages de l'Homme.* Edited by Marcel de Fréville (S.A.T.F., 1888), § 25.

thirteenth century. Brunetto divides his book into three parts—the first he describes as ready money (*deniers contans*)—this treats of 'de la nature de toutes choses'; the second as 'pierres précieuses' which are the vices and virtues; the third to which the others lead up is pure gold for it inculcates 'la doctrine de retorike' and how 'li sires doit governer ses gens qui sous li sont'. This third part is in fact another collection of instructions for a prince or seigneur, although there is much in it that applies to men of all conditions. The same dangers threaten all, for 'Aristote li tres sage philosophes et Merlins, furent deceu par feme'. Brunetto tells us frankly that his encyclopaedic book was not drawn from his own 'pauvre sens' but is like a honeycomb—'une bresche de miel coillie de diverses fleurs . . . compilie seulement des meilleurs des auteurs qui devant nostre tans ont traité de philosophie'. In one chapter alone he cites 'Seneker, Tulles, St. Bernard, Aristote, Boece, St. Mathieu, Dyogenes' and 'Macrobe'. Brunetto is nothing if not eclectic. He rates the art of rhetoric very high amongst the accomplishments of the cultured man. Figures of rhetoric are discussed at length for 'Tulles dit que la plus haute science de cité governer, si est rhetorique'. He illustrates the seventh 'flower of rhetoric' (which he calls 'demonstrance') by putting into the mouth of Tristan a stylized description of Iseult which makes us feel thankful that Béroul was blissfully ignorant of the 'arts poétiques' of his day. The encyclopedic nature of Brunetto Latini's work, dealing with peoples, kingdoms, the elements, the planets, and with the nature of animals before it even comes to the virtues, the government of a city and its lord, is characteristic of the expansion and flowering of new branches of learning in the thirteenth century. The study of nature was confined in the twelfth-century pretty much to the observation of animals and their ways. Now it blossomed forth, and works like the *Speculum* of Vincent de Beauvais found many imitators. No blame attached to plagiarism in those days. Authors made no pretence of being original. The more reputable the author, the more weighty the instructions. Aristotle himself is cited as the pedagogue in the *Secret des Secrets* or *Gouvernement du roi* composed in the form of a letter from Aristotle to Alexander, translated from a Latin version, itself translated from Greek or Syriac. We have the same kind of instructions—the necessity of cultivating *mesure*, *entendement et savoir*, *largesse*—combined with good sense as to clothing, care of health, food, etc. Interest in foreign lands and the terrestrial globe was fostered by another forgery, *La lettre du Prêtre*

Jean, which was known (in Latin) as early as 1156 and was duly translated into French, thus spreading the curiosity about this mysterious person whom Marco Polo would have given anything to locate. Works of this character multiplied and tended to supercede the ethical treatises of the previous century. But the wisdom of the ages survived in wise saws and in the proverbs which abound in medieval writings of all kinds. The memory of Cato lingered. In the charming little *Lai d'Aristote,* which tells how the Greek philosopher was inveigled into letting a beautiful woman saddle him and carry her on his back, the ignominious fate of Aristotle is put down to the fact that he ought to have remembered the wise words of Cato ('Car bons clers fu et sages hom'): 'Turpe est doctori cum culpa redarguit ipsum.' Not all the wisdom of the ages can make a man proof against Love, for Nature is stronger than 'sens et clergie'. Three times the young woman in all her beauty passed before the window where the old sage was studying, singing love-ditties as she went. At the third vision the resistance of the philosopher collapsed:

> A cest cop parchiet la chandeille
> Tote jus a terre au viel chat,
> Qui pris est sanz point de rachat.[1]

BIBLIOGRAPHY

Grant mal fist Adam. Reimpredigt. Halle 1879. Ed. H. Suchier. (Bibl. Norm.)
Estienne de Fougières: *Le Livre des Manières,* etc. Ed. J. Kremer. (Ausg. u. Abh. xxxix.)
Les Vers de la Mort, par Hélinant. Ed. Fr. Wulff et E. Walberg. Paris 1905. (SATF).
Guillaume le Clerc. *Le Besant de Dieu.* Herausg. Ernst Martin. Halle 1869.
Poème Moral.
    (1) Cloetta: *Poème moral* . . . nach allen bekannten HSS. Erlangen. 1886.
    (2) A. Bayot, *Le Poème Moral,* traité de vie chrétienne. Acad. royale de Belgique. (Textes anciens, t. I.) 1929.
Psalter (1) Oxford, (2) Cambridge. Ed. Francisque Michel, Oxford 1860.
Li Quatre Livres des Reis. Ed. (1) Le Roux de Lincy. Paris 1841.
    (2) E. Curtius. Halle 1911.
Maurice of Sully and the medieval vernacular homily. C. A. Robson. Oxford 1952.
L'Espurgatoire seint Patriz. (1) Ed. Th. Atkinson Jenkins. Chicago, 2nd ed., 1903.
    (2) Carl Warnke: Das Buch . . . und seine Quelle. Halle 1908.

[1] An allusion to an old story meant to prove that 'nature' is stronger than 'nourriture'. Three mice were released in succession before a cat holding a candle between its paws. Twice the cat resisted the temptation. The third time it proved too great. The candle was dropped and the cat rushed after the prey. See Note, lines 394–397 of Delbouille's edition of *Le Lai d'Aristote.*

La Vie de Saint Gilles. Publ. par G. Paris et A. Bos. Paris 1881. (SATF).

Prose version: E. Jones. Essai d'histoire littéraire. Paris 1914.

La Vie de Sainte Énemie. Ed. par Clovis Brunel. Paris 1916. (CFMA).

La Vie du pape Gregoire le Grand. Ed. V. Luzarche. Tours 1857.

La Vie de Saint Thomas Becket. Ed. par E. Walberg. Paris 1936. (CFMA).

Disticha Catonis. E. Stengel. Everard de Kirkham et Elie de Winchester. Marburg 1886. (Ausg. u. Abh. xlvii.)

J. Ulrich. Traductions d'Adam le Suel, etc. R.F. t. xv. 1903.

Reliable Latin Text in Zarnke: *Der deutsche Cato*.

Disciplina Clericalis. Herausg. Alfons Hilka. Heidelberg 1911. (Samml. Mittellat. Texte).

Chastoiement d'un père à son fils. (1) Barbazan et Méon: *Fabliaux et Contes*, t. ii, p. 39.

(2) A. Hilka et W. Söderhjelm. Helsingfors 1922.

Robert de Ho: *Les Enseignements Trebor*. Ed. M. V. Young. Paris 1901.

Chardry. *Josaphaz, Set Dormanz und Petit Plet*. Herausg. J. Koch. Heilbron 1879.

Robert de Blois. *Sämmtliche Werke*. Herausg. J. Ulrich. 3 vol. 1889–95.

Philippe de Navarre (= Novaro): *Les quatre âges de l'homme*. Ed. M. de Fréville. 1888. (SATF).

Li Livre dou Trésor de Brunetto Latini. (1) Ed. P. Chabaille. Paris 1863.

(2) Édition critique par F. J. Carmody. Berkeley, 1948.

Le Lai d'Aristote de Henri d'Andéli. Publ. par Maurice Delbouille. Paris 1951.

CHAPTER III

LYRIC POETRY

'L'amour', says M. Gustave Cohen (forgetting Dido, Pyramus and Thisbe, Hero and Leander amongst others) 'est une grande découverte du Moyen-Age' and he adds that the formula needed for this discovery was 'la rencontre de la mystique chrétienne et de la rêverie celtique sur le sol élu de la France'.[1] On reading these words we think inevitably of Tristan and Iseult, of the lays of Marie de France, of the romances of Chrétien de Troyes—but there is very little of the 'mystique chrétienne' about the love episodes in any of these works, and even the 'rêverie celtique' is not much in evidence. Indeed, we are reduced to the third element—'le sol élu de la France'—in most of these romantic works, and still more is this the case when we come to consider the amazing outburst of lyric poems which flooded France and spread thence over most of Western Europe in the twelfth and thirteenth centuries.

If the 'how' this movement originated is difficult to determine with any certainty, fortunately we are on safer ground as to the 'when' and the 'where' of its first appearance in Europe. The author of the earliest known lyrics in a modern language is known to us from documents. Guillaume, comte de Poitiers and duc d'Aquitaine, was born in 1071 and died in 1127. He inherited a large estate and a learned tradition from his grandfather Guillaume V who had had personal relationships with the learned Fulbert de Chartres. His grandson seems to have struck everyone by his ability to write light verses (*nugas*) and his irresponsible attitude towards women and love. From his place of origin we should have expected Guillaume to have written in a language common to the northern parts of France, but it is noticeable that all his poems are composed in a more southern dialect, in fact, in the dialect of 'Le Limousin' which during the Middle Ages gave its name to the language we now speak of as 'Provençal'. This is, perhaps, not surprising in Guillaume as Le Limousin formed part of his domains and it is more than possible that a certain lightness of character drew him naturally towards the south rather than towards the didactic north. But the interesting thing is that 'limousin' (*lemosi*) was the name given to the literary language of the poets who for nearly two centuries

[1] See *La Grande Charte du Moyen-Age*. New York, 1943. P. 106.

composed and sang the kind of poems which we know as the
poetry of the troubadours.

The fact that Guillaume de Poitiers is the first in date of the
troubadours known to us and is, to that extent, the initiator of a
new 'genre' of poetry renders it imperative to look rather more
carefully than we should otherwise have done (since this does not
pretend to be a history of Provençal literature) into the nature of
his literary output. This is not great, for only eleven poems can be
attributed to him with any certainty. Of these the majority are of
a flippant character, by an author to whom Ovid's works were
obviously familiar, whether in translation or in the original it would
be hard to say—quite possibly the latter, as it is clear that Guillaume
was of a nature to which the *Ars Amatoria* would appeal, for he was
a professional love-maker. Just as Ovid, describing himself, tells us
that 'Naso magister erat' because he was so 'doctus' in the art,[1] so
Guillaume calls himself 'maiestre certa' because he is so 'enseignatz'
in matters of love that he could advise anyone who needed instruction in the subject.[2] Many details in Guillaume's poems clearly
point to the influence of Ovid. His metaphor of the two horses (his
two lady-loves) of different temperament in Chanson III, is borrowed from the same source; his insistence on the futility of
depriving a woman of what she wants because she will soon find
a substitute, since even a sick man, if not allowed to drink wine,
would drink water rather than die of thirst ... 'Non begues enanz
de l'aiga que.s laisses morir de sei?' (VII, 3) comes straight from
Ovid.[3] So, too, his protest against keeping a woman guarded in
captivity reflects the attitude of Ovid who tells us that the husband
who objects to his wife's freedom 'rusticus est nimium'. Thus we
see that the protagonists are the same in Ovid as in the troubadour
poetry—husband, lover, wife—the first of whom (often referred to
in Provençal poems as *molheratz* = '*mulieratus*') has no right to
usurp the prerogatives of the sophisticated lover (*fin amant*). Moreover, the husband is often away and again it is Ovid who puts the
question 'Quid faciat puella? ... Vir abest et adest non rusticus
hospes' (Ars. Am. II, 369). The terms *urbanus* and *rusticus* only have
to be transposed into *courtois* and *vilain* and we are projected into
the twelfth century with its social prejudices. And these persisted,
even when the influence of Ovid, the cynical instructor in the profession of love-making, had waned, or at least been mellowed by

---

[1] *Ars Amatoria* II, 744; III, 812.   [2] *Chanson* VI. Ed. A. Jeanroy. 1913. p. 13.
[3] 'Sic interdictis imminet aeger aquis etc.' *Amores*, Bk. II.

other elements of a less crude description. For many of the ideas persisted and what Ovid had dictated to the lover (partly in jest, no doubt) became axiomatic to the troubadours. The well-known attitude of the male to the female in the so-called 'nouvelle conception de l'amour' is adumbrated in the Latin poet. It is the man who is to beg: 'Vir verba precantia dicat', and the lady who is to listen graciously to his prayers (loc. cit. I, 707 f.). Nor is it undignified (*rusticus*) for the lover to shed tears—and if they will not flow at will (as they will not always), he may touch his eyes with his moistened hand[1] (l. 659). But the courting must be strictly clandestine—not one's nearest relations or dearest friends are to be trusted (*Cognatum, fratremque cave carumque sodalem*)—a sentiment echoed by Bernart de Ventadorn (Guillaume's contemporary in the early years of the twelfth century) in the words:

> El mon tant bon ami non ai
> Fraire ne cozin ni parent
> Qu'ins en mon cor no l'azire . . .

and the wrath he feels in his heart is due to the fact that he fears to lose his love or to hear a rumour which would make him die of grief. It was, indeed, only natural that part of the game of love-making should consist in hiding ('celer') one's advances. It is well-known that this necessity of concealing the object of one's illicit love gave rise to the custom even in the earliest provençal poems of attributing a fanciful apellation to the fair one addressed (cf. the *bon vezins* of Guillaume de Poitiers, etc.).

Fortunately there is another side to the poetry of the troubadours, otherwise it would never have become the force that it did in moulding the taste of the twelfth and thirteenth centuries in France and initiating a great poetic movement in almost every country of Europe. Guillaume tells us frankly that his poems are the work of a skilled artisan who excels at his job ('Qui en port d'ayselh mestier la flor') and turns out of his workshop (*obrador* VI, 3) poems which are beyond criticism. So he appears to have learnt his trade from earlier poets. But even in Guillaume's somewhat artificial work there is something that breaks through and seems to herald a new era. There is a breath of spring, not only in the literal sense, in some of his poems which begin by hailing 'la dolchor del temps novel' (X, 1 and others). There is the suggestion of some incomparable 'joy' which a man would have to live a hundred years before he

---

[1] The author of the Old French adaptation of Ovid known as the *Clef d'Amour* improves on this: 'Et se tu ne pues avoir lermes / Tu poras un oignon tenir / Qui tantôt les fera venir.'

could possess. This *joy de s'amor* is inseparable from the lady in whom it is vested and both she and it possess miraculous powers:

> Per son joy pot malautz sanar,
> E per sa ira sas morir
> E savis hom enfolezir
> E belhs hom sa beutat mudar
> E-l plus cortes vilanejar
> E totz vilas encortezir (IX, v).

Here in Guillaume we are confronted already with the mysterious 'joie d'amour' which permeated the poetry of the Provençal poets and spread from them northwards and southwards and finally inspired the writers of the flood of sonnets that inundated Europe in the fifteenth and sixteenth centuries. Much has been written on the subject of this 'amour courtois', this 'nouvelle conception de l'amour' which characterizes the poetry of both the north and south of France in the twelfth century—which had such an ennobling effect on those concerned with it. For it was soon promoted to being a source of valour, a necessary equipment for the courtly knight, in fact, a lever by which both lover and loved one rose to almost a pinnacle of perfection. On the lover's side it must be humble, pure (though this does not preclude the sensual element), devoted, an incentive to noble actions—'quar domna fai valer ades / Los devalens' (Gu. de Cabestan). On the lady's side it must be gracious, generous and loyal—always subject to the insuperable necessity of not over-stepping the limit of *cortesia*. In fact, the lady must 'garder mesure' or she will not be worthy of the adoration of her courtly lover ('fin amant'). *Mesure* and *courtoisie* are the two qualities which raise the lovers (*les fins amanz*) above the common ruck of humanity and, if maintained, save them from ever sinking to a lower level. This exaltation is a thing unknown to the vulgar crowd and it must not become known or it would become cheap. Hence the intentional obscurity known as the 'trobar clus' which was practised by the poets in order that their pleasures should not be shared by the unworthy for it was only destined for the *élite*. Not that all the singers were of noble birth or belonged by rights to the chosen few. Guillaume was a 'grand seigneur' it is true, and, as this 'gaia scienza' developed, kings, princes, counts and nobles joined in the game. But Marcabrun, one of the nearest in point of time to Guillaume, was the son of a poor woman (perhaps it was the consciousness of his low birth that made him so disgruntled) and Bernart de Ventadorn, who composed some delightful songs—

according to Gaston Paris the only ones that make any appeal to us now—was 'de paubra generation, fils d'un sirven . . . qu'escaudava lo for por cozer lo pan del castel de Ventadorn'. It is true the *Biographies*, composed some half-century after the poets wrote, are not to be relied upon, but in facts such as these there is no reason to distrust them. It is when they invent a charming little story about a 'princesse lointaine' based on the poems the author had composed —as they did in the case of Jaufre Rudel—that they are not to be trusted.

The unreality of this kind of poetry, fostered by the artificial life at the courts and castles where it mainly flourished, carried the seeds of decay in itself. It became a mere mental exercise like a crossword puzzle. The search for the 'rime riche', the obscure or equivocal word, the almost algebraic patterns of rhymes must have made it incomprehensible to the average person of those days just as it largely is to us now. And yet Arnaut Daniel, the most 'obscure' perhaps of all, was the most admired by the connoisseurs of his time and—as is well known—considered by Dante to be the flower of the poets who composed in the 'langue d'oc'. Although for the moment we are occupied with the lyric poetry of our period, it may be mentioned here that it would be quite impossible to explain much of what developed in other branches of French literature without this brief account of 'amour courtois' and its accompanying exponent the 'fin amant'. For the idea of the courtly lover and his attitude towards his lady runs all through the romances of Chrétien de Troyes, the *Tristan* of Thomas, the 'lais' of Marie de France, and many a romance of the twelfth and thirteenth centuries. After Tristan and Iseult perhaps Lancelot and Guinevere were the most celebrated exponents of it. Even in the prose romances of the thirteenth century Lancelot could be pardoned almost anything for the correctness in his manner of love-making, and Guinevere and the 'demoisele d'Escalote' both equally insist on the necessity of secrecy in love.—'Car . . . amors descouverte ne puet pas en grant pris monter'.[1] And yet these later romances are shot through with religious and mystical elements. Whence then came this religious yet irreligious, this moral yet immoral conception of the relations of the sexes and the meaning of the central elusive idea 'la joie d'amour'. Many explanations have been attempted. Influence of Ovid, influence of feudal ideas, influence of a religious cult, whether of the Virgin Mary or the Goddess Cybele. Of late a serious attempt

---

[1] *La Mort de Roi Artu*. Ed. Frappier, p. 22.

has been made to demonstrate the influence of Arabic poets and Arabic forms on the contents and forms of the earliest troubadours through the medium of Spain. Little has been left to the originality of the first unknown poets in the vulgar tongue who may have preceded Guillaume de Poitiers. For already in Guillaume we have the feudal idea of service, the anonymity of the lady owing to the necessity of secrecy, the reference to the new season and the song of the birds, all of which features became almost stereotyped in the works of his followers, a fact which is often alleged to prove that Guillaume was not the first poet of his kind but had predecessors in the art—that the new ideas and conceptions were already in the air, though perhaps still in a vague, mysterious way. Probably no one definite source will ever be found to account for this mysterious growth. Many strands may have combined and been interwoven to produce the remarkable tapestry composed of individual poets of both the north and south of France and we may never be in a position to disentangle them. The surprising thing is that this particular type of highly artificial yet sentimental love-lyric was no passing fashion. At the end of the twelfth century the poet Pierre Vidal was singing of spring and birds, of his loyal service as 'la lei de fin amador' and how he would be gayer than a bird (*plus gais que l'auzel*) if his lady would give him 'un dous bais novel ... per amor'. At the end of the thirteenth century the stream had by no means run dry although the sentiments had become clichés and the expressions stereotyped and banal. Even so it trickled on and was destined to widen out again after a time in a different form.

It was in the second half of the twelfth century that the *chanson d'amour* of the provençal type became popular in Northern France. The poems of the group of poets known as 'l'école provençalisante' differed only in language from those produced further south. The poet Conon de Béthune, a distinguished nobleman and diplomat, wrote verses in the regulation style. It would be 'orgeus et hardimens fiers' if he were to reveal his sentiments to the 'mellor ki soit née'. Ill-luck has pursued him, but her beauty sweetens his pain and even were he to die of unrequited love, death would be sweet. He concludes with the *envoi* (addressed to an unknown friend):

> Noblet, je sui fins amans
> Si aime la millor eslite
> Dont onques cançons fut dite

'Fine amor' reigns supreme but, alas, the 'felon mesdisant' are about, spying on the lovers as another French poet, the Châtelain de Coucy, knew to his cost. The Châtelain was the 'beau ideal' of the perfect lover amongst the poets of the north. His name became so famous and his history so legendary that many songs have been attributed to him in manuscripts which undoubtedly were by other authors. He does manage to bring a little bit of variety and warmth into the well-worn themes and the story of his fate added to his popularity which was great amongst his contemporaries. Eventually he achieved the celebrity of being one of the noted lovers of the Middle Ages: 'Li chastelain de Coucy ama tant / qu'ainz por amor nus nen ot dolor graindre', writes an unknown author at the end of the thirteenth century. Another (Eustache li paintres de Reims) mentions him with other famous lovers:

> Onques Tristans n'ama de tel maniere,
> Li Chastelains ne Blondiaus autresi
> Con ie faz vos, tres douce dame chiere.

This last passage is interesting because it links together (leaving the arch-lover Tristan on one side) Blondel de Nesle and the Châtelain. Now the well-known legend attributes to Blondel the finding and ultimate rescuing of Richard Cœur de Lion from his imprisonment in Austria, which took place in 1193—this would therefore place both our poets at the end of the twelfth century. In any case it proves that the Châtelain and Blondel were looked upon as types of constant lovers. One of the Châtelain's poems in which he proclaims his constancy tells us in the two last lines of the first strophe:

> Tuit mi penser sont a ma douche amie
> Puis ke je sai mon cuer en sa baillie.
> (Ed. Fritz Fath. No. XII, 1.)

This last line possibly gave rise to the legend of the eaten heart which is attached to his name. The Provençal version of this legend, which crops up in most of the medieval literatures, occurs in one of the biographies where it is attributed to Guillem de Cabestanh. The lover, having been betrayed by a 'lauzengier', is killed by the incensed and jealous husband who 'trais li lo cor del cors'. The heart was roasted and given to the lady, who unwittingly ate and enjoyed it. On learning the horrible truth she went out on to the balcony 'et se laisset cazer ios e fon morta'. This unpleasant story is found in Italian, in Spanish, but (chiefly) in German literature, where it was filled out into a little romance (*Das Herzmære*) by Konrad von Würzburg. The earliest and the most widespread version is that which connects the tragic story with the name of the Châtelain de Coucy and doubtless it added much to his popularity, for he rapidly became a hero of romance. A less rarified atmosphere, however, soon made itself felt in the north, where the vogue for these highly stylized poems was of much shorter duration. The professional French minstrel does not live up to the high level of the princely poets of the south. Conditions were probably both harder and less artificial. Colin Muset (first half of thirteenth century) is quite capable of writing rather charming little love songs in which he tells us he cannot live 'senz joie'; that he will serve his lady 'senz dangier' for he is her 'hom liges'. He still suffers the pains of love so badly that he will probably die of love—but he will at least die 'amoureusement'. But there is a different quality in Colin's work. He is obviously the wandering minstrel, the professional, the parasite—always on the look out for the most liberal patron. We learn in a rather pathetic little poem of the reception he gets on his return home in the evening if he comes with an empty sack. If, however, he is hiding a 'sac enflé' behind him, his wife leaves her distaff and comes with smiling face to put her arms round his neck (ed. J. Bédier, XII). This is a theme we shall find later in the less sophisticated poetry of Rutebuef, but it is interesting to note how the material outlook goes hand in hand with the sublime. This was, in fact bound to be the case as the movement spread amongst other classes of society. Kings and counts and nobles do not need to beg for their bread. But the penurious minstrel or jongleur, who was entirely dependent on the generosity of those he entertained, must have often been in despair for a warm cloak or a meal. It was a humiliating position especially where a genuine poet is concerned. In Germany, where the imitation of French forms reached a height of perfection not perhaps achieved elsewhere, the same conditions prevailed. It will be remembered that Walther von der Vogelweide jubilates over the granting of a *lehn* in a poem quite as realistic as those of Colin Muset.

In the north of France the pure love-lyric never took very deep root and was more or less limited to the region of Champagne and neighbouring lands. This fact was recognized by Provençal writers who realized that the strength of the *parladura francesa* (as contrasted with the *parladura lemosina*) lay rather in a more objective attitude to love and a less purely lyrical form. For all through the twelfth century French authors had been busy on somewhat different lines and the form of poetry introduced from the Midi did not by any means find a *tabula rasa* in the north. In a romance of the first half of the thirteenth century we have some instructive allusions to songs and poems which were in fashion at the time the romance was composed. *Le Roman de la Violette* may be taken as an example of a type of romance into which lyrical passages were introduced in order presumably to relieve the monotony of a long poem in octosyllabic verse. The author, Gerbert de Montreuil, is describing the entertainment of the guests at a social gathering. Now Gerbert was composing for an aristocratic audience—he was probably a wandering minstrel with a powerful protectress, for he tells us that the 'contesse de Pontiu' will repay him liberally for his pains:

> Que ma dame est de si halt pris
> Que bien me rendra mon serviche (ll. 62-3).

In the course of his poem he gives us examples of many *chançons* which were evidently familiar to his hearers. On one occasion he makes his hero sing a song the refrain of which is taken up and sung by the other guests:

> Gerars cante, si com moi samble,
> Ceste chançon par devant tous,
> Dont clers et haus estoit li tons.
> Et chascuns d'iaus respondu a:
> 'Ensi va ki bien aime, ensi va' (ll. 715 f.).

In spite of the artificial nature of the whole romance there seems no reason to doubt that refrains of this nature were thus taken up by the audience and used in the nature of a chorus. There were many of these 'wandering refrains' tacked on to the *chansons-de-carole* or dancing songs which were in vogue at the time. The author of *Le Roman de la Rose* or *Guillaume de Dole* gives us five different versions of the opening lines of one of these *chansons-de-carole* which itself is in the nature of a refrain and was extremely popular at the end of the twelfth century. The heroine of this couplet was the notorious Bele Aalis (var. Aelis) who must have been as well known as the Biaus Robins. The song to which the refrain perhaps originally belonged has not come down to us. In fact all we actually know is that 'la bele Aaliz' got up early in the morning and washed herself. This is related in different metres:

1. Decasyllabic: 'Main se leva la bien faite Aëliz.'
2. Octosyllabic: 'Main se leva bele Aëliz.'
3. Seven syllables: 'Main se leva Aälis.'

All these forms occur in *Guillaume de Dole*, but the theme of 'la bele

E

Aelis' was developed and used by others. Her attention to her toilet is always stressed:

> Main se leva la bien fete Aëlis:
> bel se para et plus bel se vesti;
> si prist de l'aigue en un doré basin,
> lave sa bouche et sus oex et son vis;
> si s'en entra la bele en un gardin.

There are obviously great possibilities for embroidering on such a theme. All these variations leave us in no doubt as to the popularity of 'la bele Aalis'. In fact a preacher of the thirteenth century took the first couplet as the text of an allegory in honour of the Virgin![1] But Jaques de Vitry in an 'exemplum' of about the same date uses her vanity as a warning to women who 'magnam diei partem in apparatu suo consumunt'.[2]

Now there were many of these wandering refrains besides that of 'la bele Aaliz' which were attached to (or intercalated in) the dancing songs of the twelfth century and probably earlier. Some of them could be construed to mean something (e.g. *Nuls ne doit lez le bois aler | sanz sa compaignete*:); some expressed the conventional motif of the 'mal-mariée' or the ill-assorted couple; (*Dame qui a mal mari | La bele blonde a li m'otroi*; *s'el fet ami | n'en fet pas a blasmer*); some were more purely seductive, like that of the young lady in the *Lai d'Aristote*: 'Or la voi, la voi, la voi,' |; some consisted of amusical notation such as: 'Laderala duriax duron / Laderala duriax durete' (with which we might compare the English refrain of a generation ago: *Tarara boom deay*, etc.) or an even simpler marking of time: 'dodo/dodo/dodo/dodo/dodo/dodelle'. In one sense they were, of course, 'popular'. But the word 'popular' has two meanings and the appellation 'the people' is hard to define. These *chansons-de-carole* were not restricted to any one class—hence they spread rapidly far and wide. The dances might be a favourite amusement at court and castle whilst still remaining a confirmed habit amongst the heterogeneous gatherings at the May-day celebrations in the open air. For it is in these latter that the *chansons de danse* or *caroles* probably had their origin. As Gaston Paris has pointed out, the *fêtes-de-mai* were of ancient, probably pagan origin and a certain amount of licence undoubtedly marked these celebrations. It was, moreover, the spring season and the time when the minds of young men and women 'lightly turn to thoughts of love'. Even the married women were infected by the joyous season and the conventional theme of

---

[1] Le Coy de la Marche: *La Chaire française au XIIIe siècle.*
[2] *Exempla ex sermonibus vulgaribus* CCLXXIII.

the *mal-mariée* was introduced for which we should look in vain in earlier Germanic or Classical literature. But on the 'sol de France' it flourished like the green bay tree and the unfortunate husband cut but a sorry figure. We have seen this already in the more cultured court literature of the *troubadours*, but now it is the *trouvères* who are displaying their art. Shepherds and shepherdesses have become *à la mode* and occupy the forefront of the scene. Their humble status does not necessarily betoken the popular origin of the *pastourelles* and similar dramatic poems (for they are often little dramas which play themselves out in lyric form). This quasi-rustic literature early became a *jeu d'esprit* for aristocratic audiences, even if really 'popular' dancing songs had preceded them which seems more than likely. Actually two of the earliest known pastourelles are in the provençal dialect. They are due to Marcabrun, whom we have already mentioned as almost contemporary with Guillaume de Poitiers. One of these *pastoretas*, as they were called in the south, is in the form of a debate (a type well known in medieval Latin poetry) between a very prudent 'pastora' and the poet. The shepherdess rejects the cavalier's advances because of the difference in rank, ending up with the wise words:

> en tal loc fai sens fraitura (= good sense goes bankrupt),
> on hom non garda mezura,
> so ditz la gens ansiayna.

We have seen that in the courtly tradition *mezura* and *cortesia* went hand in hand; the antithesis of 'vilain' and 'courtois' runs all through the poem and it is obvious that here in Marcabrun we have a stylized form of poem indigenous probably to the region in which it existed. But it is noteworthy that this form of poem did not flourish in the south. The objective, more epic character appealed to the poets of the north where by the end of the twelfth century a large crop of lyrico-epic poems of the pastoral type had already sprung up. They remained long in favour, even returning to a limited extent to their native soil. Many of these *pastourelles* are quite charming. They are gay and humorous in spite of a certain sophistication and often succeed in producing an illusion of rusticity. Here are shepherds with their pipes and other musical instruments, alfresco meals, rustic games and dances, not to speak of disputes and sometimes scuffles. The real hero and heroine of these adroit little poems are the stock characters Robin and Marion, whose unknown early adventures (like those of 'la bele Aalis') provided one of the most popular refrains: 'Robin m'aime / Robin m'a / Robin m'a demandee / Si m'ara'. All the shepherds and shepherdesses are slightly burlesque in character, but Robin is the outstanding figure of fun. He is loyal for the most part, though unreliable at times; he is boastful and vain of his rustic feats, but a coward when a wolf threatens the flock or when he is not supported by an admiring group of friends. There is, in fact, a diminutive *geste de Robin* and the possibilities of a drama based on his character were perceived and skilfully used by the author Adam de la Halle in the thirteenth century. He found his way to the south, for Robin (though a French name) appears in later provençal poems when the fashion for the *pastoreta* revived there with an intensified aristocratic tinge. There can be no doubt as to the clerical, almost 'savant' character, of this type as we know it. M. Faral has pointed out that a pastoral poem existed in Latin and Virgil's *Bucolics* present plenty of analogies with the old French *genre*. This may explain the rather intriguing statement in the Provençal biography of Cercamon, to the effect that the poet 'trobet vers e pastoretas *a la usanza antiga*'. But an element of mystery surrounds the birth of this prolific crop of poems just as it does the origin of many another type.

The *pastourelle* had little really in common with the highly artistic and artificial forms which flourished further south. It is true that all, or most, celebrate the arrival of spring and the joys or sorrows of love, but there the similarity ends. Moreover, leaving on one side the limited number of what may be described as *chansons de malmariée*, the heroine in the *pastourelle* is as a rule an unmarried girl who is enjoying the spring weather quite harmlessly with her rustic friends. The aristocratic element is introduced from without, sometimes by the wandering cavalier, sometimes by the poet himself. This innate simplicity of plot and the lyrico-epic character of the *pastourelle* brings us quite naturally to the consideration of another type of poem which may have preceded it in date, although the few specimens we possess do not give us much to go on and dating is notoriously difficult. There is, however, a simplicity of form in the poems we are about to examine which would seem to indicate an early development. In the above-mentioned *Roman de la Violete* we have an interesting example of this type. The hero of the poem, Gerart, who is searching for his lost lady-love, hears a young woman singing a ditty which reminds him of his lady. The girl is sewing and as she sews she sings 'ceste chançon à toile': *Siet soi*, etc. There are several points of interest in this strophe—the only one of a lost poem. Obviously it is a *plainte de femme* which may have been the original theme of many of the love-poems. The personages are named, and it is the lady here who does not dare to address her lover; she is suffering from the ordinary pangs of unfulfilled longing —she can neither eat, drink, nor sleep. The form is of the simplest— four decasyllabic lines with the pause after the sixth syllable, all joined by the same rhyme and followed by a brief refrain. The other dozen or so poems of this type, which evidently went by the name of *chansons-à-toile* (or *chansons-de-toile* as they are now called), follow the same simple pattern which, one would like to think, points to a more primitive origin than that of the society poems in mock-peasant garb. The verse-form is that of the *chansons-de-geste*, the strophe monorime with the pause usually after the fourth syllable, in some cases assonance replaces the rhyme:

1. Bele Aiglentine / en royal chamberine
   devant sa dame / cousoit une chemise
   ainc n'en sot mot / quant bone amor l'atise.
   Or orrez ja
   comment la bele Aiglentine esploita.

   .   .   .

2. Devant sa dame / cousoit et si tailloit;
   mes ne coust mie / si com coudre soloit;
   El s'entroublie / si se point en son doit
   la soe mere / mout tost s'en apercoit.

There is a naturalness about these little poems which makes them perhaps the most attractive of the lyrical output in northern France. The heroine is a *jeune fille* (in most cases) and her melancholy is shown either by her absent-mindedness ('she forgets what she is doing and pricks her finger') or her tears for the absent one. Some-times there is a happy ending as in this poem and *Bele Erembor— Lors recomencent lor premieres amors*' (Bartsch I, 35). But it is rare in this type of poetry. We do not hear of the 'losengier' and his evil ways, but the mother is at times the obstacle, for she keeps a watchful eye on her daughter's behaviour:

   Mere, de coi me chastoiez?
   est ceo de coudre ou de taillier,
   ou de filer ou de broissier?
   ou se c'est de trop somillier?
      Chastoi vos en, bele Yolanz

Ne de coudre ne de taillier
ne de filer ne de broissier,
ne ceo n'est de trop somillier,
mais trop parlez au chevalier.
Chastoi vos en, bele Yolanz.

The name (*chanson de toile*) is apt for these short lyrico-epic poems—
for the maiden is generally described as busy with her needle,
though she is sometimes reading a book. This may point to a certain
religious influence as several of them are in the nature of a *plainte*
and the Virgin Mary was generally depicted, both in art and
literature, as either reading the *Psalter* or otherwise 'muliebriter
operans'. It is noticeable, too, that to the end of the eleventh or the
beginning of the twelfth century belongs a poem which was inspired
by the *Song of Solomon*. It is somewhat similar in form as it employs
the decasyllabic line in rhyming couplets, each couplet being
followed by a short four-syllable refrain. It is introduced by an
astronomical detail instead of a description of spring which indicates
its more clerical character, but as a 'plainte de femme', regretting
her absent friend and being interrogated by the poet, it bears a
striking resemblance to some of those *chansons de toile*.

Quant li solleiz / converset en Leon
En icel tens / qu / est *orbus Pliadon*,
　　Per un(t) matin,
Une pucelle odi(t) molt gent plorer
Et son ami dolcement regreter,
　　Et si lli dis
'Gentils pucelle, molt t'ai odit plorer
Et tun ami dolcement regreter
　　Et chi est illi'?

Then follows the maiden's lament for her *ami* who is 'de tel parage /
Que neüls on n'en seit conter lignage', with descriptions largely
drawn from the *Cantique des Cantiques* of which it is a paraphrase.
Nor are the watchmen (*les escalgaites chi gardent la cité*) omitted, and
thus another link appears between the ancient Hebrew love-poem
and the French medieval love-lyric which in its simplest form
exhales the plaintive lament for an absent lover. The watchman
(*la gaite*) became a stock-figure in a group of poems generally known
as *chansons d'aube* in which the lovers who have been together all
night are warned, either by a bird or a well-disposed watchman
that dawn is at hand and the lover must depart. But this brings us
back to the more courtly, artificial type of poetry which for the
moment we had left. The *aube*, or *alba*, belonged more to the

rarified atmosphere of the courts, whereas the *chansons de toile* were destined rather for the same sort of audiences that enjoyed the *chansons-de-geste*—neither exclusively courtly and aristocratic, nor exclusively popular and plebeian, but 'broadly aristocratic and in the best sense popular'.[1] The *aube*, like the *pastourelle*, became a court-pastime, but one likes to think there was a strain of something primitive in these poems too and that the 'folk-song' is not a complete snare and delusion. Some of the refrains might justifiably be attributed to a genuinely popular origin and not the least the charming little *aube* in refrain form:

> il n'est mie jors,
> Saverouze au cors gent,
> si m'aït amors,
> l'alouette nos mant.

But whatever the origin they were soon incorporated into the more sophisticated types. The 'alouette' of the poem just quoted would be replaced by the watchman and the *dramatis personæ* became stylized—like the jealous husband, the mother, the lover, or the spy. The *alba*, or *tagelied*, became popular in Germany where a song of the *minnesinger* Dietmar von Eist (or the pseudo D. von E.) gives us a sample of what was possibly the most primitive idea in this attractive form of poem which is at bottom merely a song of separation—the lament of the woman for the departing or departed lover:

> Slafest du, friedel ziere?
> man wecket uns leider schiere:
> ein vogellin sô wol getan
> daz ist der linden au daz zwî gegân.

The last verse is illuminating:

> Die frouwe begunde weinen
> 'du rîtest und lâst mich einen.'
> Wenne wilt du wider her zuo mir?
> Owê du füerest mîn fröide sament dir. (M.F. 39.17.)

Whether the bird or the watchman was the original friend (or foe) in this imagined situation of the two lovers passing the night together it is hard to say. It is the unsympathetic watchman who plays a part in the *Cantique des Cantiques*, that earliest of love songs. In the Old French, or more particularly in the poems of southern France, where the role of the watchman may not have been purely imaginary, he became a stereotyped figure only too soon. But,

---

[1] Margaret F. Richey, *Essays on the Mediaeval German Love Lyric*, 1943.

whichever way it was, the fundamental idea of the poem remains the same—it is a *lament*, often in a touching strain, of the woman who fears she may never see her lover again. This, under all the variations of detail, remains the central theme. Though not in the form of a 'separation at dawn' like the *tage-lied* we have just quoted, the little poem attributed in one manuscript to 'La Dame de Fael'[1] (though it is probably by the poet Guyot de Dijon) gives us in poignant words the grief of the woman whose husband (or lover) is setting out on a risky 'pèlerinage' to fight against the 'felon . . . Sarrazin'. Why does God allow such things? she asks:

> Sire Dex, por quei feïs?
> Quant l'uns a l'autre atalente
> Por coi nos as departis?

The stanzas are simple in form; the seven-syllabled lines follow the rhyme-scheme *ababab* and are separated by a four-lined refrain. The ideas are less stereotyped than in many of the love-poems and the effect is pleasing:

> Et quant la douce ore vente
> Qui vient de cel douz païs
> Ou cil est qui m'atalente
> Volentiers i tor mon vis;
> Adont m'est vis que jel sente
> Par desoz mon mantel gris.

It is true that the same sentiment occurs in a song of Bernart de Ventadorn ('Quant la douss' aura venta / Deves vostre païs / Vejaire m'es qu'en senta / Un ven de Paradis'), and that Guillaume d'Orange similarly enjoys the sweet breeze blowing from his own land (*Charroi de Nîmes*—Ms.D.), but the idea has not become stereotyped and the little French 'chant de départ' stands out amongst many others on account of its charming simplicity and the complete absence of any of the artificial features and stock phrases which mark so many poems of the period.

We have tried, at the risk of slightly confusing the types, to give some of the fundamental, underlying ideas which infuse so much of this almost rank growth of love poetry in France of the twelfth and thirteenth centuries. There are, of course, other types and forms, e.g. the *rotruenge* (of uncertain origin) and the *serventois* (mostly political) which must be left aside in a brief survey like the present. But there is one offshoot which is so closely connected with the

---

[1] Paul Meyer: *Recueil des plus anciens textes.* Vol. I, No. 41.

main stem that its importance cannot be overlooked. The dramatic quality of many of the poems has been mentioned, and the give and take in conversation or argument appears in most poems which are not expressly in monologue form. As the movement flowed on its course a definite type of 'debate' emerged which had a considerable vogue in northern France. Poems in the form of a *débat* or *jeu-parti* or *tençon* were the almost inevitable result of the dialectic contained in much of the artificial poetry dedicated to love in its varied aspects. The *jeu-parti* is, in fact, a rather specialized form of the wider group of 'debates' on the subject of love (*questiones amoris*) which formed the main theme of the *De Amore* of Andreas Capellanus written in the beginning of the thirteenth century. The *De Amore* was translated twice into French during this century. It treats of a number of subtle questions on love ('questions dilemmatiques') which we meet again in the poems we are about to examine. Decadence had already begun to set in, and this 'casuistique amoureuse' is, perhaps, the clearest proof of it. It was admittedly a form of game (*jeu*) which in Provence existed already under the name of *joc-partit* or *partenaire*. But it was in the north, and particularly in Picardy, that it mainly flourished, and its most vigorous growth was in the second half of the thirteenth century. If, however, the identification of one of the partners of the *jeu-parti* No. II in the *Recueil* published by Jeanroy and Brandin (S.A.T.F., 1926) be correct, one at least would date from the early part of the century. The dispute is between the 'partenaire' Gasse (who may or may not be the poet Gace Brulé, † circ. 1180) and some one he addresses as 'Sire'. This 'dilemma' may be taken as more or less typical whoever the authors may be. 'Le Sire' poses the question 'Ought I to continue to love the one who betrays me or give her up?' To which Gasse replies: 'Continue to love her.' Each then gives his opinion. Gasse (or Gace), who represents the perfect lover (*fin amant*) holds that 'Si finement de cuer l'amez / et loyal sont vostre desir / Ni a noient del repentir'. In other words, you must stick to her through thick and thin. To this 'Le Sire' replies that Gace is quite mad (*desvex*) and wants to make a fool of him, for anyone who has endured the pains of love obviously ought to enjoy its delights:

> Vilainement me confortez
> Quant j'en ai les maulz endurez
> Dont deveroie bien joïr.

Evidently the exacting rules of love were beginning to be found somewhat oppressive, and this is not surprising when one considers the gradual change in society which took place in the thirteenth century. A rich *bourgeoisie* was not likely to be so romantic or so 'refined' in character as the knightly *habitués* of the courts and castles or the minstrels who were hangers-on of these courts and truckled to the taste of their noble patrons. It is true that we find a *conte de Bretagne* among the composers of *jeux-partis* and that king Thibaut de Navarre took quite a conspicuous part in the disputes. But three-quarters of the poems of this kind known to us were composed by members of the poetic school of Arras—the Artesian poets, of whom Jean Bretel, the most prolific, and Adam de la Halle, an eminent member, were good citizens of that town without any claim to aristocratic birth. Moreover, a certain tendency to parody which belonged to a poetry of a lower level began to make itself felt. For example, the question is propounded whether, for a fortune, the disputant would be prepared to renounce for ever his favourite dish—*pois au lard*. He replies that nothing would induce him to give up the peas. He loves them 'de cuer verai' and this gives him confidence that no harm will happen to him as long as he does not forget them. No grief can gain possession of his heart so long as he sees them before him on the table. Then he sings aloud for joy:

> Tel joie ai quant on les pile
> Que j'en chant a haute voie. (Recueil cxxxviii)

The satire is obvious and it is clear that the movement, once the pastime of the rich, with its extravagancies and artificialities, has declined from its high estate.

The form of the *jeu-parti* is practically the same as that of the 'chant d'amour'. Without going into detail, which would be beyond the scope of this book, a few words must be said about this form which, by the time the movement had spread to the north of France, was pretty well fixed. Except for the earliest Provençal poets (e.g. Guillaume de Poitiers, who uses an almost classical long line), most of the composers adopted a stereotyped form of verse the origin of which is not known. The poem generally consists of five stanzas (though the number may be increased to six or seven), each stanza being grouped into a tripartite scheme by the rhymes. The two first pairs of lines, consisting of eight, seven, or even six syllables, have, as a rule, either the rhyme-scheme *ab, ab*, or simply *a, a, a, a*. Then comes the change. The third part of the scheme may be introduced by a short line, or may consist of two or three lines, possibly of greater length, but in any case with a different arrangement of rhymes. The poem generally concludes with a short 'envoi' in the form of a recommendation or salutation addressed to the recipient. This tripartite form of verse was rigorously enforced in Germany where the first two groups (*Stollen*) form the 'aufgesang', whereas the third group composes the 'abgesang'. Eventually this arrangement became the basis of the sonnet which developed in Italy during the next centuries. The rhyme schemes became more and more complicated in order to prevent plagiarism, or even copying of a form of verse which was considered most dishonourable. The language had to be pure, that is, the literary language of the courts which gradually developed into a kind of fixed norm of speech. The passage in Conon de Béthune in which he bitterly reproaches the queen ('La reine n'a pas fait que cortoise,...') and her son (Philippe Auguste) for having laughed at his slightly dialectal form of speech is well known (Chanson III). The literary language which developed in the north, as apart from the south, is clear and limpid as a rule. The same cannot always be said of the Provençal (or *lemosi*), especially when the author deliberately made it complicated and obscure in order to confuse the 'vulgar' and limit the understanding of the poem to the chosen few for whom it was meant. Even these did not always understand it, and it is fortunate that the *trobar clus* never found exponents among the poets of the north. It is interesting to note that, as Mr. Robin Flower has told us, a kind of aristocracy of letters in Ireland in the fourteenth and fifteenth centuries practised this same kind of obscurity in order to keep undesirable elements out of the bardic schools which were open only to descendants of poets. Thus history repeats itself.

BIBLIOGRAPHY

Les Chansons de Guillaume IX, duc d'Aquitaine. Ed. par Alfred Jeanroy. Paris 1927. (CFMA).

La Clef d'Amors. Ed. par A. Doutrepont. Halle 1890. (Bibl. Norm. V.)

Les Chansons de Conon de Béthune. Ed. A. Wallensköld. Paris 1921. (CFMA).

Le Châtelain de Coucy. (1) *Die Lieder des C. de C.* F. Fath. Heidelberg 1883.
(2) *Chansons du C. de C.* Ed. Fr. Michel. Paris 1830.

Le Comte de Bretagne. *Les Chansons du C. de B.* Mélanges Jeanroy. 1928.

Colin Muset. *Les Chansons de C.M.* Ed. Jean Beck. Paris 1912. (CFMA).

Le Roman de la Violete, par Gerbert de Montreuil, Publ. par D. Labaree Buffum. Paris 1928. (SATF).

Le Roman de la Rose ou de Guillaume de Dole. Publ. par G. Servois. Paris 1893. (SATF).

Les Chansons de Toile. K. Bartsch. Altfranzösische Romanzen u Pastourellen. Leipzig 1870.
  For form and use of refrains, dating, etc., cf.:
  H. Spanke. *Eine altfr. Liedersammlung.* Halle 1925.

Le Cantique des Cantiques. Koschwitz u. Förster: Altfr. Uebungsbuch. 7th ed. par A. Hilka. 1932.

La Dame de Fael. P. Meyer: Recueil d'anciens textes. No. 41.
  J. Bédier: Chansons de Croisades, p. 105.

Lais et descorts français du XIIIᵉ siècle publ. par A. Jeanroy, L. Brandin et P. Aubry. Paris 1901.

CHAPTER IV

THE ROMANTIC EPIC, OR ROMAN COURTOIS

PART I. MATIÈRE DE ROME

WHILST the troubadours of Southern France were busy with their *trobar clus* and their lyrical variations on a semi-mystical theme, poets in the north were engaged on a less rarified form of invention, perhaps better suited to their more robust nature. The languishing poet of the south might use subtle means and make tremendous mental efforts to obtain the favour of the lady of his choice who had a power over his destiny, as great as that of Fortune's wheel. But his more active opposite number in the north would have to prove his worth in more tangible ways. He must win his lady's favour by deeds as well as words—he must seek fame (*querre los et pris*) and prove his worth (*se feire valoir*) by the sword as well as by the pen, before his addresses to the fair one can be accepted. It was the combination of valour (*prouesse*) and perfect love (*fine amour*) which produced the conception of 'chevalerie' by which the Middle Ages were dominated. The physical strength and courage of a Roland or a Raoul, with its accompanying quality of excess (*desmesure*) gave way gradually before the more refined, one might say more aristocratic, ideal which gradually evolved during the second half of the twelfth century when feminine influence was making itself felt at the courts and castles of the nobility. A new conception of love and its power over men and women gradually assumed very great importance and before the end of the century had completely carried all before it. It is true that Guillaume d'Orange, according to a very old tradition, had shown a susceptibility for feminine attractions and had actually wooed and won and carried off the heathen King Thibaut's wife (Orable—later Guibourg). But Guillaume's robust method of wooing and his all-too-human quality of forgetfulness[1] were not such as to captivate the minds of the poets of this new era with its new fastidious tastes and ideals. In the early years of the century the two streams represented by the novel conception of love (which had started tentatively in the south of France) on the one hand, and the valour of the crusading knights

---

[1] Cf. *Couronnement de Louis*, l. 1433. *Trestot aveit entroblié Orable.*

on the other, were running more or less parallel. About the middle of the century they merged into one big stream and the result was epoch-making.

It is obvious that the account of the lover's progress towards the perfection henceforward required in a chivalrous wooer needed a longer form of poem to deal with all the training and testing that a youth had to undergo before he could emerge as a 'chevalier sans peur et sans reproche'. It was therefore inevitable that the purely subjective lyrical poem should be partially replaced by a more narrative form of composition which could combine the love-motif with the descriptions of combats undertaken by the hero and loved by the audience. The French always excelled in narrative literature and the success achieved by an elaborate treatment of love-episodes interspersed by combats and sensational adventures was immediate. Both in France and French-speaking England a crop of romances, epic in length but romantic in substance, sprang up in the second half of the twelfth and the first half of the thirteenth century. They are mostly of a courtly, aristocratic nature (*romans courtois*), but many are a mere stringing together of adventures (*romans d'aventure*), though the similarity in form and contents between these types is so great that it is futile to try and draw a sharp dividing line between them. It was about this time (middle of the twelfth century) that another influence began to make itself strongly felt and to affect still further the nature of the themes treated by the poets of the time. Classical influence is but slight in the *chansons-de-geste* even though Virgil and Lucan, with their epic form and patriotic ideals, carried out by great-hearted heroes, may have hovered at the back of the minds of poets trained in the average school curriculum. But of direct imitation of the classics by the French poets of the early part of the century there is little. But now the great Latin love-poet seems quite suddenly to have swum into their ken. Ovid's poems, hitherto known only to the few, began to be available to the many through translations and adaptations. Chrétien de Troyes, writing about 1170, tells us that a translation of the 'commandemenz Ovide' was amongst his earlier works besides versions of some of the 'Meta-morphoses' and other such adaptations must have existed. The stories of Dido and Medea were probably well known from tradi-tion, and now they were invested with a new interest by becoming figures in which the new love-emotions could be developed. Ovid's description of the emaciated lover who tosses about in bed and cannot sleep was taken perfectly seriously and many a medieval lover (e.g. Amadas in *Amadas et Ydoine*) was sick almost unto death. For the age of 'sensibility' has arrived and the 'roman sentimental' has become the fashion. In fact, in twelfth-century France we assist at the birth of the modern novel and the excess of emotion described is no more exaggerated in the poems of that time than it has been in romances of many a later period in France and elsewhere.

With the revolution in taste went quite naturally a change in the characters described in the works illustrating that taste. The heroes of the *chansons-de-geste* appeal to us by their naturalness, their outspokenness and their lack of subtlety—often accompanied, alas, by a lack of restraint. How often their tragic fate is, directly or indirectly, due to some rash act or some foolish vow characteristic of an ardent youthful spirit. Roland, Vivien, Raoul de Cambrai—all illustrate this. But that hero is now replaced by a polished, courtier-like young man, not deficient in courage but too conscious of what is due to his birth, his reputation and his deserts—in other words, something of a prig (cf. the hero of *Ipomedon*). The lady, too, unlike the impulsive, natural heroine of the 'chansons-de-toile', or the devoted wife of the *Chanson de Guillaume*, becomes a coy damsel, or a proud inaccessible lady determined to prove her lover to the utmost. And this is the change we find accomplished in three romances based on classical legends which form, in a sense, the connecting link between the old school and the new, between epic and romance—the *Roman de Thèbes*, the *Roman d'Enéas* and the *Roman de Troie*.

The *Roman de Thèbes*, which is probably the earliest in date of these three poems, is based on the *Thebaid* of Statius (whom the French author calls Estache) and tells the grim story of the 'Seven against Thebes'. The author is well versed in classical material—he knows Ovid well, but he knows his native literature too, for there is much that recalls the *chansons-de-geste*, particularly the *Roland* whose heroes he mentions on several occasions. The accounts of the single combats are quite in the style of the earlier epics. The weapons are the same and the author unblushingly clothes and arms his Greek heroes according to French standards. The battles are no mere tournaments—the combatants are in desperate earnest; and yet there is a difference. The knights, even whilst fighting for their cause, want the ladies to see their prowess. They hope that no peace will be made before many saddles have been emptied—'si que le veient les puceles' (l. 4152). The young knight Ator, who is described as 'flor de chevalerie', fights with his lady's sleeve on his lance. Ipomedon is well instructed in *chevalerie*. Parthenopé sends his victim's horse to Antigone declaring it is for her he has 'fait chevalerie' and she promises him a 'gent guerredon'. When the king pardons a young man for the sake of a lady friend, a cynical knight remarks:

> ... Issi vait d'amie,
> D'amor et de chevalerie,
> Si vos (referring to the other knights) le tenez a folie
> Il (the King) le tient a grant corteisie (ll. 8545 ff.).

Still more clearly does the contrast between the old and the new conventions come out in the love episode between the beautiful Antigone and her whirlwind lover, Parthenopé. When the warrior, on seeing the lady for the first time, suggests that she should become his 'amie' we read:

> 'Por Dieu', çorespond la pucele,
> 'Ceste amor seroit trop isnele,
> ... Ne dei amer par legerie,
> Dont l'on puisse dire folie,
> Ensi deit on preier bergieres
> Ou ces autres femmes legieres' (ll. 3921 ff.).

When Parthenopé presses his suit with the comforting assurance that he is a 'reis de grant tenue' she weakens, but (with almost Victorian propriety) replies:

> 'Parlez en' (fait ele) o ma mere
> Et par le conseil de men frere' (ll. 3945–6).

These may be small points but they indicate a fundamental change in convention which already breaks through in the *Roman de Thèbes*. Henceforth the heroes and heroines had to conform to a regular code of behaviour—and even to a conventional type of beauty which is prescribed in detail in many works of the period. M. Faral has made us familiar with the instructions given for these descriptions in the various 'arts poétiques' which enjoyed a vogue in the Middle Ages and became part of the stock-in-trade of the author of a 'long poem'. Nor were such descriptions limited to the subject of personal beauty. The art of 'descriptio' was soon elaborated and extended in its use, to fill out the dimensions of the romance which had to reach a recognized and respectable length like the three-volume novel of the nineteenth century. Such descriptions were not unknown in earlier works. That of Alexander in the fragmentary poem of that name (generally assigned to the early years of the century) gives in brief pattern the description of male beauty developed in many a later poem. In the *Pèlerinage de Charlemagne* we find a description of mechanical devices which forestalls in some details those of a later date. But the elaboration and exaggeration of these descriptions, used as a 'retarding motif', became an almost indispensable element in the interminable romances which tax our patience now to read and which must have been wearisome to write, even when composed at the behest of a distinguished patron or patroness. The chariot of the prophet Amphiaras in the *Roman de Thèbes* ('en un curre ert Amphiaras / Qui fu faiz outre Saint Thomas') is an example of a description of a marvellous work of art. It is ornamented with representations of the sun and moon, the planets, the firmament (all done 'par enchantement' as the author tells us), the earth, the sea; it depicts the battle of the giants, the seven arts ('gramaire i est peinte o ses parz...') and statues making music to one another as in the *Pèlerinage*. The tent of Adrastus is just as wonderful—painted with marvellous scenes, including a 'mappa-mundi' with its five zones, its kings and its seventy-two languages, its seas and its seasons—with particular mention of the kings of Greece, their histories, their prowess and their battles. It must indeed have been a work of art—as the author assures us:

> 'Mapamonde fu si grant chose,
> Qui l'esgarde pas ne repose' (ll. 4021-2).

Many of the details of these descriptions may have come direct from Ovid; others reflect the stories of wonderful things seen and related by crusaders returning from the East. But they do bear witness to that awakening of interest in an outside world, that thirst for novelty and a widening of experience which marks this second half of a century which gave birth to so much that was to grow' and mature as time went on. The form of these long romances was also something of an innovation. In the *chansons-de-geste* the decasyllabic line had (with a few notable exceptions) reigned supreme. In the romances it is replaced by the rhyming octosyllabic couplets which became almost as much 'de rigueur' as the assonancing groups of the earlier poems. The result is often very tedious, especially when the author indulges in tricks of repetition (as in the *Roman de Thèbes*) and in ready-made expressions to convey certain stock ideas. There was, perhaps, enough of new in these descriptions of strange creations and strange creatures to lure the reader on; but something more than this was needed. Their great attraction, the great hold they soon obtained over a public hungry for novelty, was

F

undoubtedly due to a more human kind of description, namely the description of incipient love, which now began to be added to the other attractions.

Le Roman de Thèbes, which was probably composed about the year 1156, is the earliest important example extant of the group of poems dealing with subjects classified loosely by the jongleurs themselves as 'matière de Rome'. The author does not name himself but opens his poem with the stock phrase of the 'jongleur' that he who knows a good thing should not conceal it ('Qui sages est nel deit celer'). But even in the dedication a new thought creeps in. When a phrase similar to the one quoted was used in earlier pious poems, the author's object was to edify his hearers. Now he writes for his own glory:

> Ainz por ço deit son sen monstrer
> Que, quant serra del siecle alez
> En seit pues toz jors remembrez (ll. 2–4).

Pride of authorship has begun to develop and from henceforth many a poem will have its authorship declared which in former days would have remained anonymous. And the author of *Thèbes*, even though nameless, has a claim to be remembered for he has written a well-ordered poem, pure as regards rhymes, filled with exciting episodes and fantastic descriptions—and not without humour. For when the old men, put to shame by the young knights, form a corps of veterans on their own, he remarks:

> Atant estes vos les enfanz,
> Li plus tendres ot passé cent anz ! (ll. 4673–4).

He ends, however, on a serious note for, when summing up and lamenting the sad end of his heroes, he remarks:

> Por ço vos di: 'Prenez en cure.
> Par dreit errez et par mesure.
> Ne faciez rien contre nature,
> Que ne vengiez a fin si dure' (ll. 10227–30).

Whether the *Roman de Thèbes* was based on the original poem or not, something of the spirit of the original has been preserved. The same cannot be said of the second poem of this classical trilogy—the *Roman d'Enéas*—which was probably composed not many years after the first. In the *Enéas* the author (also unknown to us by name) gives full rein to his imagination for it can only be called a travesty of the original. It has been said that the *Enéas* succeeded in combining Virgil and Ovid. At any rate the author succeeded in killing

the one and launching the other, for after the *Enéas* Virgil falls out
of the picture and Ovid reigns supreme in literary circles. Although
Virgil is not mentioned in the French poem it is clear from internal
evidence that the author has gone straight to the source for there
are many almost literal renderings of the original.[1] There is no
excuse, therefore, for the way in which he has handled his theme.
The beauty of the human touches in Virgil seem to have escaped him
altogether, and the characters have become commonplace. As an
example of this we might take the episode of Aeneas' visit to King
Evander in Book VIII. This episode in Virgil is full of homely,
attractive details. Evander is poor, but he is dignified in his poverty.
With delightful courtesy he beguiles the journey to the city with
interesting talk; he introduces Aeneas to his humble abode with the
noble words: 'Aude, hospes, contemnere opes, etc.' (ll. 364 ff.).
All this the translator has passed by unheeding, even the simple fare
offered by the impecunious king has became a lavish feast:

> Ne sai conte dire des mes
> Qui sovent vindrent et espes.
> Ne de bons vins et des herbez,
> Mais il an orent tuit asez (ll. 4778 ff.).

The same contrast is to be found in the manner in which the
episode of Nisus and Eurialus (Bk. IX) is treated. Without going
into detail it is no exaggeration to say that the pathos and beauty of
the passage has been completely suppressed and only the bare bones
of the story are left behind. What then, we naturally ask, has the
author added to make up for such omissions? Long descriptions,
after the style of those we have seen in the *Roman de Thèbes* (from
which he has borrowed the seven gates he gives to Carthage) were
clearly his favourite device for giving his poem the desired length
and filling out the gaps. Descriptions of palaces, of temples, of the
Capitol with its whispering gallery ('ja ni parlast hom tant an bas /
ne fust oïz eneslepas / par tot le Capitoille entor' (ll. 537-9);
of strange fish, of Camilla's horse, of the tomb of Pallas—all these
were fully in accord with the taste of the time. But the greatest
effort to please the popular taste was probably put forward by the
poet in his descriptions of amorous sentiments—of incipient love
with all its doubts and fears, of the pangs of unrequited love, in fact,
of every phase and variety of the lovers' feelings and sensibilities.

---

[1] He has sometimes mistaken the text, for 'pendent opera interrupta' (IV, 38) has been
rendered: 'pendent li mur antre-rompu'. See the author's *Enéas and the Aeneid*, Mod. Lang.
Review, t. xxix, 1935.

All this part of the poem may be called unadulterated Ovid, for the *Ars Amatoria* breaks through in almost every line. Mercifully this is not so fully developed in the Dido episode (which, as regards Aeneas, at any rate, would not fit at all into the conception of 'fine amour'). But a completely new episode is devoted to the nascent love (hardly touched on in Virgil) between Aeneas and Lavinia and we have the unedifying spectacle of the middle-aged widower Aeneas tossing about in bed, weeping and beseeching the god of Love to let him off easy:

> La nuit veillot et ert an plor
> E apelot lo deu d'amor
> E priot li molt humblement
> qu'il nel menast si aigrement (ll. 9923-6).

But it is Lavinia who suffers the sharpest pangs of love. She is suddenly wounded by Cupid's dart after having just declared to her mother that she has no use for love ('ge n'en ai cure'). It all happened unexpectedly as she stood at the window watching the Trojans pass. Hence the long monologues, the imaginary conversations with Love, the sleepless nights followed by colloquies with a more experienced mother and finally the stammering confession that it is not Turnus she loves (as her mother supposes), but Aeneas for whom she has so hopelessly fallen:

> 'Donc n'a nom Turnus tes amis?
> Nenil, dame, gel vos plevis.
> E comant donc?—Il a non "*E*"
> puis soupira, se redist: "*né*"
> d'iluec a pieçe noma: "*as*,"
> tot en tremblant lo dist en bas.
> La reïne se porpensa
> et les sillabes assanbla.
> Tu me diz '*E*' puis '*ne*' et '*as*'
> ces lettres sonent "*Eneas*" (ll. 8551-60).

It all sounds rather foolish to us now, but it was just this treatment of the so-called 'nouvelle conception de l'amour' in the *roman courtois* which constituted its charm to the twelfth-century hearer or reader. The romances of Chrétien abound in long monologues (e.g. *Cligès*), reasoned conversations between lovers and their confidantes (e.g. *Yvain*), composed with extraordinary skill and psychological insight. But it is rather depressing to see Virgil treated in this way.

Once again it is the insistence on the power of love which dominates the third poem of this trilogy—the *Roman de Troie*—a monumental work of over 30,000 lines. This power has, to a certain extent, replaced the power of death so often described in the earlier, more pious poems. For love reduces the stoutest warriors and the proudest women to a state of ignominious weakness—it knows neither sense nor moderation ('sens ne mesure') for it attacks both sexes and all ages. Here, however, we must note one great limitation to its onslaughts, for it only strikes those of noble birth. It is something which the 'vilain' cannot understand, for we move in the somewhat narrow circle of the 'roman courtois' whose characters had to fulfil certain conditions of birth and behaviour. Benoît de Ste. More, the author of the *Roman de Troie*, fulfilled all the conditions imposed upon him by his ambience. He has dedicated his work to a 'riche dame de riche rei' whom he endows with all the courtly virtues. This was undoubtedly the notorious lady Eleanor of Poitou who, after being divorced by the king of France, married the English Henry Plantagenet, duke of Normandy and count of Anjou, who became king of England in 1154. The poem was probably written to command and, one imagines, was well paid—otherwise we can hardly believe its 30,000 lines would ever have been completed. Benoît opens with the stock phrase that a good thing should not be hidden ('Salemon nos enseigne et dit / E si list om en sen escrit / Que nus ne deit son sen celer', etc.) and then launches straight into his story of the fall of Troy. Benoît bases his story, not on the account of Homer (who, as he tells us, could not have been present at the battle), but on two Latin works alleged to be translations of Greek journals kept by eyewitnesses of the events they described. One of these, Dictys of Crete, fought on the side of the Greeks, whereas the other, Dares the Phrygian, was on the Trojan side. Benoît's sympathies are with the Trojan cause—not unnaturally as the current theory all through the Middle Ages (and, indeed, up to the sixteenth century) was that the Franks were the direct descendants of the Trojans. Here, as in the two former romances we have been treating, there are many battle scenes and descriptions of single combats according to the rules of 'chevalerie' which were now codified. There are other descriptions too—of garments, of palaces, of people—only slightly less long drawn-out than those in the *Roman de Thèbes*. On the other hand there are endless conversations, arguments and moral reflections—even on the battlefield. But the outstanding feature of this lengthy poem is the space allotted to love scenes—for there are three great love episodes

here as against two in the *Enéas* and one in *Thèbes*. The truces
between the battles are filled out with these love episodes. There is
the one between Jason and Medea in which the impatient waiting
and the passionate outpourings of Medea are skilfully portrayed.
There is the one between Achilles and Polyxena in which the strong
ruthless Achilles is 'destreiz par fine amor' (l. 17547) and the author
feels obliged to apologize for his irresolute behaviour by the fact
that, if he is doing wrong, he cannot help it:

> Se il mesfait, qu'en puet il mais,
> Quant cil le *tout* sen e mesure (= tolt = takes away).
> Qui ne garde lei ne dreiture,
> Noblesce, honesté ne parage?
> Qui est qui vers Amors est sage? (ll. 18444 ff.).

But the most subtle of the three amorous episodes is one which we
find for the first time in this poem, namely the love-story of Troilus
and Briseida, which inspired later poets in other lands. The change
in a woman's feelings as she transfers her affections from one lover
to another is most skilfully described. Briseida had been so happy
with the Trojan Troilus ('entre eus n'a ire ne orguieuz') until the
Greeks demanded her return to the army in exchange for a hostage,
and the handsome Greek Diomede was sent to fetch her. She
departed from Troy amidst universal grief, in which she joined for
she had good manners ('quar n'est pas vilaine'), but the author tells
us slyly that she put on her costliest garments. These included a
beautiful robe made of shot silk (which an Indian poet, friend of her
father's, had sent from his country), and a cloak lined with a
marvellous material woven from the pelt of a fabulous animal from
the land of the Cenocefali. This is already a little ominous and very
soon comes a forecasting of events:

> Mais si la danzele ist iriée
> Par tens resera apaisiée;
> Son duel aura tost oblié
> E son corage si mué
> Que poi li iert de ceus de Troie (ll. 13429 ff.).

Then come the author's reflections on the mutability of women's
vows in which he embroiders on Virgil's remark: 'Varium et
mutabile semper femina' (*Aen.* IV, 569–70)—so cruel as applied to
Dido, but so true in this case. Women's grief is short-lived, says
Benoît, and not to be trusted:

> A feme dure dueus petit;
> A l'un ueil plort a l'autre rit.
> Mout muent tost li lor corage.

Any man who trusts them is a fool, for they forget in a day what they have loved for seven years, and they are so self-opinionated that they will never admit they have done wrong ('ja jor ne cuideront mesfeire'). And so we see the anti-feminine feeling, never far in the background in these medieval romances, peeping through quite clearly. Yet Benoît does not take a too harsh view of Briseida's behaviour, for he puts it all down to this invincible power of love against which nothing can stand. It is *Amors* which 'vaint tout et tout vaintra / Tant com cis siecles durera', and which is to blame for everything. Perhaps the example of his patroness who, after being divorced from the French king had married his enemy, had something to do with his tolerance. We are reminded of Chrétien's excuses for Laudine (in the romance of *Yvain*) in which he shows little inclination to condemn her for marrying the slayer of her husband. After all, if even Aristotle, in the *Lai* from which the above-quoted words are taken, was not proof against the all-conquering power of love, how could a poor weak woman be expected to be?

The three poems in the preceding section which treat of classical themes form a kind of group amongst themselves, but many compositions followed with a classical tinge, even if it is only some evocative names for their heroes or heroines which give the illusion of a distant, classical origin. The latter is the case with a poem generally called after its hero *Ipomedon*, in which all the names, including that of the hero, are drawn from the *Roman de Thèbes*. There are many other borrowings also from the romances we have been studying and the author shows a limited degree of originality. *Ipomedon* was probably composed about 1170 when the love-fever was at its height. But if not original, the author at least produces a finished piece of work, conforming rigidly to the rules of such poems and carrying the theme of 'fine amour' to a point of refinement not reached perhaps in any other poem. The story is of the young knight Ipomedon (whose prototype was praised for his 'chevalerie' in the *Roman de Thèbes*), who fulfilled in every detail the code of instructions laid down for love-making in the approved style. The hero sets out to win the hand of a 'belle dame sans merci' who goes by the name of 'la fiere' and who has made a vow to wed no one who does not conform to her standard of valour. Ipomedon gains access to her 'entourage' by a series of perfectly honourable deceptions and the proud one falls a hopeless victim against her will to his charms. There are innumerable contests and tournaments according to the code of chivalry of the time. Neither knows of the other's love, for concealment (*celer*) is a rule of the game. Hence many laments and soliloquies, interspersed (on the lady's side) with confidences to her maid. Here are the rapid dialogues—the form of stychomuthia brought to perfection by Chrétien; here again is the cunning device (obviously borrowed from the *Roman d'Enéas*) of the lover's name disclosed syllable after syllable by the stammering tongue of the love-sick lady. In this case the syllables are separated by a long drawn-out sigh which makes up the desired number of three: 'vas-*ha*-let', in which the intelligent maid recognizes the tell-tale form of the word *Vaslet* and so is let into her mistress's secret. *Ipomedon* does not break any fresh ground; it is conventional in thought and correct in form. It is a panegyric of 'amor fine' which reduces its victims 'de si haut si bas' and against which 'sens et raison' are powerless. It moves in aristocratic circles for the power of perfect love is greatest among the great: 'mult a grant valur amur fine / Ki seit danter rei et reïne' ... (9093 ff.). But the author has a good stock of 'proverbes au vilain' and wise saws which he brings out with good effect, and many are his reflections on the ways of women. The descriptions of combats are stereotyped and the character of the young man who sets out to become a 'chevalier eslit' and 'pris et los porchacier' is not a particularly attractive one. But the author writes well, has a sense of humour,[1] and has produced a work which is an almost perfect example of the refined taste of his time both in France and England where it enjoyed considerable popularity. The author was probably either an Englishman or a Frenchman living in England. He tells us his name ('Hue de Rotelande dit' ...) and place of origin—Credehulle, which was probably in the neighbourhood of Hereford. He wrote between 1170 and 1190 and claims that his work was translated from the Latin, but this is very unlikely and the statement was only made to give a certain *cachet* to his work. He is not out to edify but to prove to all and sundry that no one—neither knight nor learned clerk— ever 'amast cum fist Ipomedon'.

For another work of similar type but less perfect in form Hue de Rotelande again borrows his hero's name, and much more besides, from the 'romans antiques'. *Prothesilaus* is, in fact, composed of a certain number of borrowings from other works—elements of various kinds are mingled in a disparate mass and there is a profusion of narratives and descriptions. It is superior to *Ipomedon* only by

---

[1] 'Li oil lur lerment de trop rire', he tells us on one occasion (l. 7809).

reason of its length, for it boasts 12,741 lines as against the 10,578 of the latter poem. Prothesilaus need not detain us here, but another romance with classical flavour deserves mention even though its connection with the 'matière de Rome' is only a loose one.

The romance of *Heraclius* (or *Éracle*) takes us to New Rome or Byzantium. It derives a certain importance from the fact that Gautier d'Arras, the author, was a contemporary of Chrétien de Troyes and that his 'roman' may even have preceded those of Chrétien. His patron, to whom he alludes in very flattering terms, was Thibaud of Blois, brother-in-law to the lady who commandeered the story of Lancelot from Chrétien and one of the two sons-in-law of the renowned Eleanor of Poitou. It is noticeable that, though a native of Arras, he speaks very good, literary French. The poem *Heraclius* is a proper three-volume novel. Part I tells how Heraclius, as a little boy, was sold by his mother (with a ticket round his neck like a calf) to pay for the salvation of her husband's soul. He had, however, been so well taught when quite young that he was a 'connoisseur' (*conissiere*, l. 273) of three things—precious stones, horses, and women.[1] The skill thus acquired brought him promotion in the household of the Emperor of Byzantium, for whom he procured a suitable wife—the beautiful and chaste Athenais, a namesake of the historical wife of Theodosius II. Part II tells us how the emperor, against the advice of Heraclius, shut his wife up in a tower when he went away on a campaign, with the result that Athenais, bored to death, fell in love with a handsome young man who serenaded her with great persistence. By a ruse, not unlike that described in one of the stories of the *Seven Sages of Rome*, Athenais and her lover came together. Through the divination of Heraclius the emperor learned of his wife's unfaithfulness, returned to his city, and the pair were banished. Had it not been for the intercession of Heraclius, who told the emperor that it was all due to his own folly, the couple would have been put to death. Nearly all this second part is composed of dreary soliloquies and imaginary conversations on the inevitable subject of love. These gain a certain importance, however, from the relatively early date of the poem and there are one or two variations of the theme which strike an original and fresh note. When the emperor asks Athenais indignantly if she still loves her lover even after his (her husband's)

---

[1] Krumbacher, in his *Geschichte der byzantinischen Literatur* (p. 807), mentions the Greek story of an old slave (Ptocholeon) who had this threefold knowledge of horses, stones and people.

return, she replies quite simply: how could it be otherwise considering the way she had loved him:

> Sachiez que *finement* l'amai,
> Quant vous pour soie amour faussai;
> Et cil qui aime *finement*
> N'en puist partir legierement.
> Ne s'en part mie quant il vueut
> Cil qui de *fine* amour se dueut (ll. 4954 ff.).

In the case of Athenais and her lover concealment was, of course, necessary—as, indeed, it was in most of these examples of 'fine amour'—but once again Athenais gives the reason for concealment quite convincingly when she reminds us that stolen pleasures are sweet as only the true lover knows:

> Ne set nus hom qui n'est amis
> Com par est douce l'assemblée
> De deus amanz si a emblée (ll. 4615-7).

In Part II we see that 'fine amour' is already firmly enthroned in this early 'roman d'aventure'; in Part III we are back again in the atmosphere of the *chansons-de-geste*. This is not necessarily a proof that Gautier's poem was anterior to the romances of Chrétien and may have influenced his work, for the older form of epic was still cultivated and enjoyed in the second half of the twelfth century. Part III tells how Heraclius was made emperor of Constantinople; how, at the bidding of an angel, he rescued part of the holy Cross which the king of Persia, Cosdroés, had stolen from Jerusalem; how in order to do this he marched into Persia with an army and defeated the king's son in a single combat, thus avoiding much bloodshed. In the course of the duel Heraclius tries hard to convert his opponent to Christianity (... 'Paiens / car devien pour Deu crestiens / si crois en Deu, le fil Marie', 5776 ff.) much in the same manner that Charlemagne tried to convert Baligant in the *Chanson de Roland*, or Roland his youthful opponent Fernagu in the *Pseudo-Turpin*. But Heraclius himself has a lesson to learn, for, when he returns to Jerusalem expecting to enter as a conqueror, he finds the walls mysteriously closed against him and it is not until he has thrown off his regal garments and donned a hair shirt and humbled himself to the dust that God performs an 'apert miracle' for his emperor and the walls open to let him into the city in the sight of all present (l. 6409). It will be seen that *Heraclius* (or *Li Romans d'Éracle*—to give it its French name) is composed of several 'éléments disparates', a characteristic which marks most of these longer romances and which is particularly noticeable in another poem of somewhat later date, viz., *Huon de Bordeaux* (cf. infra). But there is a pious, moral tone in *Le Roman d'Éracle* which makes the otherwise interesting poem tedious and commonplace and which is as a rule conspicuously lacking in the majority of 'romans courtois'.

Turning with relief from these long, often tedious romances, two shorter poems are conspicuous, which, although still celebrating the power of love, present at least some variety in their method of treatment. The first of these—*Pyrame et Tisbé*—is more lyrical in character in that it breaks up the customary octosyllabic rhyme-couplets by introducing short lines of two syllables or two short words either rounding off one group of lines or introducing another. This is skilfully carried out in long portions of the poem and is especially effective in the case of the frequent apostrophes so much loved by medieval writers. When Pyramus, for example, in the well-known episode of the hole in the wall, utters a long plaint against the hardness of his fate, he addresses the wall:

> Ha murs,
> Tant par estes espes et durs . . .

or again:

> Parois,
> aiez merci de ces destrois

or apostrophizing Death in the style of the didactic poems:

> He morz,
> Porquoi demora cest grant torz
> Que je ne sui orendroit morz?

This artifice gives a pleasant variation to the expressions of frustrated love which is sung in the conventional manner of the period with all its stylized expressions. The story is based entirely on Ovid and need not detain us. *Amors* is the great force against which neither 'sens ne raison' can stand (l. 622), and so these young things in whom Nature had created a masterpiece (l. 68) come to the same end—proving their loyalty and that they were 'de fin cuer amant' by the fact that neither wished to go to Paradise before the other.

There is a charm about this poem of *Pyrame et Tisbé* and a naïveté about some of their utterings which is lacking in many of the poems based on Ovid's works. In the *Lai de Narcisus*, for example, the artificial outpourings so heavily outweigh the romantic nature of the story that its charm is lost. Moreover, although based on Ovid the author has merely used it as a peg on which to hang his love-theories and has completely omitted the essence of the whole story. The episode of the echo and the metamorphosis of Danes has been omitted, as well as the change of Narcissus into a charming flower at the end. Instead of this we have the usual monologues and laments, replete with love-symptoms and sighs. Once again Nature put out her utmost skill in creating the beauty of the lovers (Nature i mist tote s'entente, l. 55)—and yet the youth had no idea of love or beauty until he saw his own face in the water. Danes, on the other hand, was smitten by Cupid's dart from the very beginning, so much so that, like Lavinia, she made the first advances—of which she was heartily ashamed afterwards. Her lamentations are stereotyped, except, perhaps, for one realistic touch. When tormented by sleeplessness she thinks, perhaps, her bed has been badly made:

> La coute ne fu pas meüe
> La plume n'est pas remuée
> Ançois est toute amoncelée (ll. 196 ff.).

So she sends for her maid and heaps abuses on her head for having been so remiss. Otherwise the languishing, the apostrophes, the customary flowers of speech are all present to such an extent that one is forced to the conclusion that the authors of these love-poems drew upon the same common stock of ideas and phrases and that there was a sort of freemasonry among them from which any reproach of plagiarism was excluded.

. . .

PART II. ROMANCES OF LOVE AND ADVENTURE WITH ORIENTAL COLOURING

So far we have dealt with works in which the heroes or heroines were either characters based on classical models or created in order to conform to classical ideals. But there are other romances in which the love of adventures for their own sake, the taste for Oriental splendour, for the fabulous and the miraculous are paramount. In this group the poems dealing with Alexander the Great really belong as, already by the second century A.D., he had become a legendary figure. A romantic biography, written in Greek by one who called himself Kallisthenes, was translated into Latin by a certain Julius Valerius in the fourth century. Other translations and imitations followed and were reinforced by a forged letter from

Alexander to Aristotle describing his adventures in India—so that by the time we come to the First Crusade, which aroused an interest in the East, the legend of Alexander and his wonderful doings was in full swing. Alexander himself had become in the popular imagination the outstanding type of a heroic king, chiefly noted for his generosity (O.F. *largesce*), which was the essential royal quality always insisted on by medieval poets. Henceforth Alexander ranked with Charlemagne and eventually with Arthur as a real king and leader of his people. But Alexander died young, and although this preserved him from the decline of prestige which marked the advancing years of Charles, his untimely end became a subject for rather hackneyed moralizations:

> Dit Salemon al premier pas
> Quant de son libre mot lo clas:
> 'Est vanitatum vanitas
> Et universa vanitas.'

These are the opening words of the first known poem in the vulgar tongue on the subject of Alexander—a poem of which only a fragment remains, but just enough to show the form and nature of the work. It is composed of octosyllabic lines grouped in *laisses* of varying length (six, eight or ten lines), bound together by assonance or rhyme and composed in a language of indeterminate nature—a kind of Franco-Provençal. We learn from a German translator that the author was a certain 'meister Elberîc', elsewhere called 'Elberîc von Besenzun', about whom nothing more is known. The poem has been dated as early as 1100, but without any definite proof. We may note the description of male beauty which is familiar from many descriptions in the *chansons-de-geste* (and which it is interesting to compare with that of Baligant in the *Chanson de Roland*):

> Clar ab lo vult beyn figurad,
> saur lo cabeyl recercelad.
> plen lo collet et colorad
> ample lo peyz et aformad.
> lo corps d'aval beyn enforcad
> lo poyn et bras avigurad.
> fer lo talent et apensad.

Clearly this was a stereotyped description—so, too, the instruction given him by the wise masters in rhetoric, music, etc., and it is regrettable that the *Fragment d'Alexandre* breaks off just before we can learn whether the line 'Parler a dames corteisement d'amor' which occurs in a French version of later date was in the original or not, as it would help us in dating the poem. The legend of Alexander became extremely popular. Besides the decasyllabic version just mentioned there was a continuation by Lambert le Tort who amplified the wonderful stories he found in the *Epistola Alexandri*, thus pandering to the prevalent taste for marvels. Other versions followed both in verse and prose by various authors, one of whom, Alexandre de Bernay, gave his name to the duo-decasyllabic lines in which it was written. These were followed by two poems of little literary value entitled respectively the *Vengement* and the *Vengeance Alexandre*, and further prose versions swelled the stream. But the point we wish to stress is that all these versions were pure *romans d'aventures*. There is practically nothing of love in them and nothing of religion. They are full of the wonders of distant lands. *Inde la majeure, Babylon, Persia, Carthage* have begun to capture the imagination and run the love-themes very close. The thrilling exploits of Alexander in the East and the marvellous beings he encountered fired the imagination to the exclusion of everything else, even of love.

Other poems, however, managed to combine the sentimental and the sensational which did not inevitably exclude one another—indeed, sometimes they enhanced one another. 'En Babiloine la cité / Furent dui ome renomé' had sung the author of *Pyrame et Tisbé*, and at once the attention was arrested. 'En Babiloine fu menée' the author tells us when relating the fate of the heroine of *Flore et Blancheflore*—a poem which enjoyed great popularity in France and elsewhere. Pyramus and Thisbe had ended tragically in accordance with the classical tradition, but at the end of the twelfth century and the beginning of the thirteenth a more romantic spirit reigned, and in most cases, after separations and terrible hardships the lovers were reunited. There is a general similarity between most of the poems. Love, Death, Fortune, are the deities invoked. In spite of the growing power of the Church, God is rarely mentioned except as the God who is on the side of the lovers, and Paradise does not weight the scales when balanced against the loved one. In fact, we are still in a more or less heathen atmosphere, the *aetas ovidiana* which followed on the more Homeric age of the heroic epic with its national heroes and its faith in God. The author of *Flore et Blancheflore* makes this quite clear although his subject is not a classical one. It is the story of two children (whose names give the title to the poem) brought up together, who at an early age read and wrote Latin and enjoyed heathen books on love:

> Livres lisoient paienors
> Ou ooient parler d'amors.

After describing their forcible separation by unfeeling parents the poem develops into a quest, for the heroine was spirited away to Babylon and her lover set out to find her. The search ended in a brief clandestine reunion which nearly ended disastrously. But so great was the charm of the pair ('Plus biaus ne fist onques Nature', l. 2776) that even the heart of the 'amiral de Babiloine' was melted and he ended by forgiving them and loading them with gifts. The author was clearly well-versed in current literature. He mentions the model lovers Paris de Troyes, Parthenopé, Ipomedon, Antigone, Ysmaine, all of whom he doubtless knew from the romances of *Thèbes* and *Troyes*, which poems he rivals in some of his descriptions of marvellous works of art. The account of the elaborate tomb erected to deceive Flore into thinking that Blancheflore was dead equals any description of wonders and mechanical devices in earlier poems and is even more fantastic. Fortunately this poem too, like some of the earlier ones, is not without its touch of humour, for Flore, who is hoisted up to the tower where Blancheflore is imprisoned, hidden in a basket of flowers, jumps out at the wrong moment and frightens another young woman nearly out of her senses. But for the most part, except for its extravagancies, the poem is intended to prove that, although 'the course of true love never did run smooth', all ends well if the lovers are but loyal to each other.

We are already some way removed from the fatalistic outlook of a Medea, a Dido, or even a Thisbe, but the power of love remains undiminished. A lighter, gayer element has crept in, and though we still hear of 'Amour qui tout vaint', yet in the same poem—*Aucassin et Nicolete*—we learn that God loves the lovers ('Dix ... qui les amans aime', XXVI, 12) and we know that a happy ending is in store. It is impossible to classify *Aucassin et Nicolete* for no other work quite like it has come down to us. It differs in form from most of the romances for it is partly in prose and partly in verse—short lines of seven syllables which have a gay ring but, if one can judge from the musical notation, were chanted to a rather monotonous melody. There is a dramatic element also in this *chante-fable*, for there is a great deal of quite animated conversation. As, however, there are never more than two interlocutors at the same time, it has been suggested that in all probability it was declaimed by one person. Sometimes one has the impression that it is a story told to children, for the conversation is so naïve and childlike that it makes us smile. The contents, however, do not altogether support this theory, and it is noticeable that the language (i.e. the prose) is extraordinarily like that of a quite sober chronicler of the thirteenth century, Robert de Clari. The story, like those we have been considering, is that of two very young people ('deus biaux enfans petis', I, 3) frustrated by parents whom, in turn, they elude. After many vicissitudes, including some surprising adventures, they eventually come together in happy union. The story is so well known that it is enough to point out one or two unusual elements in it. There is more than a hint of parody in the descriptions of combats, of the king lying in childbed and of his wife waging a war in which the opponents fight with cheeses, baked apples and mushrooms. There is a sympathetic description of a 'vilain' who is distressed at losing one of his oxen, not for his own sake, but for that of his old mother, who is lying sick 'on the straw itself' (*si gist a pur l'estrain*, XXIV, 58) because her miserable mattress has been dragged from under her to pay their debt; there is the pastoral scene with the shepherds, which hits off very nicely their irresponsible yet mercenary attitude towards their employers, and there is the tirade against paradise, where all the dirty and ragged old hermits and priests keep company with the lame and the sick whilst all the joyous folk go to hell. There is, moreover, the picture of the heroine (so much more energetic than her slightly spineless lover) roaming the lands 'a guise de jongleur' dyed dark with some herbal mixture and carrying her 'viele', in search of her lover. These pictures were not necessarily original—we have a similar description of a 'vilain' (though a much less sympathetic one) in Chrétien, there are ribald references to paradise in lyric poems, and there is a description of a maiden stained dark with herb juice and singing her way through strange lands in *Bueve de Hantone*. But no one can fail to be struck by the charming way these episodes are related in *Aucassin et Nicolete* whether they were sung or said: 'or se cante; or dient et content et fabloient'; or by the lyrical quality of some of the songs; or by the picture of Nicolete framed in the window looking at the blossoming rose and listening to the birds. The author, whether scholar or wandering minstrel, was a poet and an artist and, although only one copy of his work has come down to us, one can hardly think he was less appreciated in his own day than in ours. It gave rise to at least one imitation, a perusal of which serves to show what the somewhat hackneyed theme could become in the hands of a mere versifier. The *Chanson de Clarisse et Florent* relates how the daughter of Huon de Bordeaux (see infra) underwent a series of misfortunes similar to those of Nicolete and for the same reason. Many of the episodes and sometimes the actual words in which they are described (although the poem is in octosyllabic couplets) betray the hand of the imitator and the poem need not occupy us further except as yielding a proof of the public craving for exotic stories and adventures. For it was turned into a prose romance and printed several times together with Huon de Bordeaux and translated into English by Lord Berners in the first half of the sixteenth century.

Undoubtedly *Clarisse et Florent* owed some of its popularity, however, to the fact that it was a continuation of the justly popular romance: *Huon de Bordeaux*. This romantic epic dates from the early years of the thirteenth century. It is a worthy production wherewith to close this heterogeneous section. The tripartite character which we have noticed in other poems gives variety to this work also, for it combines epic, fairy tale and romance. It begins, almost like a *chanson-de-geste*, with a characteristic scene at Charlemagne's court in which the ageing emperor wishes to crown his feeble son. The stock characters of counsellor Naime and the disloyal traitor are present and into this milieu is introduced the gallant youth Huon who has had the misfortune inadvertently to kill the emperor's son on his way from Bordeaux to the court. As a penance for this crime (accidental though it was) he is sent by a vindictive emperor to the king of Babylon, from which Charles undoubtedly hoped he would never return. His instructions are threefold: (1) to kill the first knight he meets at the court, (2) to make love to the emperor's daughter by kissing her thrice, (3) to bring back a bunch of hairs from the emperor's beard and four large molar teeth. All these incredible feats he performs with the help of the fairy-king Auberon and his magic horn, hauberk and bowl. Much has been written about the Germanic myth of Alberich, both in ancient and modern German literature. He has been immortalized (under the more modern form of the name Oberon) by Wieland, by Shakespeare and by Weber. But what marks his character and endears him to us in *Huon de Bordeaux* is his humanity and his pathos rather than his magic qualities. He feels

G

bitterly the hardness of his fate, for it was a spiteful fairy who condemned him at his birth (like Peter Pan) never to grow into a full-sized man. In spite of his diminutive size (he is three feet high) he is fabulously beautiful ('biaux com le soleil') and has all the thoughts and feelings of a man. 'Je sui un hom comme un autres carnés', he says pathetically on one occasion. He has a deep affection for Huon (the origin of which is not explained in the poem) and feels it deeply when the latter brings misfortunes on himself through his own folly. For Huon, after a serious start, turns out to be a bit of an adventurer and acts frequently out of sheer bravado and quite against Auberon's orders. He is, as the author tells us, on several occasions 'de leger cuer', and so brings misfortune on himself and others, thus giving the author an excuse for introducing more hair-raising adventures. We know all the time, however, that with the help of Auberon's horn and hauberk all will come well in the end, that he will marry Esclarmonde and they will live happily ever after. There is relatively little of love, however, in the poem and the idea of 'fine amour' is conspicuously absent. It would not have conformed at all to Huon's hasty temperament. But it is impossible to give in a few words any idea of the wealth of adventure, the fierce battles in which even the horses take part, the mysterious happenings such as portents and omens, and more than all of the psychological interest of the poem. The author was well acquainted with literature in the vulgar tongue—he refers at length to the story of Ogier le Danois whose son was killed (by Charlot, the emperor's son) at a game of chess; to Tristan and Iseult, to Oliver and Roland and to the traitor Macaire. He even makes a rather obscure reference to Charlemagne's secret sin of which we hear in the legend of St. Gilles. But he remains quite original and, although we might like to cut down his poem by a third (the latter part is purely a concession to popular taste) yet the other two-thirds have outstanding merits and the poem repays a close study. Auberon, 'le petit ome', is an unforgettable figure, with his loyalty, his hatred of lying and his readiness to forgive—ignoring the imperfections of others in his anxiety to relieve them from the difficulties those very imperfections had caused. He brings a moral element rather surprisingly into the poem, as no one can drink out of his magic bowl unless he has made his peace with God—a different version of the *Lai du Cor*. Huon, although light and unreliable, is able to pass the test because he had visited Rome and made full confession to the pope. Emphasis is laid throughout the poem on the necessity for confession—perhaps a reflection of the volume of penitential writings subsequent to the Third Lateran Council of 1214 in which the need for confession was emphasized. This, combined with much internal evidence, would point to the first quarter of the thirteenth century as the probable date of this interesting poem.

PART III. MATIÈRE DE BRETAGNE

It is unlikely that the romances based on classical subjects could ever have enjoyed great popularity outside a limited circle. The subjects were, in a sense, too erudite, the scenes of action too distant, the miraculous devices too complicated for the average mind. Even the added attractions of Babylon, of *Inde la majeure* or of Persia had a remoteness that taxed the imagination rather severely. The *Matière de Rome* was, in its very nature, destined for a less heterogeneous audience than the more familiar *Matière de France*. A change in taste and certain unique conditions of social and cultural life in France had made Charlemagne and his knights seem a little crude, and the constant fights between heathens and Christians had begun to pall. The stage was set for something new. But the *Matière de Rome* did not entirely foot the bill. It was too remote and too far removed from the national consciousness. It was left for the *Matière de Bretagne* to step in and fill the breach—and this it did to perfection.

It is well known that King Arthur (whose renown was to rival that of Charlemagne) was introduced into a generation avid for novelty by the Welshman, Geoffroy of Monmouth, in his famous *Historia regum Britanniae*. This was translated into French rhyming couplets by the poet Wace in 1155 under the title of *Li Roman de Brut*. In this epoch-making work, not only King Arthur and the knights of the famous 'round table' ('... la reönde table / dont Breton dient mainte fable') were introduced into French literature, but a whole fantastic world of giants and dwarfs, of magicians and fairies, located in the legend-soaked regions of Wales, Ireland, Cornwall and Britanny, loomed into view and were seized upon by the popular imagination. The Breton fashion swept everything before it. Breton customs, Breton heroes and Breton legends became the rage. For a moment the fate of the new matter may have hung in the balance and the attractions of Rome and Byzantium been hard to displace, especially in the minds of those who had actually been to the East. But the new matter triumphed and the *Matière de Rome* practically disappeared. There is an interesting romance dating from the early years of the second half-century which shows a certain hesitation between the two worlds and the process of transition from East to West. The poem *Ille et Galeran* by the same Gautier d'Arras who had already composed the romance of *Heraclius* (cf. supra), opens its narrative with the words:

> Sachiez que deus Bretaignes sont,
> Et genz diverses i estont
> Li Englois sont en la grigneur
> Mais li Normant en sont seigneur,
> En la meneur sont li Breton (ll. 135–9).

The author proceeds to tell the story of Ille (the son of Eliduc) and Galeran, the sister of Conain, duke of 'Bretaigne la meneur'. In his former work Gautier had introduced his hero as son of a 'senateur de Rome'; the heroine was the finest woman in Rome and the story stretched out from Rome towards the East, finishing up with a campaign in Persia. Perhaps Gautier had become sensible of the changing taste when he boldly introduced the hero and heroine in his second romance as natives of Brittany and disguised his characters under Breton names such as Conain and Hoel. Yet much of the story takes place in Rome and the interest between Rome and Bretaigne is pretty equally distributed—Bretaigne, however, always emerges victorious and the author never fails to denigrate the Romans on every possible occasion:

> Car Romain sont vilain gaignon . . . (l. 2067)

or

> Car j'i voi mout felons Romains . . . (l. 4073).

The Bretons, on the other hand, are consistently praised ('Li Breton sunt chevalier buen') and Ille, who is spoken of as 'li Brez naïs', is the perfect knight—'li Brez qui tant fet a loer', etc. The story itself, moreover, keeps up the rivalry for it presents the problem of the man with two wives—one of whom resides in Brittany, the other in Rome. It is an ancient problem, familiar in the stories of Tristan and Iseult, of Jason and Medea, and, if we wish to go further back, of Jacob, or indeed of Abraham. Ille, the hero of Gautier's poem, has, in spite of a less exalted birth, been accepted by the duke of Brittany as a husband for his sister, and they are happily married. The husband's skill with arms, his horsemanship ('almost as if he

had been born on horseback') and his noble appearance made up
for his inferior rank. But one day, with a view to increasing his
prestige in his lady's eyes, he undertook a quite unnecessary joust
out of pure 'desmesure' and had the misfortune to lose an eye.
Thus disfigured he feared to lose his aristocratic lady's affection and
slipped away to hide his shame in other lands—in spite of his wife's
comforting reassurances and the delicate way in which she accounted
for his misfortune:

> As preuz meschiet mout plus souvent
> Qu'il ne fait a la gent faillie;
> La preude gent est assaillie
> De mainte grant mesaventure;
> Teus est proece et sa nature (ll. 1880–84).

In almost identical words Perceval's mother in Chrétien's poem
accounts for the misfortunes which had happened to her husband:

> Que les mescheänces avienent
> As prodomes qui se maintienent
> A grant enor et an proesce (ll. 429–31).

But even this encouraging thought did not prevent Ille from making
his escape, for he reflected sadly: 'Que feme a molt le cuer volage /
Et mue souvent son corage'—reminding us again of Chrétien and
his reflections on women. On his arrival in Rome, whither he has
taken his way, he finds everything in disorder, for the Eastern
emperor was invading the land of the feeble king of Rome. Ille
performs marvels of valour and the king offers him half his kingdom
if he will stay and marry his daughter. Alas for his peace of mind,
for the king's daughter is attractive and has already fallen in love
with him. Both king and pope press for the union, not knowing
that Ille is married already, and Ille is torn in two. He is filled with
pity for the wife in Brittany he has so lightly deserted and at the
same time pity for Ganor who is so loth to lose him. 'Pitié de ça,
pitié de là', cries the demented man, for Ganor has fainted in his
arms. He tears himself away, however, with a promise to return,
and gets in touch again with his wife Galeran, who has been travelling far and wide in search of him. They return to Brittany where
Galeran bears him three children, but, at the birth of the third—
when in danger of losing her life—Galeran vows to enter a convent,
and she carries out her vow, thus freeing Ille to marry Ganor and
become king of Rome. It is rather an artificial solution of a
knotty problem, but one of the characteristics of 'fine amor' (about

which the author has much to say) was that it throve on dilemmas and difficulties. Each of the ladies must have longed for the death of the other, but as the author very truly remarks:

> Car morz qu'on vuet vient a enviz:
> Ainçoiz muert amez que haïz (ll. 5269–70).

The remark is characteristic of the author, for he has many shrewd things to say about women and love, about human feelings in general, and he grows almost eloquent about the harmfulness of 'desmesure', envy and 'janglerie'. We get the impression that this native of Arras was familiar with court life and its failings. He was well-versed in current literature. He mentions 'le roi Artu' (though only in the one expression, 'ainc puis le tens le roi Artu'); he has all the usual tags about Nature (the creator of beauty), about 'fine amor' and its problems, about ladies watching the battles from their windows (as in the *romans antiques*), about 'chevalerie' and 'courtoisie'. He is familiar with the *chansons-de-geste*; he mentions Roland, Oliver, Agoulant and Estout de Lengres, and the battle scenes are described with the usual phrases. Various allusions, both in the poem under discussion and *Heraclius*, show a certain (though vague) knowledge of history, although the poems can only really be designated 'romans d'aventure'—perhaps the first of their kind. Gautier is, in fact, a many-sided writer, and from the very fact of his work containing so many disparate elements, it becomes an important pivot in the evolution of literary taste and deserves more attention, perhaps, than would otherwise be its due.

Gautier's work falls in a period of great literary activity. The third quarter of the twelfth century is remarkable for the output of works of high literary value. Marie de France, Béroul, Chrétien de Troyes were all busy with their respective works, the exact relation and chronology of which it is so hard to determine with certainty. Gautier has much in common with them all. In fact, in one instance he and Marie de France give us different versions of the same story—for the story in *Ille et Galeran* is almost identical with that of *Eliduc*, one of Marie's best known 'lais'. Gautier, as we have seen, treats it somewhat heavily and at great length, but with much acumen and knowledge of human nature. Marie treats it lightly and charmingly, with few reflections, but introducing a beautiful example of almost unbelievable feminine unselfishness to which there is no counterpart in Gautier's poem. It is noticeable, too, that the husband is much more to blame (though Marie herself does not blame him) in *Eliduc*, for he has no pity for the wife he has left behind and is not troubled by scruples, whereas Ille feels the full force of the dilemma—'car il est amez d'eles deus' (3370). Marie does not regard the question as a moral one but merely as a matter of propriety and ignoring the laws:

> Kar n'est pas bien ne avenant
> De deus espouses meintenir
> Ne la lei nel deit consentir (Eliduc, ll. 1128–30).

These are the author's words. Eliduc himself has no such scruples; he accepts his first wife's self-sacrifice joyfully ('unques nul jur ne fu si liez'), when she offers to give him up to the beautiful girl he is in love with and whom she voluntarily restores to health and strength for his sake. Her retirement into a convent is in order to leave her husband free to live in 'parfite amur' with his new wife, not, as in Gautier, because she fears her life is in danger. Gautier dilates on women's unfaithfulness; Marie makes one of her heroines say: 'Mult est fole qui humme creit' (1084). Marie adds a pleasant touch of magic, for it is by placing a little red flower (brought in by a weasel to revive its dead mate) in the mouth of her apparently dead rival that she is brought back to life—an episode that would be quite out of place in Gautier's solid poem. Indeed, the real interest lies in observing the differences between the two poems rather than in trying to prove which copied which. The difference of length (Gautier's *roman* is roughly six times as long as Marie's narrative *lai*) is, of course, bound to govern the nature of the contents, for Gautier, like Chrétien, with whom he has so much in common, has of necessity to fill out his poem with descriptions of battles, episodes and adventures, psychological explanations and reasonings in order to bring it up to its necessary length. Marie, on the other hand, confines herself to the one central theme, the subject and the matter of which she claims to have derived from 'un mut ancien lai bretun'.

Much has been conjectured and written about these Breton lays. It would look as though originally they were songs sung to musical accompaniment on the harp—but, unfortunately, no specimen has come down to us, even if it ever existed. We have, however, many examples of the narrative form of lay which must have varied in character. In Thomas' *Tristan* (cf. infra, p. 103) Iseut sits in her room and sings 'un lai pitus d'amour'. Actually this was a lament for the tragic fate of Guirun, to whom, amongst others,

was attached the well-known story of the eaten heart (cf. p. 53) or
herz-maere. The charming description of Iseut as she plays and sings
seems to fit in with the description of this plaintive lay:

> La dame chante dulcement,
> La voiz acorde a l'estrument;
> Les mains sont beles, li lais bons,
> Dulce la voiz, e bas li tons.

The combination of the visual and the audible, the beautiful hands
and the sweet, low voice tuning in to the instrument is inimitable.
The singer, moreover, seems to have composed ('fait') the *lai* (a
good one—'li lais est bons') which recalls a similar passage in
Marie's *Chevrefoil* where Tristan himself, who knew how to play
the harp, composed ('en avoit fet') a new lay to remind himself
perpetually of the joy he had experienced at meeting Iseut in the
forest. So this was a joyful lay, not a 'lai piteux d'amur' like that of
Iseut and such as one generally expects from those who suffer the
pains of 'fine amor'. From examples such as these it must be
assumed that originally the word *lai* might apply either to the tune
or the contents, or both, of the short poem—much as our word
'song' in modern English.[1]

The pure 'narrative' lays[2] of which a good many French ones
have come down to us were poems of varying length in octosyllabic
verse, mostly having as their background an alleged Breton locality
and the romantic history of Breton characters, although others with
classical subjects such as the lay *De Narcisus* and *Li Lai d'Aristote*
exist. Opinion has swung back and forth as to whether or not the
word Breton had any authentic meaning or was used merely to
describe a dim and distant past—as we might say 'in the olden days'.
However this may be, the lays form a delightful literary genre, even
though of small dimensions, of which Marie de France is the chief
representative. One lay of early date, however—perhaps previous
to those of Marie—ought to be mentioned before looking at those of
Marie herself. This 'lai', too, was composed by the hero:

> Seignors, cest lai trova
> Garados, qui fait l'a.

The actual story, which is in lines of six syllables and bears marks
of an earlier date than those of Marie, is recounted by someone who

---

[1] Cf. 'noter un lai' applied to the rhythmic sound of blows on a helmet in *Cligès*.
[2] Even though the lays are not strictly epic in form, yet owing to their subject matter they
must find their place in this chapter.

calls himself Robert Biquet. A stranger came to King Arthur's court with a magic horn (hence the title usually given of *Le Lai du Cor*) on which is inscribed the test that no one can drink out of it unless his wife be absolutely faithful. The king insists on all his knights being subjected to the test. The married ladies, including the queen, all turned pale at the thought; the young unmarried girls tittered and smiled surreptitiously at their lovers. All the knights fail, and then King Arthur has a try, for he has no qualms as to the result in his own case. Alas, the wine ran out, all over him and down to his very feet:

> Mes sour lui le versa
> Contreval dekes as pez.

The king was furious and, snatching up a small dagger or knife (*cnivet*) would have stabbed his wife on the spot had not his knights restrained him and taken away the knife. When, however, the failure to pass the test proved universal, Arthur suddenly saw the humour of the situation, burst out laughing, accepted the gift of the horn with joy and rewarded Garadoc, who was the only one to pass the test, with the gift of the town of Cirencester. This was the Garadoc who composed the lay ('c'est lai trouva') which Biquet recounted. It will be noted that the scene of this episode is laid at King Arthur's court; Arthur himself and his unfaithful spouse are introduced, as well as several of his best known knights—Gauvain, Ywain, and Giflet. Strangely enough, only one of Marie's 'lais' (*Lanval*) takes us to Arthur's court and the two knights, Walwain (Gauvain) and Ywain are expressly mentioned here also. Here, too, the queen plays a sorry role—in fact a more ignoble one than is usual in the Arthurian legends for she plays the part of Potiphar's wife to a young stranger (Lanval) who has come to the king's court. *LANVAL*
Lanval has been neglected both by the king and his entourage. He is befriended, however, by a benevolent fairy who, after clearing him from the charge brought against him by the queen, carries him off to Avalun, after which he is never heard of again:

> Od li s'en vait en Avalun,
> Ceo nus recuntent li Bretun,
> En un isle que mut est beaus
> La fu ravi li dameiseaus.
> Nul hum n'en oï plus parler,
> Ne jeo n'en sai avant cunter.

This lay is one of the most fantastic, perhaps we may say one of the most Celtic of Marie's lays—although she shows a good knowledge of legal procedure and a capacity to realize the loneliness of an unknown stranger at court:

> Hume estrange descunseillez
> Mut est dolent en autre terre,
> Quant il ne seit u sucurs quere (ll. 36–9).

Is this a 'cri de coeur' on Marie's part? We know nothing about her except what she tells us herself in her works. These are threefold in character, for besides the 'lais' she composed a collection of fables and a saint's 'Life' entitled the *Espurgatoire S. Patrice*. In the *Prologue* to the *Fables* she tells us that fables, for example those of *Esope*, always contained some grain of wisdom in the moral, or 'essample', which followed them, and was the most important part of the poem. Hence, although there might be some things in them unsuitable for her to recount, yet, at the request of one 'ki est flurs de chevalerie, / D'enseignement, de curteisie', she had undertaken to rhyme them for she could not refuse the request of such a man ('tel hume'). In the *Epilogue* to the collection she tells us her name, so that she shall not be forgotten: 'Marie ai nun, si sui de France', and adds that she had composed them 'Par amur le cunte Willame'. In the *Prologue* to the *Lais* there is a more important identification to be made for she addresses her patron:

> En l'honour de vus, nobles reis,
> Ki tant estes pruz e curteis,
> A ki tute joie s'encline
> E en ki quoer tuz biens racine,
> M'entremis des lais assembler ... (ll. 43–7).

What can we gather from all this? The 'nobles reis' was probably Henry II of England, in spite of the fact that the words 'vers qui tute joie s'encline' do not seem quite applicable to Henry's troubled life. Such expressions were, however, rather stereotyped in the case of patrons. Did Marie write in England or in France? At the lively court of Eleanor of Poitou during her sojourn in Poitiers, or was she an exile and more or less a prisoner at the more sombre court in England? This might explain her rather pathetic words in the above-mentioned prologue to the effect that the best way to forget grief is to undertake some difficult task ('grevos ovre comencier'), and that with this in view she had decided to translate some good story from Latin into French. This, however, she had abandoned because so many others had done it, and had then decided in preference to rhyme and turn into 'ditties' the 'lais' she had heard sung and told, even though it had meant hard work and using the midnight oil on many occasions (Prologue to *Lais*, 28–42). All this is very interesting as regards her motives, but does not enlighten us much as to her identity which must remain something of a mystery, although a quite plausible view would make her the half-sister of Henry II who ended her life as Abbess of Shaftesbury in, or about, 1216. In this case Henry would be the noble king to whom her lays were dedicated and they must therefore have been written before 1189, the year of his death. All this, however, is conjecture, but once again it is 'court-literature' with which we have to do. Marie was certainly well educated and well read, which would fit in with the circle of learned men that Henry gathered around him. She knew French and English well; she was at home in Latin and she probably had a bowing acquaintance with Celtic even if we doubt the existence of the Celtic originals of her poems. Undoubtedly at Henry's court there would be minstrels and poets of French, English and Breton extraction, and Marie would draw inspiration from various sources. Some of her themes spring from English soil—for instance, the charming episode of Tristan and Iseult in the forest; probably, too, the story of the were-wolf <u>Bisclavret</u>. Other themes, such as that of the 'mal-mariée', probably had their origin in France. In the two 'lais' <u>*Guigemar* and *Yonec*</u> we have the familiar picture of the young wife shut up for safety in an unapproachable tower and a jealous old husband ('vieil gelus') for whom the author has nothing but bitter words. In each of these poems, however, the fairy element plays an important part—an element very reminiscent of Irish, Welsh and Cornish legends even in the present day. The white hind which brings about the lovers' meeting in *Guigemar*, and the bird into which the lover is transformed in *Yonec*, strike one as completely un-French in character and point to a contamination of Celtic and French themes.

Marie has great sympathy for a young wife kept in durance vile by an unreasonable, jealous brute of a husband, but none at all for a wife who is disloyal to a good one. In *Equitan* it is the wife who is to blame. This lay is more in the nature of a 'fabliau'. A wife, happily married to a worthy man, accepts a king for her lover. It is true she is flattered and cajoled rather unduly by the king. But she hatches a horrible plot by means of which her husband will step into a bath of boiling water and be killed. The plot miscarries, however; it is the king who steps into the bath and the husband

BISCLAVRET

GUIGEMAR

YONEC

who pushes his unfaithful wife in after him. Marie, who dearly likes a moral, closes with the words:

> Tel purchace le mal d'autrui
> Dunt li mals (tut) revert sur lui (ll. 309–10).

BISCLAVRET

We find the same moral in practically identical words at the end of one of her animal-fables, in this case referring to the wolf who, in his effort to destroy the fox, lost his own skin. In *Bisclavret*, too (of which name she gives the Norman equivalent *Garwaf* or *Garualf*—English *werewulf*), the disloyal wife, who hides her husband's clothes, thus preventing his change back into human form after his weekly three-day transformation into a wolf, is severely punished. Like the wife in *Equitan*, she has taken a lover without due justification, for her husband was a noble knight, beloved of all, and the couple were devoted to each other ('Il amot li et ele lui'). But, partly out of fear and partly out of temptation, she betrays him cruelly, and he, for a space of some years, is denied the privilege of assuming his human form. She is severely punished, however, for when her wolf-husband sees her one day flaunting herself at the king's court:

> Nul hum nel poeit retenir;
> Vers li curut cum enragiez.
> Oiez cum il est bien vengiez!
> Le nes li esracha del vis.
> Quei li peüst il faire pis? (ll. 232–6).

What indeed? Nor does she alone suffer for her misdeeds. She had a family by the man for whom she had betrayed her husband, and the women-folk of her lineage could be recognized by their unfortunate appearance for:

> C'est verité, senz nes sunt nées
> Et si viveient esnasées (ll. 311–13).

LE FRESNE

In *Le Fresne* we have the same poetic justice in the case of a spiteful woman who accuses a friend of unfaithfulness to her husband on account of having given birth to twins, and then has twins herself. This theme occurs again in a poem of the early thirteenth century entitled *Galeran de Bretagne*, in which the conventional ideas and style of the 'roman courtois' are reproduced in a rather exaggerated form. Here again we are up against a potential love-dilemma, for the hero discovers at the last moment that he has married the wrong twin, and the marriage, celebrated one day, has to be dissolved the next in order that he may marry the right one. But this brings us to one of the features of Marie's outlook on life. Marriage vows and conscience scruples for her weigh nought when weighed in the balance against pure love ('fine amor'). But the course of true love rarely runs smooth, even though God be on the side of the lovers— hence the pathos of most of her lays. In the lay of the *Deux Amants*, both lovers lose their lives as a result of a cruel test to which the 'amant' is subjected. He must carry his 'amie' up a steep hill in his arms without resting on the way. In spite of the maiden's efforts to reduce her weight (perhaps the first example of slimming), and the strengthening potion carried by the young man, the attempt fails and both lovers perish. In another charming short lay which Marie herself calls <u>Chevrefoil</u> (*Goteleaf* as she tells us, in English), we have an episode of the Tristan story showing the impossibility of separating true lovers in life or in death. Their love entails great suffering and this should not surprise us:

> Ne vus esmerveillez neënt
> Kar ki eime mult leälment
> Mult est dolenz et trespassez
> Quant il nen ad ses voluntez (ll. 21-4).

Tristan, banished from the court, is lurking in the forest near the path the royal procession would follow on its way to a festival at Tintagel. He has cut an inscription on the bark of a tree meant for the eyes of Iseut only and ending with the appealing words:

> Bele amie, si est de nus:
> Ne vus sanz mei, ne mei sanz vus (ll. 77-8).

Lovers *must* come together, even though it entail risk for themselves and suffering for others. The jealous husband need not excite any pity if he deserves his fate. But not all neglected husbands are bad. What is, then, the solution? The king in *Equitan* sees no reason why he and the seneschal should not share the latter's wife:

> 'Si bele dame tant mar fust
> s'ele n'amast u dru n'eüst!
> . . . Li seneschal, si l'ot cunter,
> Ne l'en deit mie trop peser;
> Sul ne la peot il nient tenir,
> Certes *je voil od li partir*' (ll. 79-85).

Obviously the idea of 'sharing' (*od li partir*) with a lover was not very likely to appeal to a normal husband. But when there were several lovers to one woman the difficulty became even more acute. In *Chaitivel* Marie tells the story of a lady of such beauty and refinement that no knight could see her without desiring her. The lady could not love them all, nor did she wish to kill them all ('El nes pot mie tuz amer / Ne ele nes vot mie tuer'). There were four noble knights, however, in Brittany who stood out amongst the others, and all of whom the lady loved. The difficulty was to choose the one she loved most, and this was so difficult that she carried on a secret intrigue with each of the four ('Bel semblant feseit a chescun', l. 56). This she did by means of messengers and tokens, so that when they went into battle each carried something of his lady-love—one a bracelet, one a sleeve and one a banner—and each cried out her name as he rode to the attack. They all performed wonders in the tournament and still she did not know which to choose. It was all very difficult, but the dilemma did not materialize as the matter was decided for her. The knights, each striving for her admiration, 'trop folement s'abaundonerent'. Three of them were killed and the fourth badly wounded. One might have thought this would clear the matter up, but this would not have been in keeping with Marie's idea of 'fine amur'. The lady went to see the wounded man and comforted him greatly—'Mes les autres tres regretot / E grant dolur por eus menot' (179-80). The survivor suffered so horribly from not being granted the 'joie d'amur' now that he was the only one left that he pleaded with her to call the lay which she was about to compose to commemorate her grief *Le Chaitivel* (thus describing himself), instead of *Quatre Dols*, as she had intended to call it in memory of the four. The little poem ends rather quaintly with the same words employed by Gautier at the end of *Éracle*:

> Plus n'en oï, ne plus n'en sai,
> Ne plus ne vus en cunterai.

They were probably employed to round off many a story at that time, especially one that ended rather abruptly as this one does.

It is obvious that Marie had very decided views on love, quite personal to herself. There is hardly a trace of religion in the lays, a characteristic they share with most of Chrétien's romances. In Gautier's poems, on the other hand, there are prayers and moralizations, characteristic perhaps of an earlier decade. Marie's outlook is non-moral—she just proceeds with her story without pausing to explain. Gautier in *Ille et Galeran* feels obliged to explain that Ille is free to wed Ganor because he cannot be married to a nun. Marie, in *Eliduc*, simply does not trouble to discuss the question. Love, and loyalty to the demands of love, are her ideals. Cruelty and envy are her bugbears. Love without pain is impossible, hence the pathos that runs through her poems. Love, alas, is so unreasonable—it knows neither 'sens ne reisun', and the more perfect (*fine*) it is, the more it brings in its train 'meinte dolur'. But it brings many a moment of ecstasy for it was the joy that he experienced in a brief meeting with his 'amie' that made Tristan indite the lay that Marie recounts:

> Pur la joie qu'il ot eüe
> De s'amie qu'il ot veüe
> ... Tristram ki bien saveit harper
> En aveit fait un nuvel lai (*Chèvrefoil*, 107 f.).

Only one of Marie's lays ends with the comfortable words 'they lived happily ever after'. This is the one entitled *Milun,* of which ~~MILUN~~ the hero was born in South Wales and England is the background where the action takes place. It is a rather colourless story of two lovers who correspond by means of a tame swan that takes their messages back and forth. A son born of their intercourse, before the heroine was married to a wealthy countryman, having been smuggled away to Northumberland, grows up into a perfect knight, beloved of all for his generosity, honourable and courtly. When he went overseas 'pur pris querre' he was called 'Sanz Per' by those who did not know his real name. Unawares, he meets his father in a tournament and unhorses him, but remounts him when he sees the grey hairs beneath his helmet. Recognition follows and the son joyfully accompanies his father back to his own country. When he hears all the story of the lovers and how the swan carried their messages, he declares he will kill the lawful husband of his mother and bring the parents together. Mercifully this unjust act is rendered unnecessary by the timely death of the husband and the lovers are brought together without any fuss by the affectionate son:

> Unc ne demanderent parent:
> Sanz conseil de tut autre gent
> Lur fiz amdeus les assembla,
> La mere a sun pere dona.
> En grant bien e en grant duçur
> Vesquirent puis e nuit e jur (ll. 527-32).

Even the lay of the nightingale—*Laüstic*—has not such a satisfactory ending, although the lovers are chaste and only correspond through the medium of the nightingale's song. The ill-natured husband kills the bird and the only consolation vouchsafed to the sorrowing lover is that of carrying about with him for the rest of his days the dead

MILUN

bird which his 'amie' has sent him enshrined in a little case made of precious stones. In both *Laüstic* and *Milun* it is noticeable that the lovers are more restrained in their actions and the husbands less acutely jealous. Hence the milder fate which awaits them in both stories. Where the actions of the lovers are aggressive and the husbands justifiably outraged, the ending is bound to be tragic, and the 'lai' consequently composed 'De la pité, de la dolur / Que cil suffrirent pur amur' (*Yonec* 553–4).

YONEC

Tristan

Of the 'pity' and the grief caused by love, of the exquisite moments of enjoyment which make it all worth while, no better example can be found than the love-story of Tristan and Iseult which first appeared and quickly seized upon the imagination of poets and hearers alike during this fruitful period of which we have been speaking. It is not going too far to say that, in spite of all the research that has been done on the subject, the core of the legend (the tragic love-potion) and the original inventor still lie buried in obscurity. It has no parallel in Celtic literature nor in Germanic in as far as our knowledge of these literatures goes. There is nothing in classical literature to correspond to it, indeed the whole spirit of the legend seems nonclassical in character. The idea of two noble individuals, one a queen and the other a glamorous knight, wandering miserably in the forest, feeding on herbs, never spending two successive nights in the same place, losing their own self-respect and the society of their fellows, is so unspeakably tragic that even the moments of rapture ('Por la joie qu'il ot eüe', as Marie says) must barely have sufficed to make up for the anguish they suffered. Yet such is the skill with which the poet Béroul has portrayed this legend that it is impossible to read his *Roman de Tristan* unmoved and not to feel oneself on the side of the lovers—who, owing to their sinful condition and their material suffering, did not get the good of either this world or the next. As the hermit tells Girart de Roussillon in a parallel situation contained in the epic of that name:

> Ne vos sai conseiller, deus vos aiüt
> Car icest siecle e l'autre aves perdut (lls. 7416–7).

But Girart was a harder nut to crack than Tristan, who was ever a sensitive lover, less ruthless in his actions than that old rebel Girart and more capable of remorse. And yet one is amazed in Béroul's poem at the shameless deceit and untruthfulness of the lovers, which enabled them to carry on their clandestine love for 'un an ou deus' without arousing King Mark's suspicion—in spite of the fact that

'amors (by which the author means *fine amor*) ne se puet celer'
(l. 575). Surprise, too, cannot but be felt at the attitude of the king,
who, only when pushed by the three jealous, vindictive barons, can
be induced to take any action against his wife and his favourite
nephew. Through all the different episodes of which Béroul's poem
is composed Mark's character remains consistent:

> Ne set qu'il die, sovent erre (l. 612).
> Le rois n'a pas coraige entier
> Sempres est ci et sempres la (ll. 3432–3).
> Tu es legier a metre en voie (l. 4144).

In fact, in King Mark and the hero himself, as depicted in Béroul's
poem, we see a striking illustration of the character which Giraldus
Cambrensis attributes to the Welsh of his day: 'Gens . . . sola
instabilitate stabilis, sola infidelitate fidelis.'[1] The story of *Tristan et
Iseut* as it can be pieced together from the five basic versions (the
Anglo-Norman poem of Thomas; the poem of Béroul with the
nearly related German version of Eilhart von Oberge, the two
shorter poems, each known as *La Folie Tristan* and the prose-
romance of somewhat later date) is so well known that we may be
pardoned for not reproducing it in detail here. The poems of
Thomas and Béroul have both unfortunately survived only in a
fragmentary state, the fragment of Béroul being of considerably
greater length than that of Thomas. The latter poet, who professes
to base his work on the story of a 'conteur breton' called 'Bréri'
(cf. infra) bears marks of courtly influence to a much greater degree
than that of Béroul. There is a charm of naïveté in Béroul's narrative
which is lacking in Thomas' more courtly poem in spite of the fact
that Thomas' version may be the earlier in date. In the former the
lovers seem like a pair of irresponsible children, to whom ideas of
right and wrong do not occur. They lie and commit perjury
without turning a hair. And yet, when they are caught 'en flagrant
délit' and the king unwillingly decides to punish them, we all
exclaim with the author: 'Ha! Dex, qel duel que la reïne / N'avot
les dras du lit ostez!' (ll. 749–50). The reason may be partly because
of the hateful character of their accusers—the loathsome dwarf and
the jealous vindictive barons—which acts as a foil throughout to
the gentleness and the 'pure love' of the hero and heroine. King
Marc himself, in spite of his weakness and sudden bursts of anger,
shines in comparison with these villains, for when he finds the lovers

---

[1] See Tanqueray: *Med. Aev.* Vol. VI, No. 1, Feb. 1937.

H

asleep in the forest and notices their emaciated and pathetic state, he actually places his glove over Iseult's face to protect her from the glare of the sun. For such an action we can pardon him much even though by this action, as well as by the removal of Tristan's sword, he emphasizes his feudal rights. In the trial by ordeal, moreover, (the *escondit*) in which Iseult vindicates herself by an oath, the king gives the impression of letting himself be convinced by means of an almost palpable ruse and we are grateful to him for his simplicity. Owing to a break in the continuity of the poem and a certain inconsistency in the fate attributed to the three wicked barons, a second author has been postulated for the later part of Béroul's poem—but the style of the two parts is so similar and the fact that in a recited story it would be very easy to overlook what had happened in an earlier section, make it tempting to vindicate Béroul as author of the whole poem. Moreover, the scene at the ford, in which Tristan, disguised as a leper, carries Iseult across the muddy stream and thus enables her to perform her *escondit*, is described in such a humorous, realistic way that we are loth not to give Béroul the benefit of the doubt as regards its authorship.

But who was this Béroul and whence did he derive his tale of the love-potion and its dire results? As before mentioned, there would seem to have existed some previous version, albeit a composite one, from which Béroul and probably the authors of the other versions drew their matter. The *Folie Tristan* (Ms. of Berne), which is closely connected with Béroul's poem has a pleasant way of repeating 'Don't you remember?' (*ne vos membre?*) as he recalls each incident. There is reason to think that most of these incidents were assembled in a common version to which our poets had access, whether in a long poem—an *Urtristan* or merely isolated lays is a matter for conjecture. Whatever was the origin of the main theme —the love-philtre—there are many features in the poem which point to a Celtic origin—Béroul's version alone gives us a feeling of primitive conditions, of wild scenery, of fantastic characters such as the king's dwarf—a sort of malignant leprechaun with his little body and big head, and the thorn tree whence he tells his malicious secrets (ll. 1320 f.). Then there is the description of the marvellous 'arc-qui-ne-faut' and the references to Cornish places (Tintagel, etc.) and the characteristics of the Cornish people. How, then, and at what date did the story of the *lovendrinc* come to France, both North and South? Tristan was already known as the type of the perfect (if tragic) lover to the troubadour Bernart de Ventadorn who, in a lament for his absent lady, sang:

> 'Plus trac pene d'amor
> de Tristan l'amador
> que-n sobri mahnta dolor
> per Izeut la blonda.'[1]

The lady for whom Bernart indited this poem has been not unreasonably identified with Eleanor of Aquitaine, in which case the date would be 1154 when Eleanor went to England as Henry II's queen. Many other allusions could be cited to show that Tristan (*li courtois Tristans, Tristans li preux, Tristans li amoureux*) was the lover *par excellence* and that 'the fair Iseult' (*Iseut la bloie*) could take her place beside Helen of Troy. But the creator of this wonderful pair of lovers remains lost in obscurity and whether he was a wandering Celtic minstrel or a French poet at the court of Poitiers will, perhaps, for ever remain unknown—*Ignoramus et ignorabimus*. Geoffroy of Monmouth himself tells us, in one of his genealogies, of a certain Blegabred who surpassed all previous singers and seemed a 'very god of all minstrels' (Bk. III, ch. xix). There are references to a 'famosus ille fabulator Bledhericus' in Giraldus Cambrensis; to a *conteur* 'Breri' who related the stories of the kings and counts of Brittany in Thomas' *Tristan*; to a 'Bleheris' who was born in Wales but told his story at Poitou:

> . . . Bleheris
> Qui fu nes et engenuis
> En Gales dont je cont le conte
> Et qui le racontoit au conte
> De Poitiers qui amoit l'estoire
> Et en tenoit en grant memoire
> Plus que nul autre ne faisoit . . .

in Wauchier de Denain, one of the continuators of Chrétien's *Perceval*. It is well known that the court of Poitou was the French centre of the 'matière de Bretagne' and it must have played an important part in the spread of the legend, wherever it originated. But none of these names really gets us very much further and the subject is rendered yet more complicated by references in Provençal literature to a poet *Cabra*, who might be identical with the *li Kieures* mentioned in a twelfth-century mystery play as having composed verses on the love-story of Tristan and Iseult, and the *La Chievre*

[1] Cf. Ed. C. Appell, Lieder No. 44.

cited in the *Roman de Renart* (as having related the Tristan love-story which he couples with that of Paris and Helen of Troy) :

> Seigneurs, oï avez maint conte
> Que maint conterre vous raconte
> Comment Paris ravi Elaine
> Le mal qu'il en ot, et la paine
> De Tristan dont la Chievre fist . . . (*Rom. de Ren.* part II).

With these tributes to the popularity and the high esteem in which the love-story of Tristan and Iseult was held in the second half of the twelfth century we must leave the matter to further conjecture, adding only that many another lay of *Tintagel* or of *Tristan* or of *King Marc and Iseut* besides those which have come down to us, must have undoubtedly been composed and related and sung. We have in our account been rather biased, and concentrated attention on Béroul and his poem because it is difficult not to believe that Béroul conveys the atmosphere of the original story and represents the combination of the Celtic and Norman elements, as yet untouched by the more cultured influence of the French courts, better than any of his contemporaries. But the courtly romances in their Arthurian setting, with their 'Questiones amoris' or 'dilemmas of love', were already in existence.

Much of the literature which flourished in the second half of the twelfth century in France (and to a certain extent in French-speaking England) is of an extraordinarily artificial character. Just as the lyric poems of the time (particularly in Provence) emanated from kings and princes and their hangers-on, so in the north it was the social atmosphere of the princely courts which was the fertile soil whence so much aristocratic literature sprang into existence. Yet, though it was an unnatural growth, its influence was widespread and long-lasting. Indeed, it has never quite disappeared. The dedications of the different works and poems often give us a clue as to their origin. In England, Henry II gathered learned men and writers around him. Diffuse authors of Welsh-Norman extraction chronicled his reign. His wife Eleanor brought French ideas and doubtless a French suite to the English court when Henry became king in 1154. Eleanor's daughters by her first husband, Louis of France, were active at the French courts—Blois, Poitiers, Troyes and Arras were all centres of literary activity where the newly-invented dialectics of love were hotly discussed and the *sic et non* of Abelard's Treatise was diverted to very unspiritual propositions. The most outstanding figure in all the literature of romance

which flourished in the second half of the twelfth century is undoubtedly Chrétien de Troyes. Although this does not cover all
his literary activities, we might with justice call Chrétien the great
exponent of the 'question dilemmatique', a form of amusement
much in favour amongst the aristocratic highbrows of that time.
This will be best illustrated if we glance at his works in rapid
succession. Six major works have come down to us, and judging
from the opening words of one of his most famous romances—
Cligès—the story of Erec and Enide would seem to be the first
considerable tale at which he tried his hand. It is true that he
mentions in the same list of his previous compositions an ambiguous
'Del roi Marc et d'Iseut la blonde', but there is some ground for
thinking that this lost work was more in the nature of a lay. The
poem *Guillaume d'Angleterre* has been intentionally omitted. It is
sometimes attributed to Chrétien de Troyes but it is obviously an
imitation, particularly as regards language. The author's only claim
to be identified with the poet of Troyes is the fact that he was
named Chrétien. We turn, therefore, to *Erec et Enide*.

Erec et Enide is the story of the faithful wife who has to undergo
a series of trials inflicted by an unreasonable husband to prove her
love. It is a time-honoured subject and the suspicion in the husband's
mind is due in Chrétien's poem to his wife's fear that her spouse will
'wax craven and utterly do away with his renown in knighthood'
if he spends too much time dallying with his wife at home. This
very real danger is envisaged already in Geoffroy of Monmouth.
Says the jolly Cador, duke of Cornwall, when Arthur is doubting
what reply to send to threats from Rome: 'For where use of arms
is none and nought is there to do but to toy with women . . . and
suchlike follies, none need doubt but that cowardice will tarnish all
they once had of valour and honour and hardihood and renown.'[1]
The clash of loyalties became really acute, however, when honour
and love began to be idealized as they were in the time of Chrétien.
The lady's claim on a man's time and energy (as many a troubadour
found) was very exacting during this period of novel problems, and
a 'young man married' was in grave danger of becoming 'a man
that's marred'.[2] We have then in *Erec* quite a different situation from
that in much of the lyric literature of the time, or in the lays of
Marie de France. It is no longer the Ovidian triangle of husband :

---

[1] Geoff.: *Historia*, Book IX, ch. xvi. (Transl. Seb. Evans.)
[2] Cf. Shakespeare's *All's well that ends well*—Act II, Scene 3:
'He keeps his honour in a sealed-up box
Who hugs his kiksy-wiksy here at home.'

lover : wife. When asked whether she is the 'fame' or 'amie' of
Eric, Enide replies promptly 'Et l'un et l'autre'—and in spite of
marital trouble and misunderstandings the spouses are happily
crowned together in the end. How different this is from the fatal,
tragic love-passion of Tristan and Iseult, and the constant references
in Chrétien's romances, generally in a very derogatory sense, to the
actions and behaviour of those lovers, makes us wonder very much
as to the nature of his own treatment of the legend.

The question of 'waxing craven' (or becoming 'recreant' in the
knightly language of Chrétien's time) on account of love was
indeed a very real one, but there were many more of these 'questiones amoris' to occupy idle minds in the abnormal conditions of
this period, as we may see from the work of Andreas Capellanus—
the *Tractatus de regula honeste amandi*, another product of the reigning
taste. In this same poem of *Erec et Enide* there are at least two other
problems of behaviour. Enide herself has a difficult question to
decide: Should a wife disobey her husband who has forbidden her
to speak when she sees danger and death threatening him unless he
is warned? Whichever decision she makes, it will probably be the
wrong one. Why did she not preserve 'un bon teisir' when, on
one occasion, she spoke and her husband came back wounded
almost to death?

> Ainz teisir a home ne nut
> Mes parler nuist mainte foiiée (ll. 4630–1).

Alas, Perceval's experience was exactly the opposite as we shall see,
but these dilemmas were often real and one can never foretell the
consequences of a difficult decision. 'La force d'un conseil gist au
temps', as Montaigne says, and this is specially so in delicate questions involving the emotions.

A dilemma of a somewhat different kind faces the knight Mabonagrain in a mysterious adventure entitled *Joie de la Cort* which occurs
towards the end of the same poem. Should a man be loyal to a
promise made to his lady even if it means killing his best friend?
(cf. ll. 6104–5). This again must be solved by the rules of 'amour
courtois', for the lover would be 'faus/et foimantis et desleaus' if he
sought a 'vilaine delivrance' from his vow. In this case a new
element makes its appearance, for Mabonagrain had promised his
lady to remain in an enchanted garden surrounded by a wall of
impenetrable air until such time as he was defeated in single combat
by some daring rival. However much he might regret the vow,

he must not even let a shadow of regret appear upon his face (ll. 6083–8). A grizzly row of heads on stakes bore witness to the fact that hitherto the combats had ended in his favour and that the spell was not yet broken. The land and the whole court were suffering from an absence of 'joie'; all looked eagerly for a stronger man who should defeat the strong Mabonagrain and deliver the sorrowful region. Then Erec, the deliverer, came and defeated the knight and 'joie' returned to the court and the people sang for joy and the ladies composed a lay ('un lai troverent') which they called 'Le Lai de Joie'. The author tells us it was not much known ('gueires seüz'), and this can hardly surprise us as the whole episode of the *Joie de la Cort* is completely fantastic and 'other world' in character. Its importance must not be overlooked, however, for the idea of the 'bespelled' land appears in various forms in Chrétien's works from now on and plays a fundamental part in all the later developments of the history of the Holy Grail.

In *Erec et Enide* there is much that strikes the reader as very Celtic in character. Not only the idea of the spell and the deliverer, or the knights waxing craven, but the whole poem with its genealogies (so loved of Welsh chroniclers), its lists of knights with Celtic names, its eulogies of Arthur and his 'largesce', its reference to Merlin and the currency,[1] and the description of the magnificent coronation at the end—all take us back to Geoffroy of Monmouth or his translator. Tinged as the episodes may be with the superficial manners of the French courts, there is nothing yet of the stylized description, the skilful thrusts and parries of imaginary or real conversations, in spite of the dilemmatic problems which form the basis of the work.

We are probably justified in taking *Cligès* as the next in date after *Erec* of Chrétien's romances. It shows a development in Chrétien's treatment of love which is very instructive. The poem opens with the well-known list of his earlier works including (besides *Erec*) a translation of the 'commandemenz Ovide', various adaptations or versions of classical stories, and a version of the Tristan story which he entitles 'Del roi Marc et d'Iseut la blonde'. None of these works except *Erec et Enide* has survived. After this enumeration Chrétien informs his audience that 'chevalerie' and 'clergie' having passed from Greece to Rome, had now found their resting place in France. He then proceeds to his story, starting, in approved fashion, with the history of Cligès' parents. His father, Alexander, we are told,

[1] See Merlin's Prophecy in Geoff. of Monm.

was son to the emperor of Greece. As a young man he decided he would like to go to England in order to 'se faire valoir' at the court of King Arthur 'de cui si granz est li renons / De corteisie et de proesce' (ll. 152–3). His father furnished him with money and clothes in abundance and sent him off with a last warning against being 'mean' (*chiche*) and a panegyric of 'largesce'—'que largesce est dame et reïne / Qui totes vertuz anlumine', etc. Cligès and his little company are well received by Arthur and the admirable Gauvain becomes his best friend. Chrétien is more enthusiastic in *Cligès* about Arthur's court than in his other romances. Noticeable also is the knowledge he evidences of English localities—not only Southampton (*Soz Hantone*), Dover and Totnes, the well-known ports of embarkation, but of Windsor (*Guinesore*), Winchester (*Guincestre*), Canterbury, Oxford, and Wallingford (*Gualinguefort*). His descriptions of some of these places and of the discomforts of the sea journeys in *Cligès* give one the impression that he had made the journey to England and possibly even accompanied Henry II on some of his frequent circuits. An expedition related in the romance, made by Arthur into Brittany, necessitated a sea journey in the course of which Alexander (Cligès' father) and the queen's companion Soredamors fall violently in love. Then we are plunged into one of the most artificial sides of Chrétien's writing which must have been one of his concessions to the taste of his times and of his predominately feminine audience. Each lover utters a 'pleinte' consisting of scores of lines composed of artificial and rather silly reflections on the eyes (and their function), the heart, Love personified and the state to which the lover is reduced, interspersed with descriptions of Cupid's dart, the beauty of the loved one and the pains of uncertainty. For the rule of concealment (*celer*) had to be observed, even when there was not the slightest need for it. The secret came out at length, however, through one of Soredamour's hairs which had been introduced into the texture of a shirt intended for the future lover. Had Alexander known of it, says the author, he would have treated it like a shrine ('sanctueire') and worshipped it day and night (495–6). Whether the golden hair was a reminiscence of the hair of Iseult with which King Mark fell in love it is hard to say, but it is noticeable that throughout *Cligès* the story of Iseult is never far from the poet's mind. He seems unable to keep off it and each comparison he makes between his heroine and Iseult is to the latter's disadvantage. It is difficult to believe that, as has been suggested, Chrétien was so shocked by the

immoral Tristan story that he had to write an *Anti-Tristan*. The
wife who pleads for, and obtains from a magician, a potion which
renders her marriage nugatory so as to reserve herself for her lover
is no more moral than the wife who, under the influence of an
unwished-for potion, deceives her husband. She certainly excites
our sympathy much less. Moreover Phenice, the heroine in *Cligès*,
indulges in yet another ruse—that of the 'fausse mort', or apparent
death produced by another potion which enables the lover to obtain
the coveted lady who has been preserved intact for him by the
former magic potion. How artificial it all is. Did Chrétien's
audience really like it? It would seem so: for, judging from allusions
to it in other works, it was the most popular of his stories. It must
be said that the story is well told. Chrétien's vocabulary is rich and
his narrative style so vivid that, even when he is indulging in
stereotyped descriptions of love-symptoms or beauty, we are
somehow lured on. Moreover, in *Cligès* a sense of humour breaks
through. When the three physicians from Salerno have done their
worst to arouse the apparent corpse, pouring molten lead into her
hands and beating her unmercifully, a multitude of curious ladies,
who have been peeping through the windows, become so incensed
that they break in by sheer weight of numbers and, seizing the
doctors, hurl them from the windows to their death. Whereupon
the author remarks 'Ainz miauz ne firent nules dames' (l. 6050).
It is true the story was probably not original. It is told in a slightly
different form by one of the Seven Sages in *Marques de Rome*. There
was also a legend of a similar kind about Solomon's wife which
may have been the ultimate source. But Chrétien has told it in his
inimitable way and again we must believe that it suited the taste of
the audience for whom it was meant.

And so we come to Chrétien's third considerable work which,
although unfinished, must have been written before *Yvain* as several
allusions to it occur in that romance. *Le Conte de la Charrete*, as it
is called in the prologue, would seem to have been less popular in
its own day than *Cligès* and it certainly requires great determination
to read through now. It is the least well-constructed of Chrétien's
romances and it is often difficult to identify the characters. This was
no doubt partly intentional—for one of the author's tricks of technique was to keep people guessing. It is long before it is announced
that 'li chevaliers', the hero of so many adventures, is no less than
Lancelot. It is often hard to distinguish between the different actors
and to unravel the intertwined episodes. There is a reason and

perhaps an excuse for this. Chrétien, who tells us in his prologue that the 'sens et matière' for his story had been given to him by Marie de Champagne, has obviously tried to combine one of the more absurd dilemmatic love-questions with the theme of a quest—in this case the quest for Arthur's queen. The 'rape' (or carrying off) of Guinevere seems to have been traditional. In the *Vita Gildae* (written before 1129)[1] the heathen King Melwas of Somerset was the abductor; in Geoffroy of Monmouth it is Mordred, Arthur's nephew, who robbed his uncle of his spouse; in Chrétien's poem it is Meleagant, a fearless brutal knight:

> Nus ne fust miaudres chevaliers
> Se fel et desleaus ne fust;
> Mes il avoit un cuer de fust
> Tut sanz douçor et sanz pitié (ll. 3180 f.).

He was in fact a very devil, and there were many unhappy captives in his domain who could not get back to their own country until the advent of a deliverer who would break the spell. For the land where these people were held prisoner and to which the queen had been spirited away is described as 'the land whence there is no return':

> Et si l'a el reaume mise
> Don nus estranger ne retorne (ll. 644-5).

The queen herself seems to be in the secret for, when at the outset King Arthur so compliantly lets her be carried off, she murmurs:

> 'Ha! Ha! se vos le seüssiez,
> Ja, ce croi, ne me leississiez
> Sanz chalonge mener un pas.'

The fact is Guinevere herself is 'fée' and seems to have been destined for these abductions. Hence a certain vagueness as to who was actually her deliverer and even a possibility that Arthur himself may have been her first kidnapper. If so, he was following in the footsteps of his father, Uther Pendragon, who, with Merlin's help, penetrated into Tintagel Castle, transformed into the shape of the husband of the beautiful Igerne who eventually became his wife and the mother of Arthur himself.[2]

It is into this confused and confusing account of Lancelot's quest for Guinevere that Chrétien has introduced the motif of the love-dilemma. In his hasty pursuit of the queen and her ravisher, Lancelot

---

[1] Cf. Webster, *Guinevere*, p. 3 (Massachusetts 1951), for bibliography on the subject.
[2] Cf. Geoff. of Monmouth, Bk. viii, ch. xix.

rides his horse to death and, in order to continue his journey, mounts a tumbril (*charrete*) of the kind used for conveying malefactors to the gallows, by which means he arrives at the castle where Guinevere is confined. It was a bitter pill to him to travel in such unworthy fashion and for two split seconds ('deux pas') he hesitated. Then, in this difficult 'jeu-parti' between Love and Reason, Love carried the day and he mounted the cart. The reproach and shame of this follows him all through. When the lacerated, exhausted knight, having crossed the sword-edged bridge and worsted Meleagant, appears smiling before the queen, longing for a gracious word, she will not look at him, or even acknowledge him because of that momentary hesitation before he mounted the tumbril. She is punished deservedly for her hardness when she hears a rumour that Lancelot has committed suicide. But the rules of 'fin' amor' were outraged by the hesitation, in spite of the fact that Lancelot had worshipped some of her hairs (found in a comb on his journey) as if they had been a shrine (*sanctueire*) and bowed to the room in which Guinevere was lying 'con s'il fust devant un autel' (l. 4736).

Such were the concessions that had to be made to a ruling fashion which was probably just at its peak when Chrétien wrote and was as extravagant as it was artificial. But there is a deeper meaning in Chrétien's *Lancelot*—a hint that he was feeling his way to the less worldly story that was shortly going to occupy him. For the idea of a quest demands purpose of heart and determination. Lancelot pursues his quest through many perils and temptations, never turning aside for any danger, never brooking any delay. The queen is imprisoned and the land is under a spell. He must ever press on to achieve what he has begun. As one of the young ladies, whose allurements he resisted, says of him:

> 'Il viaut a si grant chose antandre
> Qu'ainz chevaliers n'osa anprandre
> Si perilleuse ni si grief,
> Et Deus doint qu'il an vaigne a chief' (ll. 1287 f.).

The 'grant chose' may have had a deeper meaning than appears at first sight for the sort of 'Harrowing of Hell' which Lancelot achieved brought release and joy to many. The delivery of the land was no small thing quite apart from the freeing of the queen, which actually gave Lancelot an opportunity of disloyalty to Arthur, thus introducing the subversive element of feminine love into the harmony of the great king's court. To qualify for the Deliverer, Lancelot had many cruel tests to pass, such as the marvellous bed on which he was struck by a burning lance and the 'pont-de-l'espee', with its lacerating edge; he resisted temptations of the flesh and boldly tackled superior numbers. But we have to admit that it was no lofty aim which drew him on. It was the queen he was after; the queen about whom he thought in his protracted 'rêverie' (*panser*) and the sight of whom revived his strength in his single combat with the adversary. Thus we have a rather curious twofold effect of Lancelot's quest which is quite in keeping with what we have mentioned of its inception. For Chrétien, although writing to order, cannot keep the more serious side of his character entirely in abeyance.

It is difficult indeed to say how much is due to Chrétien's invention in the *Conte de la Charrete*. There must have been many well-known tales and legends current amongst educated people of his time— some classical in nature—ravishments, quests to the underworld (the story of Orpheus was well known), ominous staghunts (or boar-hunts as the case may be) and other such. These stories may have easily coincided with similar Celtic legends of an equally fantastic kind. A German version of Lancelot's quest for the kidnapped Guinevere, the *Lanzelet* of Ulrich von Zatzikoven, has certain points in common with Chrétien's romance but makes no mention of the 'charrete' or the guilty love of Lancelot and Guinevere. The author claims to have based his work on *ein welschez buoch von Lanzelete* taken to Austria by Hue de Morville, one of the hostages for the release of Richard I in 1194. Whether this French original preceded or followed Chrétien's romance it is hard to say. Exact dating of individual poems in this period is almost impossible, and it is to be feared that serious commentators have sometimes adjusted their dating to suit their particular theories. But it is reasonable to suppose that in Chrétien's case, even if the quest for the queen with its other-world character is traditional, the story of the tumbril, the dilemmatic love-question and the love affair between Lancelot and the queen were introduced 'by request' and perhaps proceeded from the fertile imagination of the youthful countess who gave Chrétien the 'matière et sens' of his poem.

It is interesting to note that Lancelot, with his French-sounding name, was a relatively late member of the species of freemasonry which existed amongst Arthur's knights. In *Yvain* or the *Chevalier au lion*, perhaps the most finished product that has survived of Chrétien's work, we are back amongst the old group—Kei, Gauvain,

Sagremor, etc., each with his customary role. Kei is even more spiteful than usual; Gauvain is the 'sun of knighthood' by which all 'chevalerie' is 'anluminee'; Queen Guinevere is a kindly, gracious lady, and King Arthur as 'fainéant' as usual, for he is described as taking a nap whilst his knights are discussing an important adventure. The story is well known and need not detain us long. It is woven again around the dilemma of the clash between chivalrous adventure and domestic bliss. This difficult question had already been treated in *Erec* where the wife suffered bitterly for a few indiscreet words. In *Yvain* it is the husband who suffers, for, having been granted a year's leave by his newly-married wife, he forgot to come back at the appointed time and both his mental and physical sufferings were acute. But, besides this time-honoured difficulty, the heroine, Laudine, was also faced with a dilemma, for the man she loved was the man who had killed her husband. The skill with which her maid Lunete inspired good sense into her mistress' mind, the poignancy of Laudine's own soliloquies and the reflections of her husband's murderer (Yvain) are told with an unerring penetration into the human mind—especially the feminine which, without being unduly harsh, he treats with a certain cynicism. This part, we may assume, was Chrétien's own, and his psychology of love is only matched by his mastery of language which moved his contemporaries to admiration and has not lost its charm to-day. Other episodes, such as the magic basin, the faithful lion, the role of dwarfs and giants were to be found in earlier literature. Another favourite motif of Chrétien's should, however, be mentioned—namely that of the spellbound land. This is the subject of the 'pesme aventure' which corresponds somewhat to the 'Joie de la Cort' in *Erec*. In the enchanted 'chastel' in *Yvain* thousands of young girls employed in sweated labour were awaiting a deliverer and the joy of these 'chaitives desprisonees' was as great as if he had been God come down from heaven (ll. 5781-2). This constant reverting in Chrétien's romances to the idea of a region 'under a spell' and the necessity of a deliverer gives a seriousness to the author's writings even when treating the dialectics of love. Moreover, a fresh note is struck in *Yvain* when the author complains that true lovers were no longer to be found, and the love that he qualifies as 'amor saintisme' towards the end of the poem is the disinterested love between two men, in fact, between Gauvain and Yvain, who unwittingly fought a duel on behalf of two quarrelsome sisters.

Had they recognized each other it is needless to say they would not have fought:

> Qu'amors qui n'est fausse ne fainte
> Est precieuse chose et sainte (ll. 6050-1).

We come to *Perceval* (or *Le Conte del Graal*, as it is headed in the manuscripts)—Chrétien's last great work, which remained unfinished and has left us all guessing as to what his solution of the problem would have been. For here we have a very different theme from any of those treated in his former poems. True, the motifs both of the dilemma and the spell are at the centre of the plot, but it is the training of the deliverer which is the real subject of the 'conte'. The poem opens, in approved fashion, with a proverb ('Qui petit seme petit quieut', etc.) followed by a panegyric of Phelipe de Flandre—a much better man, we are told, than Alexander, for his gifts were inspired by charity: 'Que (=car) li don sont de charité/ Que li bons cuens Phelipes done.' From him, too, Chrétien tells us, he received 'the book' with the instruction to put into rhyme 'le meillor conte. . . . Qui soit contez au cort real / ce est li contes del graäl'. We are then launched straight into the history of the small boy (whose name is not revealed as 'Perceval le Gallois' till much later) who was brought up purposely in ignorance by his mother in order to keep him out of temptation. Chrétien shows a remarkable knowledge of child psychology here—the boy's delight at the bird-song, his persistent curiosity at his first sight of knightly armour, his keenness to set out for Arthur's court where such armour is bestowed and even his unwillingness to turn back when he sees his mother fall as she watched him set out. Chrétien obviously knew that 'cet âge est sans pitié'. His education began early, for his mother gave him rules of conduct which he quoted on every possible occasion, until a wise knight (*li prod'om*) gave him fresh ones and advised the simple youth not to quote his mother any more. The instructions (*anseignemenz*) of the 'prodom' were of a knightly character but included a famous warning which the 'distichs' of Cato had popularized—namely, the danger of being 'trop parliers':

> 'Et gardez que vos ne soiiez
> Trop parlanz ne trop noveliers;
> Nus ne puet estre trop parliers
> Que sovant tel chose ne die
> Qu'an li atort a vilenie,
> Et li sages dit et retret:
> 'Qui trop parole, pechié fet' (ll. 1648-54).

Everyone who knows the story will remember that it was this piece of advice which caused Perceval to refrain from asking the meaning of the bleeding lance and the sacred dish (or grail) when they passed before his very eyes, thus failing to break the enchantment which held the fisher-king and the land under a disastrous spell. It was the dreadful fear of *vilenie* (cf. l. 3211) which kept him tongue-tied, but 'I fear', says the author, it will do him harm':

> Par ce que j'ai oï retreire
> Qu'ausi bien se puet an trop teire
> Con trop parler a la foiiee (ll. 3249-52).

Another dilemma, but not of love this time. 'It must indeed have been hard for the simple youth to know what to do, but he was thinking of himself and not of the afflicted king and hence 'plus se test qu'il ne convint'. The moral tone—even at times the religious tone—is much more marked in this poem than in Chrétien's other works. The 'conte' is, in fact, a kind of 'chastoiement' and contains sayings and instructions drawn from the *Disciplina clericalis* of Petrus Alfonsi and the *Disticha Catonis*, both of which must have been known to the author.

The first section of the part devoted to Perceval actually closes with Cato's description of Fortune (quoted by the 'leide demoisele'):

> 'Ha, Percevaus, Fortune est chauve
> Derriers et devant chevelue'.

It is noticeable, however, that so far it is only the utilitarian aspect of Perceval's delinquency that is emphasized—the fact that he has missed a good opportunity with unfortunate results. He has not broken the spell: the king would remain in his misery and the land would still be under a curse and many lives would be lost before the true deliverer came along. At this point (l. 6519 ff.) Perceval disappears from the scene and for some 2,000 lines the worldly-minded Gauvain fills the stage. When Perceval makes his appearance again after the lapse of some five years he is a sadder and wiser man. During those five weary years he has become an accomplished knight, but he has forgotten God:

> Einsi les 5 anz anplea
> Qu'onques de Deu ne li sovint (ll. 6237-8).

The consequence is that he has nothing but 'enui' in his heart. It is time now for the religious part of his education. On one of his aimless journeys he was stopped and admonished by a group of pilgrims for carrying arms on Good Friday and induced to pay a visit to a hermit. This holy man completed the instruction which his mother and the 'prodom' had begun. Weeping bitterly, Perceval told the hermit the sad story of his failure to pass the test and learn the meaning of the bleeding lance and the 'graäl.' This failure the hermit attributed to his cruelty in connection with his mother's death—not to his simplicity in obeying the 'prodom's instructions as was indicated in the earlier section of the poem. Perceval learnt, however, that his mother's prayers had saved him from a still worse fate. He learnt, also, that it was the hermit's uncle 'qui del graäl servir se fet' (l. 6419)—not with material food, but with 'une sole oiste':

> Tant sainte chose est li graäus
> Et il est tant esperitaus
> Qu'a sa vie plus ne covient
> Que l'oiste qui el graäl vient (l. 6425 f.).

The hermit then enjoined 'penitence de ton pechié', mixed with a few items of 'chevalerie'. He then whispered in his ear a prayer containing some of the most sublime names of God—only to be used in case of dire emergency (ll. 6481-8). After showing signs of true repentance and sharing the hermit's meagre food and lodging for a night, Perceval received Holy Communion and from that point he passes completely out of our sight:

> De Perceval plus longuemant
> Ne parole li contes ci (ll. 6514-5).

His name is not mentioned again in the poem.

It is almost tragic that this story of human development and deep spiritual meaning breaks off at such a crucial point and that the poet has felt it necessary to interlard it with some of the most fantastic adventures and feats of the incomparable Gauvain. But a poet must live, and 'the book' (the traditional 'livre' or 'estoire' of the poets of that time) had been given him by the generous Phelipe de Flandres whose gifts would hardly be justified did the poet not conform to the taste of his court. Hence the interval whilst Perceval is lost to view is filled with the fashionable sort of episodes. There is the story of the two quarrelling sisters, the younger of whom champions the cause of the unrecognized knight (Gauvain) against that of the elder sister's fiancé—not a very pleasing episode and the replica of one already treated in *Yvain*. One would like to know if these two unloving sisters (twice described by Chrétien) were drawn from life. There is one episode, however, described in Chrétien's best manner which must not be overlooked. This is the description of the impromptu battle between Gauvain, assisted by his girl friend and a crowd of townspeople led by the mayor and the corporation ('le majeur et les eschevins'), who besiege them as they sit unsuspecting and amusing themselves in a room of the palace. Gauvain has to snatch up the chess-board wherewith to defend himself and the lady hurls the chess-pieces (which are fortunately extra large and hard) at the foe with great effect. She was a valiant ally for she tucks up her skirts and swears like a trooper:

> Si s'est estrainte et escorciée
> Et jure come coreciée
> Qu'ele les fera toz destruire . . . (l. 6003 f.).

With this episode the Gauvain interlude ends, but it is taken up again later and there are further adventures with damsels and mysterious knights of which Gauvain is the hero. The main feature of this section, however, is the introduction of the mysterious castle inhabited by ladies ('dames et damoiseles'), including Arthur's mother, Gauvain's sister, and many others, who are held captive by a spell which can only be broken by a knight who passes the test of the 'lit de merveille' (described at great length and quite fantastic), the savage lion and other perilous encounters. Gauvain, the matchless, if irresponsible, knight, boldly undertakes and accomplishes all these tests, but the poem breaks off before the episode is completely finished. It will be noticed that this spell can be broken by Gauvain, the perfect courtier-knight. This is but another example of Chrétien's psychological acumen, for there is no trace of a mystical meaning here. The 'anchantemant' are such that a knight who has 'tot le los du mont' and is 'sanz vilenie' can remove them and so enable the ladies to recover their property, the young girls to get husbands, and the young men to attain the rank of knight. Gauvain was eminently the right person to break this spell, which is quite different from that involved in discovering the mystic truth of the 'saint graal'.

It is interesting to watch the development of the mysterious spell-motif which runs through Chrétien's romances. In the first in date—*Erec*—we have the enchanted garden guarded by the invincible knight. But the deliverance, through the valiant Erec, affects not only the garden but the land around and more especially the sad inmates of the court. Hence the name 'Joie de la Cort'. In *Cligès* the motif is absent and everything revolves around the two pairs of lovers. In *Lancelot* it is another mysterious spell which allows people to enter the enchanted region but renders them unable to leave it. 'Facilis descensus Averni', etc.—but unlike Avernus, this nether region can be 'harrowed' and the deliverer—Lancelot— is almost mobbed by the grateful crowd who—be it noted—all come from the Kingdom of Logre (King Arthur's England). In *Yvain* we have a more restricted idea of a 'chastel', but none the less, the deliverer is worshipped almost as if he were God come down from heaven. Finally in *Perceval* it is a land which, in addition to its ruler, lies under some strange ban. And once again it is England. Like Uther Pendragon in *Geoffroy of Monmouth*, the king (*roi-pêcheur*) suffered from a mysterious malady which prevented him from moving without assistance; he watched with concern the island (England) being 'well nigh all laid waste'. Here, however, the likeness ends, for Uther was poisoned and it was his son Arthur who brought prosperity back to the land with his strong lance, his invincible sword and his shield painted with the image of holy Mary. There was nothing new, of course, in the idea of a spell— there was the Celtic idea of the 'geis', there was the classical riddle of the sphinx, the Anglo-Saxon idea of the deliverer (in *Beowulf*), and— perhaps most important of all—the vision of Christ, the Harrower of Hell, delivering the spirits in prison. Many of such ideas and legends may have been at the back of Chrétien's mind when he sketched in embryo the moral development of one destined to become a benefit to mankind. There can be no doubt that in *Perceval* Chrétien was turning definitely more towards the mystical meaning of life. It would be futile to reiterate here the theories as to the origin of the grail itself. Its source in Chrétien's own brain is far from being an impossibility in view of the skill with which he handles the love-problems and invents their solutions. For, beneath the ephemeral fashion of the 'question dilemmatique', the stylized description of love-symptoms and the superficial attitude towards social rank, there is something much deeper in Chrétien's mind which will keep breaking through. At heart, despite the yielding to contemporary pressure, a concession probably due to the necessity of making a living, Chrétien's attitude towards the true values of life were not what a superficial reading of his works might suggest. He acquiesced seemingly with the accepted meanings of the overworked terms *corteisie* and *vilenie*, but we frequently get a glimpse below the surface: 'Je sui un hom' declares the poor hideous creature who guarded the beasts in *Yvain*. 'En ceo fist ele com corteise', he says of Enide when out of consideration for a miserable girl's feelings she tried to go and speak to her alone, and his sympathy with the poor, maltreated, overworked girls in 'la pesme aventure' is obvious. So, too, it is obvious that Perceval, whether he was destined for the role of deliverer or not, has to undergo a severe training before he can achieve true moral worth as distinct from the worldly perfection of a Gauvain or a Lancelot. We have seen how, for Perceval, the dilemma was not concerned with a love-problem but with a right judgment as to when to hold one's tongue—a difficult question indeed. It must be admitted that Chrétien seems to have enjoyed dealing with these 'questions dilemmatiques'. They hardly existed for Marie de France for whom 'pure love' overruled all other questions and cut across all conventions. We have a definite example in Gautier d'Arras where he describes the difficulties of his hero in *Ille et Galeran* both as to whether he has a right to expect his lady to be faithful when he has been disfigured, and how he himself is to be faithful to two loves (cf. supra). But it was Chrétien who brought the discussion of such problems to a pitch of perfection which none of his followers ever reached and which, though prompted by a passing fashion, greatly conduced to his popularity in his own day. For this was a kind of escape literature. It would be absurd to ignore the background against which Chrétien's literary activity stands out:—the political struggles of those thirty years (1160–90), the misery in England and her continental possessions (so often mentioned in contemporary works) which was bound to accompany these struggles; the marriages, the repudiations of marriage, the intrigues, the dashings to and fro between France and England of the harassed king and all his suite (including the queen); the murder of Thomas à Becket and the horror it occasioned. For it was not in France proper that this ferment of thought and expression was going on. It was in the domains of Henry Plantagenet and the neighbouring countries. Whilst the French government under Louis VII was quietly consolidating itself in Paris and Suger was composing his chronicle, the Norman and Anglo-Norman aristocracy, the beaux-esprits of Champagne and Guienne were indulging in these games of the intellect with practically no regard for the ideals of a St. Bernard or the approval of the Church. But by the end of the century a change was coming—mere lip-service to the tenets of the Church began to be found inadequate. The necessity of confession, penitence and penance was recovering its influence over men's minds and Chrétien's tentative suggestion of some holy thing (*si sainte chose*) of spiritual import (*si esperital*) was seized upon by his followers and developed in the early thirteenth century into that mystical vessel of grace, only to be obtained through purity and renunciation that we find in the prose *Queste del Saint Graal.*

BIBLIOGRAPHY

Parts I and II

Amadas et Ydoine. Ed. J. R. Reinhard. Paris 1926. (CFMA).

Ipomedon. Hue de Rotlandes *Ipomedon.* Kölbing u. Koschwitz. Breslau 1890.

Hue de Rotlandes *Protesilaus.* hgg. von F. Kluckow. Halle 1924.

Roman de Thèbes, édition critique, par L. Constant. 2 vol. Paris 1890. (SATF).

Roman d'Enéas. (1) Texte critique par J.-J. Salverda de Grave. Halle 1891.

(2) Texte critique par J.-J. Salverda de Grave. Paris 1925–31. 2 vol. (CFMA).

Roman de Troie par Bénoît de Sainte Maure, publié par L. Constant. 6 vol. Paris 1904–12. (SATF).

Gautier 'Arras, Œuvres, *Ille et Galeran et Éracle.* Par E. Löseth. Paris 1890.

Poème d'Alixandre. Förster-Koschwitz: Altfr. Uebungsbuch, pp. 238–46.

Bartsch-Wiese. Chrestomathie 12th ed. 1927, pp. 12–14.

C. Appel. Prov. Chrest. 6th ed. 1930, pp. 13–14.

Floire et Blancheflore. (1) Publié d'après les mss. avec Introd., des notes et un glossaire par M. Edélestand du Meril. Paris 1856. (Bibl. Elzévirienne.)

(2) Éd. crit. d'après le ms. fr. 1447, par M. Pelan. Paris 1939.

(3) *Li Romans de F. et B.* in beiden Fassungen. F. Krüger. Berlin 1938.

Huon de Bordeaux. F. Guessard et Ch. Grandmaison. Paris 1860. (Anc. poètes.)

Aucassin et Nicolette: (1) *Auc. u. Nicolete neu nach den Hss.* herausgeg. von H. Suchier. 9th ed. Paderborn, 1921.

(2) *Auc. et Nic. Chantefable du XIIIᵉs.* Éd. par Mario Roques. Introduction détaillée, etc. 1925. 2nd ed., 1936. (CFMA).

Clarisse et Florent. Publ. by M. Schweigel with other poems. Marburg 1891.

Pyrame et Tisbé. (1) Barbazan et Méon. *Fabliaux et Contes* II, p. 326 ff.

(2) Texte normand du XIIᵉs. édition critique, par C. De Boer. Amsterdam 1911.

(3) *Piramus et Tisbé,* poème du XIIᵉs. Ed. C. de Boer. 1921. (CFMA).

Part III

Geoffroy of Monmouth: *Historia regum Britanniae.* E. Faral: La Légende arthurienne. Tome III. Documents. Paris 1939.

History of the Kings of Britain. Transl. S. Evans. Everyman's Library 577.

Wace: *Li Roman de Brut.* Ed. I. Arnold. 2 vol. 1938–40. (SATF).

Gautier d'Arras. See supra, Pt. I.

Marie de France. *Lais* edited by A. Ewert. Oxford 1944.

Die Lais der M. de F., hgg. von K. Warnke. 3rd ed. Halle 1924.

Die Fabeln der M. de F., hgg. von K. Warnke. Halle 1898.

Selected fables edited by A. Ewert and R. C. Johnson. Oxford 1942.

Le Lai du Cor. Ed. by Fr. Wulff. Lund 1888. Restitution critique.
See Dissertation by H. Dörner. Strasbourg 1907.

Béroul: (1) *Li Roman de Tristan par Béroul et un anonyme.* Publ. par E. Muret.
Paris 1903. (SATF).

(2) *Le R. de T.* poème du XIIᵉ siècle, éd. par E. Muret, 1913. 4th ed. 1947.
(CFMA).

(3) *The Romance of Tristan* . . . ed. by A. Ewert. Oxford 1939.

Thomas: *Le Roman de Tristan par Thomas,* publ. par J. Bédier. Paris 1905 (SATF).

Folie Tristan. Les deux poèmes de la *Folie Tristan,* publ. par J. Bédier. Paris 1907.
(SATF).

La F.T. de Oxford. E. Höpffner. Paris 1943.

La F.T. de Berne. E. Höpffner. Paris 1949.

Chrétien de Troyes. Sämmtliche erhaltene Werke . . . hgg. Wendelin Förster.
4 vol. Halle 1884–99.

CHAPTER V

STORY-TELLING IN THE MIDDLE AGES

BEFORE the stories of Arthurian heroes were grouped together to form the collective and somewhat tendentious cycle of the Holy Grail, there is ample evidence in France of the craving for story-telling which is common to people of all ages. No one who has read the more outstanding examples of epic literature in the twelfth and thirteenth centuries can doubt the ability of their authors to tell stories which would enthral their hearers or readers as the case may be. The author of the *Chanson de Roland* is a born story-teller; the various episodes in the life of Guillaume d'Orange, the tragic fate of Raoul de Cambrai, even though wrapped in slow-moving epic form, were of such a nature as to move the hearts and hold the attention of the hearers, probably by their narrative quality rather than by their poetic form. We know from contemporary evidence that this was the case. The author of the poem known as the *Poème Moral* (end of twelfth century; see supra, p. 19) tells us that the church service was barely ended before the congregation would rush out to listen to the 'jugleire' reciting the story of Charlot and Ogier, of how Roland killed Fernagu and how Aiol was mocked on account of his rusty armour. Even the *Lives of the Saints* provided many a piquant episode—for, although these stories generally had a moral character and were composed with the edification of the hearer in view, the moral is sometimes lost sight of—or is of rather an inverted nature. There is the popular story of Eppo the thief (of which we have versions in several languages) who was saved from the gallows by the Virgin for having repeated five 'Ave Marias', and a corresponding number of 'Paternosters' every time he passed a church, even if he was actually on the way to commit a robbery or a murder. By another curious inversion the cult of the Virgin which had been partly responsible for the almost idolatrous glorification of woman in the court poetry (*poésie courtoise*) was probably partly the cause of a considerable anti-feminist reaction in literature. It was a reversal of the symbol AVE into its equal and opposite EVA. The abuse heaped upon the sex for a sort of monopoly in ruse and guile became a favourite ingredient in many of the short stories of the period. The celibate atmosphere of the monastery and

124

the priesthood may have contributed to this, but the tendency was very widespread and brings us to our first considerable group of stories told for their own sake.

The popular collection of tales which became current in almost every country of Europe, known as the *Histoire des Sept Sages de Rome*, is indicative of several tendencies in the literature of the time which bore considerable fruit during the following centuries. The first of these tendencies is seen in this thirst for short stories—mere tales, fabulous or otherwise, and not long enough to be tedious. The second was the liking for a framework into which stories could be inserted at will and slipped in and out, or multiplied as required. The third is a lack of care for the outward form—for skilful versification, or pure rhymes; for the stories in this collection are told in prose even where a verse-form had been first in the field. The Latin version of this legend of the 'Seven Wise Men of Rome', which is generally known as the *Historia de Septem Sapientibus*, was translated into almost every European language and enjoyed an enormous popularity. This Latin version has been shown to have been based on an earlier Old French prose version—itself a rendering into prose of a rhymed version which preceded it. Whether this was the earliest version or whether it was in turn based on a Latin original, who can say? In any case the germ of the story is the guile and wickedness of a cruel stepmother—a fact which might point to a secular origin, though possibly this part of the legend is merely a version of the biblical story of Potiphar's wife. One of the earliest evidences we have of its popularity in France is the work known under the name of *Dolopathos*, or *Opusculum de rege et septem sapientibus*, which can be dated as belonging to the end of the twelfth century. The author refers to himself in the preface as 'frater Johannes qualiscumque in Alta Silva monachus'. This Latin version was the basis of a long, diffuse French poem of 12,901 lines composed by a certain Herbert, a poet at the court of Philippe Auguste who died in 1223. The *Dolopathos* contains what would seem to be the basic form of the legend, padded round with monkish reflections, moralizings and ejaculations. The framework is here in its simplest form—a young prince is accused by his stepmother of making love to her and conspiring against the king; he is condemned to death and only saved by the manoeuvre of his advocates, the Seven Sages of Rome, who, by relating a story a day, delay the execution of the sentence until the truth comes out. The stories include the tale of the faithful hound (familiar to modern readers in the poem of *Beth Gelert*), a story from Herodotus, a version of the 'pound of flesh' story (familiar through Shakespeare), the story of the children changed into swans (probably of Celtic origin) and the story of the woman who pretended to throw herself down a well to deceive her husband, which was very popular in the Middle Ages and was used by Molière.

The Latin *Historia* has the same framework but has double the number of stories, as alternate stories are told by the stepmother in order to persuade the king to execute his son without delay. In some versions each of the sages tells two stories and so the number is again increased. This idea of 'le pour et le contre' may not have been in the original but the repercussions of the general idea of stories fitted into a framework were almost incalculable when we think of the *Decameron*, the *Heptameron*, the *Canterbury Tales* and the *Arabian Nights*. In any case the popularity of the *Sept Sages de Rome* was immense if we may judge from the number of manuscripts, of printed books, of translations, of chap-books, to which was added the story of the 'Seven Wise Women'—just as 'les neuf preux' had to have their counterpart in 'les neuf preuses'. Nor was its popularity confined to the West, for in other versions (generally designated the 'oriental group' (including a Persian, a Hebrew and a Syrian version), a teacher of the name of Syntipas or Sindbar has the role of story-teller and the Seven Sages dwindle in importance. In some of the occidental versions the role of teacher falls to Virgil but he does not usurp the function of the story-tellers. It was all very ingenious as a method of accumulating stories. The object of the original ones was to illustrate the vice and guile of women; the opposing tales were introduced to show the folly of hasty decisions. But the object was often forgotten and the stories became mere stories for their own sake with little regard for the moral lesson they were supposed to inculcate. However, the ending was always the same—the intriguing stepmother after defeating each of the sages in turn and making the weak king change his mind just as many times, is vanquished in the long run. She receives the due reward of her sins, and the honour of a virtuous youth is vindicated.

It is not surprising that *Les Sept Sages de Rome* had a sequel. In *Marques de Rome* the misjudged prince has become king and has a favourite 'seneschal' (Marques by name) who is the son of Cato, one of the seven. He is persecuted by the queen in much the same way as his predecessor had been. It is to be noticed that the Seven Sages have begun to fall from their high estate and lose their prestige also owing to the malice of a jealous woman. There is a pathetic scene in which they are all found lying asleep round a pear tree, their cheeks wet with tears on account of their neglect. They are partially reinstated, however, and their intercession for Marques when he falls from favour is as successful as in the case of the young prince. *Marques de Rome* is full of adventures and the actual stories do not play such an important part. In fact they are only introduced towards the end of the 'roman'. But the episodes are well related and there are some interesting passages in which philosophical questions are treated (e.g. the discussion on *sens* and *reison*). The language, too, is colourful and abounds in expressive phrases. In fact, *Marques de Rome* deserves attention both as a narrative and as a treatise on human nature. It was deservedly popular and may be read with advantage still. This is more than can be said for the further sequels—*Laurin, Cassiodorus, Péliarménus* and *Cador*, which are tedious and aimless. The Seven Sages of Rome deteriorated rapidly, just as did the Seven Sages of Greece in the days of their decline. There is, however, one noticeable detail in *Laurin*, the most readable of the three, which consists in the fact that the story is brought into the orbit of King Arthur and his knights. This brings us to another collection of tales quite different in character but alike in providing pabulum for the hunger for stories which characterized the age.

Chrétien de Troyes, besides being a great artist and a connoisseur of the human heart, bequeathed to the French nation a group of fascinating personalities and a mysterious emblem which were bound to have far-reaching results. He had, moreover, left an unfinished poem of an enigmatical character—*le roman de Perceval*. In this romance we have the first known reference in French literature to that 'sainte chose', the Holy Grail. King Arthur and his knights had been introduced to the public (*circ.* 1155) in Wace's translation of Geoffroy of Monmouth's *Historia regum Britanniae* and in this translation we find references to the fruitful idea of the round table ('... la reönde table / Dont Breton dient mainte fable'). Chrétien does not actually mention the round table, but Arthur and his court provide a centre in the romances from which the knights set out on their various adventures and towards which they gravitate like bees returning to their hive. The accounts of their adventures are very different from the tales told by the Seven Sages although the later additions to this collection (in *Marques de Rome* and *Laurin*) do approximate to their style and even incorporate some of their elements. Now Chrétien's works were destined for court audiences and were, for the most part, secular in character with the exception of the unfinished *Perceval* which opens the door to more serious treatment. This opportunity was seized by Chrétien's first continuator, Robert de Boron, who pursues the subject of the Holy Grail and provides a history of its early adventures and how it was brought to Britain by Joseph of Arimathea. He gives us a notion of the 'secrets du graal', its guardians, and the mystical importance attached to it, thus providing a 'trait d'union' between Chrétien's predominantly secular account and the subsequent mystical and religious character it assumes in later works. There was quite enough in Boron's work combined with Chrétien's stories of King Arthur's knights to form a compact mass which, like a snowball, increased in size and volume as it rolled along. 'La légende du Graal', as M. Pauphilet has said, 'est un développement continu, une incessante création.'[1] Quite when and how the development took place it is hard to say, but before many years had elapsed vast compilations in prose had arisen in which the tales of Lancelot, of Perceval and even of Tristan and others not originally connected with the Round Table, overlap and intertwine, though each gives prominence to its own hero. Perhaps it was the possibility of adding new stories, of reviving popular heroes and following them in their careers, of writing sequels and thus giving them a kind of cyclic character, which accounted for the immense popularity of these collections in the Middle Ages. However this may be, the conglomerations of adventures known as the *Prose-Tristan*, the *Perceval* in prose (or *Perlesvaux* in a later version) achieved a great degree of popularity to judge from the number of manuscripts—even though they constituted a 'masse indigeste' of material difficult to disentangle. The *Prose-Tristan* does not really add much to our appreciation of the legend and tragic history of Tristan and Iseult. The *Prose-Perceval*, in which the hero loses his original character and finally accomplishes his task, is full of inconsistencies but keeps alive the characters which play their individual parts on the constant background of the main story. The *Cycle de Lancelot*, however, offers certain features of intrinsic value and some of its component parts have proved of lasting interest. The Lancelot-cycle or *Cycle de Map* (so called because of an erroneous attribution to Walter Map) comprises five romances—the *Estoire del Graal* (or *Grant Saint Graal*), *Merlin*, *Lancelot*, *La Queste del Saint Graal* and the *Mort Artu*. All are full of knightly adventures

---

[1] See Pauphilet: *Le Legs du Moyen-âge*, p. 109.

and prowess, of strange forests and mysterious apparitions. A glance at the last two, in many ways the most characteristic and engrossing, will give some idea of the tendencies and methods of these works. The *Queste*, in which we have the subject of the search for the grail adumbrated by Chrétien de Troyes, is the most purely religious and celibate in character of the five romances composing the cycle. An air of melancholy and frustration broods over it. There are many tears and little laughter. It portrays the Christian life according to the monkish rules and is a kind of protest against the life of chivalry and love which the romances had advocated and sung. But it is more than this. It embodies a noble idea of a universal brotherhood combined with a deep insight into character which the many adventures do not obscure. The 'Table Round' is no limited conception. It is round because it symbolizes the whole round world. It is a centre to which 'de toutes terres ou chevalerie repère, soit de chrétienté ou de paiennie, viennent li chevalier'. The story opens on the eve of 'Pentecoste'—a time much celebrated in the romances as the psychological moment for romantic adventures. The companions of the Round Table are assembled at Camelot in the year of our Lord 453. An air of expectancy, one might almost say an ominous air, seems to brood over the knights for the whole country is under a kind of spell. There have been for a long time past mysterious happenings, rather sinister portents, and a certain 'malaise' is apparent among the companions for they have failed to perform the last test to which they have been subjected. They have seated themselves at table in a mood of somewhat frustrated expectancy and have just finished their first course when things begin to happen. A beautiful youth accompanied by a dignified old man mysteriously enters the hall. He is introduced by the 'preudome' as 'celui par cui les merveilles de cest païs et des estranges terres remaindront' (= *will cease*). The youth promptly proceeds to the one empty seat known as 'le siège périlleux' which has been set aside and labelled as being destined for the one who shall deliver the land from the spell. The youth is in effect Galahad, and he tells them he has come to stir them up to undertake the *Queste* which is waiting to be accomplished in order to 'achever les aventures del Saint Graal'. And so they set out. The number of knights who volunteer for the quest is 150. King Arthur (less adventurous than of yore) and Queen Guinevere let them go with regret, for well they know that many of them will not return—especially does the king grieve over the departure of Lancelot and Gauvain, whom he loves

more than all the others. And here we perceive the skilful irony of
the author, for it is Gauvain who is so eager for the quest and
Lancelot who, throughout the whole cycle, is disloyal to the king.
In fact, there is a complete reversal of the roles of the individual
knights for Lancelot, despite his prowess and experience, can never
achieve the quest. He is 'plus durs que pierre, plus amers que fuz,
plus nus et plus despris que figuier'; for in spite of all the gifts with
which Nature had endowed him, he is not warmed by the fire of
the Holy Spirit. Lancelot confesses his sin freely: 'je suis morz de
pechié d'une moie dame que je ai aimée toute me vie, et ce est la
reine Guenievre, la fame le roi Artu.' Alas, Guinevere is equally
guilty and she has never been to confession since her marriage. So
Lancelot cannot even be short-listed for finding the grail in spite of
his many tears and the many sermons and interpretations of hard
sayings and ominous dreams to which he has to listen. Gauvain, the
knight 'sans per', the valiant, the courteous, who plays such an
important part in Chrétien's romances, is also relegated to the
background, though for different reasons. He is the typical worldly
knight, never failing in valour or gallantry, a model of politeness,
but he, too, is rejected as regards the finding of the grail, for he
cannot face the pain of penitence—'de penitence faire ne pourait il
la peine souffrir'. This character had already been sketched by
Chrétien, but here we have, as Monsieur Pauphilet has said: 'la
chevalerie courtoise, jugée selon l'esprit cistercien'. The idea of
chastity is again prominent. No knight on this quest might be
accompanied by his wife or his lady-friend for the devil knew that
the easiest way to entice a man into sin was by means of a woman,
as had been the case with Adam the first man, Solomon the wisest
man, Samson the strongest, and Absalom the fairest of mortals.
One glance from Guinevere's eyes had been the dart from the
enemy's quiver which had deflected Lancelot from the path of
virtue and caused his fall into the sin of 'luxure'—the most dangerous
sin of all. The three elect who attain the end of the quest are
Galahad, Perceval and Bohort (*li dui virge et li tiers chaste*), types of
the Christlike celibate, the simple-minded seeker and the laborious
saint. The story is long, often tedious, but it lures us on as one
anecdote follows another. Dreams and visions abound giving rise
to interpretations and sermons. The knights move to and fro in the
'gaste foreste' in search of adventure—'une heure arriere et autre
avant'—and are quite distressed if they cannot meet with one. But
on the whole there is no dearth of aggressive knights, holy hermits,

damsels (either angel or fiend) or charitable elderly aunts, so that the interest seldom flags. There is much that partakes of 'le merveilleux', strange ships glide to and fro with no apparent means of locomotion—one of them being Solomon's ship (*la nef de Solomon*) which mysteriously kept alive the sacred tradition from the 'tree of life' to the cross for which it supplied the wood. Magic castles and creations of the devil appear and vanish at will. It is rather a light relief when twelve damsels, disappointed at Bohort's refusal to satisfy their desire because he values his own soul more than their lives, throw themselves from a high rock, but vanish into thin air before they reach the bottom. The final scene of the finding of the grail, the apparition of Joseph and the deaths of Galahad and Perceval leave us with an impression of pure fantasy and religious mysticism; but, in spite of the melancholy that pervades the *Queste*, owing to the narrator's skill, we are left waiting for more—for clearly the end was not yet and a sequel was indicated.

In the *Mort le Roi Artu* the melancholy deepens in spite of the fact that the religious element, so prominent in the *Queste*, has entirely disappeared. There are no more tears of penitence and confession. But, as the Round Table disintegrates, a certain pessimistic, almost fatalistic, note creeps in. It is distressing to see the knights killing one another, for victory gives no sense of satisfaction when it is erstwhile friends and companions who are fighting. It is tragic in the extreme when Lancelot gives the death-blow to his former friend Gauvain, since their love and admiration for one another has never really ceased. Indeed, Lancelot almost abases himself to bring about a reconciliation, but Gauvain, incensed by the death of two of his brothers, forces the king, against his better judgment, to continue the war against Lancelot and his clan (*meisnie*). What lay at the bottom of the fraternal slaughter was actually the unquenchable love between Lancelot and Guinevere which, in spite of temporary misunderstandings, shone like a steady flame. After having been spied upon and caught 'en flagrant délit' they are parted for the moment. Lancelot, however, appears with his followers just in time to save Guinevere from the flames to which she had been condemned. In a scene, reminiscent of Béroul, Guinevere is carried off to the neighbouring forest, but the estrangement between Lancelot and the king now develops into open warfare between the 'Round Table' and the 'lignage du Roi Ban' to which Lancelot belongs. It is a tragic war because it is between friends, for Lancelot had been trained at Arthur's court to which he had added lustre for many a year. King Arthur sinks deeper and deeper into melancholy as one after another his knights are slain. It could not be God's will that such tragedies should happen. It is Fortune with her dire wheel who is responsible. There was a hint of this when the knights returned from the quest and Gauvain was asked by the king how many knights he had slain. He has to confess to the number of eighteen, but this was not owing to his valour, he declares, but because 'bad luck' (*mescheänce*) happened to him more often than to the others. And now the king, as misfortunes crowd upon him, sees himself in a vision seated by Fortune on the top of a high wheel, only to be hurled to the bottom with such force that he is stunned by the fall. As he falls he hears Fortune remark that everyone, however high he is placed, must fall in the end. It is indeed a case of 'de si haut si bas', for he had been the ruler of many kingdoms and his court the admiration of the world. His dignified death and disposal of his famous sword give a certain nobility to his end, but his last tragic act is unintentionally to squeeze the life out of one of his knights in a last final embrace.

What then caused the unparalleled vogue of this rather melancholy collection of stories which, with its almost pagan character, seemed only to illustrate the wisdom of the Greek sage's advice: to regard the end of a long life? It surely was due again to the skill of the narrator in the disposal of his matter and the consistent delineation of the characters he portrays. The story of the love of Lancelot and Guinevere is as poignant in its last stages as that of Tristan and Iseult which in many points it resembles. Lancelot, who during the quest had abjured his love, falls again when temptation is renewed, for he had no will to resist. He had not been back at court a month, the author tells us, before his love flared up again and this time he showed it openly whereas before it had been hidden. Guinevere was irresistible, for her beauty was so great that everyone was amazed at it. Although at this time she was fifty years of age, yet nowhere in the world could her equal be found, which caused some knights to declare that, as her beauty did not fade, she was the fount of all loveliness. Lancelot himself, although no longer in the prime of life (we are told that he was sixty-eight), still had such a power of attraction that his men adored him and the young lady of Escalot died of an unrequited passion which Lancelot had rather shamelessly kindled. The king himself is a somewhat enigmatical character for, although he has lost any control over his knights and is weak and lachrymose, he is capable of great anger and (like King Mark) is ready to burn his wife when her sin is exposed. And yet, when she returns to him after her proven faithlessness and her flight, he receives her with open arms and they are as happy together 'as if God had come down to earth'. On one occasion he actually excuses the lovers on the ground that 'sens ne reson' cannot stand against 'force d'amor'.

La Mort le Roi Artu, to give it its full name, is a beautiful story well told. The language is both fluid and colourful and carries the reader along without a hitch. It is, in fact, an outstanding piece of story-telling and many are the episodes which remain fixed in the memory. There is the scene in the garden when Lancelot climbs up and enters the queen's bed-chamber by the window; the grievous duel between Lancelot and Gauvain in which the latter is nearly victorious because it is fought about the hour of noon when Gauvain's strength was always at its greatest; there is the beautiful scene when the 'lady of Shalott' comes floating down the stream and the king and all his knights descend the steps to gaze upon her as she lies dead in the boat; and there is the impressive scene in which the famous sword Escalibor is thrown into the lake and a hand is seen rising out of the lake as far as the elbow which seizes the sword and waves it upwards three or four times before disappearing again into the water; and then the curtain falls on the final scene when the mysterious boat comes for Arthur and he is wafted away out of the sight of his watching, grieving knight. All these scenes are familiar to the reader through later versions, but this only proves the skill of the first narrator who started the ball rolling.

In a framework such as this adventures could be multiplied at the discretion of the writer for the story is capable of continuous development. The same is true of another 'genre' of literature which provides an almost equally adaptable framework for the story-teller's art. A chronicle could easily become a store-house of miraculous happenings and anecdotes. Not only in his *Life of Saint Cuthbert* did the venerable Bede (if we go back no further than the eighth century) give rein to his story-telling bent. His *Historia Ecclesiastica* is a treasure house of pleasant tales of Alban, of Caedmon, of Cedd and Aidan. There are mysterious happenings and visions, too, though their tone is completely different from that of the adventures in the *Queste*. Although monasticism was at its height, the strictness of the Cistercian rules was as yet unknown and the doctrines of repentance and penitence do not cause such floods of tears to flow in spite of sermons and instructions. History, ecclesiastical and otherwise, flourished from the eighth century onwards. It is valuable, not only for documentary importance, but for the stories and legends which enliven its pages, for it is 'history tinged with legend and invention' and it is often hard to draw a hard and fast line between the two. Paulus Diaconus (*c.* 720–90), in his *History of the Lombards*, relates many a pleasant 'yarn. There is that of Gunthram's dream and the lizard that came out of the king's mouth and led the way to the hidden treasure; there is the story of the fly whose leg the king cut off, not knowing it was an evil spirit, and of the boy Grinwald, mounted on a large horse and killing his captor with his little sword, which may well have inspired a well-known episode in the *Chançun de Willame*. Still more irresponsible is the work of Liutprand of Cremona who wrote his *Antapodosis* in the tenth century as an act of retaliation for supposed injuries done him by the king. Here we have the story—worthy to be compared with any *fabliau*—of the woman who out of avarice hid the precious belt in her own body and it was only discovered to her confusion by a string which was hanging out. This unpleasant story appealed so much to the author that he embellished it with a little poem in equally bad taste. Liutprand's contempt for women is so great that he is a forerunner not only of the *fabliaux* but of the type of story told in the *Seven Sages of Rome*. In the eleventh century Richer's chronicle provides a pleasant mixture of fact and fiction, but it is not till we come to the twelfth century that we find that prince of story-tellers, Geoffroy of Monmouth, in whose *Historia*, as we have seen, fiction so far outweighs fact as almost to belie its name. There were, of course, other legends in the *Historia* besides those of King Arthur's Court. We have the story of King Lear and his three daughters; of the Irishman who cut a steak from his thigh to appease his uncle's hunger, and other tales which crop up again in later works. Geoffroy's good fortune consists in having had a competent translator of his Latin work, for in 1155 appeared the translation into French by *Wace* which became the source from which many of the stories we have been considering first sprang and found their way into practically all the countries of Western Europe, so that King Arthur, having been once 'launched', had a greater and more international vogue even than Charlemagne himself.

Beside the brilliant story-telling of Geoffroy of Monmouth other chronicles, or quasi-chronicles, pale in comparison. His mantle, to a certain extent, fell on Geoffroi Gaimar, who lived at a time when the recent appearance of the other Geoffroy's romance of British history was at the height of its fame. But Gaimar as a romancer cannot be mentioned in the same breath as his predecessor. His chronicle (*Estoire des Engleis*) is a history of the Anglo-Saxon kings but extends into Norman times and ends with the death of William Rufus. Its historical value does not concern us here, but merely the fact of his using a historical framework in which to insert his own stories or elaborate those of others. Visions and signs abound as they do in all chronicles of this period, and the author obviously revels in anecdotes, amplifying and embroidering those that he found in his sources. He incorporates into his history well-known stories such as those of Haveloc the Dane and Hereward the Wake. The latter story, based on contemporary history, is well known. The former, founded on national English traditions coming down from the time of the Danish wars, is more remote and therefore lends itself better to legendary treatment. The hero Haveloc belongs to the town of Grimsby and the Danelaw and seems to have been a historical person (or possibly two persons merged into one) of the name of Olaf (or Anlaf). Gaimar has inserted the story into the gap between his two main sources, viz. Geoffroy of Monmouth's *Historia* and the *Anglo-Saxon Chronicle*. Clearly local legends were introduced into this story of a dispossessed prince who was brought up as a boy by the honest fisherman Grim (hence the name of Grimsby) and employed, when a young man, as scullion in the court of a neighbouring king. Now it happened that this un-scrupulous king was at a loss how to dispose of an orphaned niece who had been committed to his care, in such a way as to be able to seize her inheritance. Knowing nothing of the origins of his scullion Cuaran (as Haveloc was called at his court), he married his niece to him, thinking thus to rid himself of both her and her pretensions. For a time this ruse succeeded, but, warned by a dream, the young couple returned to Grimsby, where Haveloc was recognized by a daughter of the fisherman who had adopted him. He thus became aware of his birth and he and his wife (*Argentille*, by name) made their way over to Denmark where, with the help and support of an old friend of his father's and many discontented subjects of the present king, he regained his kingdom and all ended happily. So much for the historical tradition. But now, added to this, comes the legend. Haveloc, though graceful in form and of a generous

K

disposition as became his high birth, was of almost supernatural beauty and strength, and no one could stand up against him:

> Bel vis aveit e beles mains
> Cors eschivid (= *slender*), suef e plains:
> Beles jambes ot e bels piez.
> Li suen semblanz ert tut tens liez.
> Mais pur co que hardiz esteit
> N'aveit vadlet en la maisun
> Si li faiseit ahateisun
> E sur lui cumençast medlées
> Qu'il nel ruast jambes levées (ll. 105-14).

For this reason the king had made him his 'jugleür'. But the king knew nothing of an even more supernatural gift which marked him out as a mortal with a destiny. One night, as he lay asleep on his back, his wife noticed that a flame issued forth from his mouth:

> Une flamme vit qui issid
> Fors de la buche sun marid
> Qui encore ert tut endormid (ll. 242-4).

Haveloc was ashamed of what his wife had seen—but Argentille realized that the flame indicated some great destiny, and she asked immediately: 'Amis, u est li tuen lignage?' (l. 304). Moreover, she had just had a dream in the best tradition of one of Merlin's prophecies. She dreamt that they were in a grove between the sea and the forest, when a huge bear rushed to attack her husband. Then wild boars came up from the sea and attacked the bear. There were foxes with the bear and many of these were killed as well as the bear itself, into which a wild boar drove its teeth. The remaining foxes ran up and straightway did obeisance to Haveloc with their tails between their legs as if to beg for mercy. As Cuaran (or Haveloc) approached the sea all the big trees in the forest did homage to him (*de tutes pars li enclinerent*). As the wood fell back the sea mounted and Cuaran was in danger again. But two lions approached and fell on their knees before him and, when Cuaran mounted a tree for fear, they came and knelt before the tree. It was at this point that Argentille awoke and perceived the flame. Other wonders marked out Haveloc, of the kind loved in the English-Welsh legends and in the lives of insular saints. Bede tells us in his *Life of St. Cuthbert* how the otters did obeisance to him on the sands, and the crows humbled themselves before him in the air, and the sea itself showed its willingness to obey his behests. And yet the story must have appealed to Frenchmen just as much, for as well as the account of Gaimar and an English poem on the subject we have a *Lai de Haveloc* written probably by a Frenchman living in England, in which the story is treated in a more sophisticated manner reminiscent of the lays of Marie de France, though based ultimately on Gaimar's story. Gaimar makes his own contribution to accepted legends, for instance, the rather aimless episode of the runaway dwarf that he adds to the story of Aelftruda and Ethelwold. He mentions the 'arc-qui-ne-faut' familiar to us from Béroul's *Tristan*, and to the story of Taillefer of Hastings' fame (whom he makes a formidable juggler throwing up and catching his sword so skilfully that the English think it is by 'enchantement') he adds that of his horse which rushed at the English open-mouthed (*goule baée*), as if to eat them, as he had been trained to do by his master, thus spreading terror in their ranks. Obviously Gaimar delights in these stories which increase in number as his work proceeds. Contemporary conditions in England with the divided allegiance which prevailed were a fruitful source of adventures. Outlaws abounded and their feats and fates provided much material, especially in the case of *gentiz homes* like Hereward and Haveloc, who caught the popular imagination.

Geoffroy Gaimar wrote his *estoire* in octosyllabic verse, as did Wace, the translator of Geoffroy of Monmouth. How popular these semi-historical stories about outlaws were we can judge from their persistance. Some 100 years later the author of a prose romance related the story of another outlaw, Fulk-Fitzwarin, who lived in the reigns of Henry II and John. Fulk, or Fouque, with his 'meinie', is worthy to rank with Hereward the Wake and Robin Hood. Here again we find adventures, disguises, marvels and dragons piled on top of one another, but the much later date at which the chronicle was written naturally gave the author access to many episodes in the *Chansons de geste* (e.g. the quarrel during the game of chess) and elsewhere which he did not scruple to use.

This kind of fabulous chronicle-writing has taken us chiefly to the north-west of the territory in which French was spoken, and the effect of the pronunciation on the texts written in Norman England will have been noted in the brief extracts given. The syntax was not greatly affected and there is little to distinguish the language in which the *Lai de Haveloc* was written from the normal central French. As the twelfth century advanced, a kind of literary language developed and parallel with this development went a more reliable form of chronicle—both in Latin and in French. This was partly due to the fact that the Crusades gave birth to the most lively histories of this period and they tended to be written by those who took part in the actual happenings. This is not to say that the authors added nothing on their own account. The Latin chronicle of the 'Anonymus' who told the story of the First Crusade is full of dreams and portents, saints appearing on the battlefield and suchlike details which appeal to the popular imagination; Ambroise, who tells the history of the Third Crusade in French verse, gives such graphic details about what he has seen that he does not need to add much of his own invention; Robert de Clari, who writes of the Fourth Crusade, likes to give rein to his imagination and enlarge on the gruesome end of traitors or relate the wonders of Constantinople, but his chief merit lies in the light he actually throws on current events. It was not till these dramatic events began to form part of past history that the element of fiction was really introduced and fabulous stories began to accumulate round some of the notable characters of the preceding century. Perhaps the most outstanding example of this is the prose work known as the *Récits d'un ménestrel de Reims* which is indeed 'fiction tinged with history'. As a chronicle of events it is completely unreliable, but as a collection of stories to be poured into the ears of gatherings of receptive listeners in any locality it could hardly be beaten.

This work was written about the middle of the thirteenth century and forms an excellent climax to the list of quasi-historical works which flourished in this story-telling age. The author is a 'conteur' rather than a 'chroniqueur' and he knew well what would please his audience. The anecdotes follow one another in quick succession, interspersed with historical data, some true and some false. Many of the stories may have been current legends and they serve to show the kind of matter by which a 'raconteur' could please his audience. Each fresh incident or change of subject is introduced by the constantly recurring phrase: 'Ci vous lairai ester du' . . . 'si revenrons à . . .', which seems to prove that even these prose works were composed for auditors rather than readers. After a few facts, mostly inaccurate, the anecdotes begin with the piquant story of Eleanor of Poitou who, considering her first husband (King Louis of France), not worth a 'pomme pourrie', made advances to Sultan Saladin of whose goodness and prowess and liberality she had heard so much. Saladin, flattered by her offer, sent a boat to fetch her, but she was betrayed by one of her demoiselles, caught with one foot in the boat and brought back in disgrace (II, 7 f.). After some interesting but highly inaccurate details about Gui de Lusignan and his wife, in which Sultan Saladin plays a magnanimous part, the 'ménestrel' turns his attention to King Richard of England, and we have the well-known story of Blondel, the king's favourite minstrel, who found out where his master was imprisoned by playing an air they used to sing together outside the castle in which the king was confined. The story is well-told as befitted a story told by one minstrel about another. Some more stories about Richard, some good, some bad so as to please his varied audiences, are followed by the fantastic story of an envoy sent to the besieged army in Damietta packed up in a little egg-shaped vessel made of skin, well lined and sewn up, with a hole like the turret of a submarine through which the inmate could breathe. The tiny vessel floated up to the ramparts but was caught there in a net and the passenger taken prisoner. This fabulous adventure is followed by an unpleasant tale about the opulent bishop of Beauvais and some very flattering ones about Sultan Saladin which conformed to the popular taste of the times, for the Sultan had gradually become an almost legendary figure. These latter are too good and too characteristic to pass over in silence. There is the story of Saladin's visit to the 'ospital de Saint Jehan d'Acre' to test the charity of the inmates. Dressed as a pilgrim, feigning illness and loss of appetite, he asks for soup made from the foot of the Grand Master's favourite horse. Very sadly the Grand Master ordered the horse to be killed, and it was already lying bound on the ground and the knife was raised for the stroke when Saladin called out 'Tien coi, ma volonté est assevie...je vueil mangier char de mouton', and the horse was led back to the stable. The 'ospital' was rewarded by a generous annual grant for buying shrouds or warm coverings for the sick. The remarkable account of Saladin's eleventh-hour conversion to Christianity, his death and burial beside his mother at Acre is probably equally fictitious. The Emperor Frederic's quarrel with the Pope is related, ending with the sad fate of his envoy—'li granz clers Perron de la Vigne'— who, accused wrongly of having betrayed his master to the Pope, was degraded from being chief counsellor to the Emperor and paraded about the streets on an ass accompanied by a varlet who proclaimed his disgrace concluding with the well-known words (so often applied to those raised by Fortune's wheel) 'de si haut si bas'. Such are the stories, often accompanied by moral reflections or proverbs, or even moralizing fables (such as that of the wolf and the goat, which seems to be the author's own invention, or that of the linnet which was contained in other collections of moral tales), all adapted to the taste of his hearers, to which he pandered at the expense of truth even more than his predecessors had done. These are but samples of the matter which was provided by an author for a public avid for stories meant to be enjoyed, without troubling about a moral such as always followed the relating of the *exempla* which enlivened the sermon in church.

It may be objected that a collection of stories such as we find in the *Queste* and, indeed, the whole idea of this legend, inculcated a moral lesson and had a deep significance. But does this bear looking into? The faithfulness and steadfastness of the love of Lancelot for Guinevere, though it was the fatal obstacle to his finding the grail, was a palliative for his sin in the eyes of his friends and was even condoned by the king as we have seen, because nothing can stand against 'force d'amor'. One feels that God is on the side of the lovers—as Béroul tells us in the case of Tristan and Iseult—and very soon they became dear to the public as outstanding examples of the victims of *fin' amor* with all its accompanying exquisite misery and pathos. We are up against that strange inverted morality again, which pardoned the sinner if he abode by certain accepted ideas of religious devotion or chivalrous love, however deceitful or blameworthy he might be in other respects. Guinevere herself tells us in the *Mort Artu* that 'amor descouverte n'est pas fine amor' and how strongly this idea had taken root in certain circles can be judged by the popularity of the little romance of *La Châstelaine de Vergi* which may be based on a court scandal in the thirteenth century or may be a pure work of fiction.

This poem has come down to us in eight Mss. of the thirteenth and fourteenth centuries and seven of the fifteenth and sixteenth—a tribute to its success. Froissart ranks the love of the heroine with that of Tristan and Iseult, of the lady of Fael and the Châtelain de Coucy. The story relates the tragic fate of two lovers who met regularly under the vow of secrecy. The scene is laid in Burgundy:

> Si comme il avint en Borgoigne
> D'un chevalier preu et hardi
> E de la dame de Vergi . . . (ll. 18–20).

The young man was a great favourite of the duke; the young woman was his niece. For a long time their love was 'douce et celée', but alas! there was a Potiphar's wife again. The duchess made love to the knight and was convinced by the manner of his reply that he had an 'amie' hidden away somewhere. Furious at his refusal of her love, she told her husband that the young man had made love to her and she begged the duke to protect her honour. The duke, desirous of finding out the truth, urged the young man, on pain of banishment and exile, to confess the truth. The lover was now up against one of those 'questions dilemmatiques' so common in this kind of literature—either he must be banished from his loved one, or he must divulge his love. Either course is equally dreadful. After much hesitation he chooses the latter. The duke, in spite of his protestations of secrecy, under great pressure from his wife gives way and betrays the lovers. The tragedy is now inevitable. The duchess, in conversation with the young châtelaine, makes a cunning reference to the little dog which acts as go-between to the lovers. Horrified at her lover's treachery in betraying or 'discovering' their love, the girl kills herself after a long and touching lament:

> 'Ha! amis, dont est ce venu?
> Que poez estre devenu,
> Quant vers moi avez esté faus?
> Je cuidoie que plus loiaus
> Me fussiez, se Deus me conseut,
> Que ne fust Tristans a Yseut...' (ll. 753–60).

Never could she have been so disloyal as to 'descouvrir' their secret even if God had given her earth and heaven and paradise in exchange. She apostrophizes 'fine amor' in her perplexity:

> 'Ha! fine amor, est ce donc droiz
> Que cel a ainsi descouvert
> Nostre conseil, dont il me pert?' (ll. 806–8).

But she generously pardons her lover and dies gladly of her own volition:

> 'Douz amis, a Dieu vous commant'!
> A cest mot de ses braz s'estraint,
> Li cuers li faut, li vis li taint.

Naturally the young man follows her to the grave. He picks up a sword and strikes himself to the heart. The duke draws the sword from the dead knight's body, rushes into the hall where his wife is dancing ('grant oirre droit a la carole') and cuts off her head in the presence of all his court. The author ends this triple tragedy with an exhortation to all lovers to conceal their love:

> Et par cest example doit l'en
> S'amor celer par si grant sen
> C'on ait toz jors en remembrance
> Que li descouveirs riens n'avance (ll. 249–52).

It all sounds rather silly to us in a more prosaic age—but it shows us how seriously these rules of conduct were taken, in a code which became almost a religion for a certain section of society. It is a relief to turn to another short story which would presumably make an appeal to a more general public than that which enjoyed the *Chastelaine de Vergi*. The attractive poem known as the *Tombeur de Notre Dame* tells the story of a poor juggler who, finding the work of tending cabbages in the garden of the monastery to which he had retired too hard, took refuge in the chapel and performed his acrobatic tricks before a statue of the Virgin Mary as being the very best he had to offer. Thus we have come round full circle in this rather diffuse chapter. For, as in the case of Eppo the thief, the Virgin detected the spark of real devotion hidden beneath a rough exterior and invisible to all except herself owing to a questionable mode of life. Just as she had saved Eppo from the gallows, so now the Virgin stooped in pity and wiped the poor juggler's brow with 'une touaille blanche' that she held in her hand. The story is pleasantly told with other attractive details into which space forbids us to go.

BIBLIOGRAPHY

Le Roman des Sept Sages. (1) Deux redactions publiées par P. Paris, 1876. (SATF).
    (2) J. Misrahi: *Le Roman des Sept Sages*. Paris 1933.
    (3) A. Hilka: *Historia Septem Sapientum*. Heidelberg 1912. (Samml. Mittellat. Texte IV.)
Dolopathos de Jean de Haute Seille. A. Hilka. 1913. (Samml. etc. V.)
    Le Dolopathos en français. C. Brunet et A. de Montaiglon. Paris 1856. (Bibliothèque Elzévirienne.)
Le Roman de Marques de Rome. Hgg. von J. Alton. Tübingen 1889.
Chrétien de Troyes and Wace. See Bibl. ch. iv.
Robert de Boron: *Li Roman de l'Estoire dou Graal*, éd. par W. Nitze. Paris 1927. (CFMA).
The Arthurian romances, Vulgate version, edited by H. Oskar Sommer. 7 vol. Washington 1909–13.
La Queste del saint Graal. (1) Ed. F. J. Furnival. Roxburghe Club, 1864.
    (2) Sommer (see supra), Tome VI.
    (3) A. Pauphilet. Paris 1923. (CFMA).
La Mort Artu. Roman du XIIIᵉs. publ. par Jean Frappier. Paris 1936.
La Mort le roi Artu. Ed. J. D. Bruce. Halle 1910.
Geoffroi Gaimar: *L'estorie des Engleis*. See Bibl. ch. viii.
Le Lai de Haveloc and Gaimar's H. Episode. A. Bell. Manchester 1925.
Gesta Francorum. See Bibl. ch. viii.
Robert de Clari. See Bibl. ch. viii.
Récits d'un Ménestrel de Reims. Ed. par N. de Wailly. Paris 1876. (SHF).
La Châtelaine de Vergi. Ed. by F. Whitehead. Manchester 1952.
Del Tumbeor Nostre Dame. E. Lommatzsch. Berlin 1920.

CHAPTER VI

SECULAR AND MIDDLE CLASS LITERATURE.
FABLIAUX, DITS, FABLES, AND *BIBLES*

WACE's version of Geoffroy of Monmouth's *Historia*, which inspired so much of the literature which flourished in the second half of the twelfth century, appeared in 1155. Roughly contemporaneously with this, the first known 'fabliau' (*Richeut*) was probably rhymed. This somewhat repellent poem gives a realistic picture of types and social conditions, which, judging from its skilful treatment, can hardly have been the first of its kind. A greater contrast can scarcely be imagined than that between the behaviour of the unscrupulous 'procureuse' and her clever but equally unscrupulous son, and that of the knights and ladies with their artificial and romantic ideas about honour and love. Both were in all probability exaggerated, but they represent two different social environments, each with its specific outlook on life, and we are justified in casting a glimpse at the soil out of which these widely divergent, yet contemporary types were produced, to see whether different forms of 'escape' literature were needed in the contrasting conditions which characterized the century.

For some thirty years following the appearance of Wace's Chronicle the cultural activity in the courts of Anjou and Blois (in spite of struggles for power, marriages, repudiations, intrigues and the like) was at its height, with well-born knights and ladies vying with one another in their intellectual and amorous enjoyments, whilst in Normandy tournaments were in their heyday. One can truthfully speak of a 'floraison littéraire' in the feudal courts of north-west France during those years which has left its mark on subsequent European literature and which, though aristocratic in essence and secular in character, was romantic in the extreme. In the south of France, too, the troubadour poetry was still in full swing, for amorous and chivalrous ideas were still in the ascendant. But what was happening in Paris and its neighbouring provinces? Was the Île-de-France untouched by these glamorous activities and the exceptional culture of the Anglo-Norman and Anglo-Angevin kingdoms?

Actually in Paris and other cathedral cities of northern France another spirit was awakening which was gradually to carry all before it. Paris itself, for political reasons, developed in quite a special way. It became a true capital growing larger with every forward movement of the monarchy. It became, moreover, a commercial city like the great markets of the twelfth and thirteenth centuries. It had its fairs, like Troyes, Bar, Provins, Lagny and Bar-sur-Aube.[1] The original crusaders had not thought in terms of commerce, but gradually the idea of trade spread from the commercial cities of Italy and crept northward to Flanders, the centre of the North Sea trade. Then the class of merchants emerged—originally poor, landless adventurers, nomadic folk, who saw their chance of making a fortune, became the creators of personal property and were inspired by a greedy spirit of self-seeking. They were intruders into the social system with its three estates of knights, priests and peasants. Hence the confusion of the merchant with the rich 'vilain' which we so often find in the literature of the period. The rich 'vilain' who, by reason of his (probably) illicit gain, was considered a suitable husband for a well-born maiden, became one of the butts of the satire of the time. We find him in the *Vilain mire*, in *Les trois boçus*, and many another 'fabliau'. Least of all was the successful climber liked by the penniless student, the lay-clerk, or, indeed, the educated (or semi-educated) man of any description. The same century which saw the rise of these merchant adventurers witnessed the foundation of the universities (especially Paris) where, from the days of St. Bernard and Abelard, all kinds of questions came under discussion. It was in Paris, in Provins, in Amiens that these new social forces emerged, each with its own difficulties, its own problems and its own standard of living—utterly different from those in the princely courts, but just as vocal. Of the literature now under discussion the authors are largely indigent, semi-literate, witty ex-students, unfrocked monks and wandering scholars, a product of the university towns who had their headquarters at Paris: 'l'esprit moyen' (says Michelet), 'qui se forme de bonne humeur gauloise et d'amertume parlementaire, entre le parvis Notre Dame et les degrés de la Sainte Chapelle.' It is, indeed, just in such spots that the clash would take place between the eager merchant intent on piling up stocks (sometimes with the help of the moneylender) and the mocking, casual, penniless student who,

[1] Cf. *Le Dit de l'Endit rimé*. Edition of Barbazan and Méon, from which most of these examples are taken.

with those of his like, frequented the fairs of the towns where a merchant population had sprung up. Amongst these Paris occupied the first place[1] but Provins was a very good runner-up[2]—in fact, it might almost be looked upon as a rival, so great was its importance in those days. Provins had, under a series of outstanding counts, an extraordinary, though ephemeral importance in the twelfth century. It was a centre of commerce, especially famous for its cloth and wine. Jews and moneylenders dwelt there, encouraged by the kings and barons who profited from their commerce. Moreover, the Templars had there an establishment which was very worldly in character, and the fairs were so prosperous that money abounded both in clerical and commercial circles. Pilgrims and students flocked thither—the latter attracted, perhaps, by the presence of Abelard who for a brief time took refuge there from his persecutors in Paris. This ephemeral importance of Provins is interesting as it explains many allusions in the 'fabliaux' and the town was presumably the birthplace of Guiot de Provins who in his *Bible* reproduces many of the characteristics which marked this famous market whilst it was ruled by a succession of pious princes who made concessions to clergy and merchants alike.[3] It is easy to understand that in such a centre the stingy priest would become as unpopular as the merchant or 'riche vilain'—indeed, more so as the latter had at least become a capitalist by his own efforts and industry.

These, then—namely the cunning priest who had grown fat on his stipends and the rich vilain were (apart from women—the perennial target for abuse in scurrilous literature and sometimes even gently castigated for changeableness and cruelty in more polite forms) the chief objects of ridicule and abuse in the 'fabliaux'. And nearly always at the bottom of the spite with which they were attacked lay the rankle of the fact that they had amassed wealth. An instructive 'fabliau' pits one against the other. In the *Bouchier d'Abbéville* the 'bouchier', who is, in fact, a wealthy and respected figure in his town and obviously a grazier of some importance, is insulted and treated as a 'vilain' by a priest whom he begs for a night's lodging on his return home from the market: 'Vilains! Sire' (he says indignantly), 'qu'avez vos dit? Tenez-vos lai hom en

---

[1] 'Premier est Paris amenteüe
Qui est du monde la meillour' (*Dit de l'Endit*, ll. 80 f.).
[2] Apres parlerai de Provins . . . (Ibid., l. 86.) Brunetto Latini, in his *Trésor*, quotes a proverb: Nos devons bien croire que cest hom est bons drapiers por ce qu'il est de Provins. (Livre III, Pt. 1.)
[3] For a description of Provins and its prosperity in the twelfth century consult Bourquelot: *Histoire de Provins*.

despit?' But, although he offers to pay well for the night's lodging, the priest is adamant. Thereupon the 'bouchier', who learns that the priest is a sheep-owner on a large scale, plays a clever trick on him. By stealing one of his sheep, he obtains a meal, a bed, and finally the price of a fine fleece, by the offer of which he had already seduced first the priest's paramour (*prestresse*) and then the lady's maid. No wonder the priest, on finding out the extent of the ruse, remarks 'De ma manche m'a ters mon nes' (*He has wiped my nose with my own sleeve*). The 'fabliau' is the work of a clever raconteur. The language is never extravagant. The priest is described simply as one 'qui molt goulouse autrui avoir' (l. 136) and the poem ends with a neat 'question dilemmatique' as to who should keep the fleece:

> Chascuns en die son voloir:
> Liquels doit miex la pel avoir
> Ou li prestres, ou la prestresse
> Ou la meschine piperesse?

Another favourite subject was the fate of the priest who seduced the wife of a 'bourgeois' or a 'vilain' as the case may be. Whether the priest was discovered alive or dead by the enraged husband mattered little, for his body or corpse suffered impartially the most revolting humiliations. But the attacks on the priests and the Roman hierarchy generally were nearly always, as in the case of those on the rich peasants, directed against the amassing of wealth and the greed and avarice which marked them. One is amazed at the impunity which such attacks enjoyed, but attacks on the Church were not yet identified with heresy.

It would be unprofitable here to delve again into the mysterious source of these stories. Bédier has shown with an overwhelming weight of evidence that we need not go to India or Persia to account for them. His idea of the 'polygenesis' of most of the fables and legends appeals to the simple unbiased mind. 'L'esprit laïque ... et son compère l'esprit bourgeois', says Bédier are what inspire them. 'L'esprit laïque'—yes, most certainly, but 'l'esprit bourgeois' brings us up against a difficulty. For they are so *anti*-bourgeois, so *anti*-capitalist, so obsessed with the hatred of wealth and money-making which were precisely the characteristics of the 'bourgeois' community of that time. It was easy to abuse women and feminine guile; it was the fashion to rant against those who had risen to power and privilege in the only effortless way possible in those days, namely by ecclesiastical preferment and the deception of simple folk. But, popular as these subjects were, the grievance which crops up in the majority of 'fabliaux' and kindred stories is the eternal one of the 'have-nots' against the 'haves':

> Honiz soit li hons, quel qu'il soit
> Qui trop prise mauvais deniers
> Et qui les fist fere premiers . . .

So speaks the author of *Les trois boçus* in which the beautiful daughter of a poor but worthy citizen is given in marriage to a hideous dwarf 'por l'avoir qu'il ot amassé'. It was no wonder that the dwarf became suspicious or the wife vindictive. It was money which was at the root of the evil, and the one who is humiliated in the end is the money-grubber—be he priest or knight, seneschal or 'vilain'.

In the pleasant little 'conte' entitled *De Brunain la vache au prestre*, a simple peasant, who had heard in a sermon that God repays good deeds double, takes his ox Blere and presents it to the priest. The avaricious priest is delighted and yokes it to his own beast Brune. But the peasant's ox being the stronger animal of the two, drags his yoke-fellow back to the home of his former master, who joyfully exclaims: 'Voirement est Diex bon doublere . . . or en avons deux por une.' So the victim is again the priest 'qui a prendre bée toztans' (*who is always out for all he can get*). It is the same story everywhere. The grapes may have been sour, but for the authors of these stories wealth is the most fickle of jades. In the *Bourse pleine de sens* it is a rich but very stupid merchant who has to be chastened; in *Le cuvier* another rich merchant is deceived by an unfaithful wife. When he wished to lift the bath under which his wife's lover was hidden, he was rudely told to let well alone. In the rather amusing story of the *Provost a l'aumuche* a steward who had been caught in the snares of wealth (*richece l'avoit sourpris*) tried to increase his store still more by concealing a nice piece of fat bacon beneath his tall cap (*aumuche*). Unfortunately he got wedged by the crowd of guests near a big fire and the fat melted and ran down his face to his great discomfiture. This makes the author wish that all the possessors of illgotten gain should suffer likewise.

It would be tedious to go through all the 'fabliaux' in which the rich man comes off worst—whether he be a 'riche chevalier sot', or an influential steward, or a rich go-getting merchant, or simply a 'riche vilain'. And here it must be noted again that the term *vilain* is no longer the simple rustic. It is constantly interchangeable with the appellation 'marcheänt' who is supposed to have the same predatory instincts. It is, in fact, used about almost anyone who is out for gain and does not behave 'like a gentleman'. We have, however, the genuine rustic in the *Dit du Buffet*, in which a greedy and hard-baked seneschal ('felon et aver et recuit') is humiliated by a poverty-stricken cowherd ('un bouvier qui vient de charrue'). But it is the seneschal who is the true 'vilain' as the author admits, for he had grown as fat as a pig at his master's expense and was overbearing and mean to those beneath him. It is worth looking a little closer at the *Dit du Buffet* for the author is conscious of his ability and his duty to instruct others:

> Qui biau set dire et rimoier
> Bien doit sa science avoier
> A fere chose ou l'on aprenge . . .
> . . . l'en devroit bien escouter
> Conteör quant il set conter.
> Por coi? Por ce c'on i aprent
> Aucun bien, qui garde s'en prent (ll. 23 ff.).

Then he proceeds to describe the characters with genuine insight. A good-natured count, who only laughs at the well-known misdeeds and goings-on of his wicked steward, is about to hold a court and has invited all and sundry to a free feast. If the 'escuier, chevalier et dames', says the author, had been as anxious about their souls as they were about their bodies, there would have been no torments for them in hell. A rustic was also tempted to come and try his luck at getting a free meal. He was dirty and unkempt but full of native wit. The steward, out of sheer vexation at his daring to come, first gave him a *buffe* (or buffet) for his cheek and then told him to sit on a *buffet*, which he would only lend him and which must be given back at the end. After the feast the cheerful count offered a 'robe d'escarlate nueve' to the minstrel or juggler who would make them laugh the most. Some played the fool, others sang or fiddled or told risqué stories. When all had finished, our peasant came forward and to everyone's amazement gave the seneschal a fearful box on the ear with his horny hand, saying that it was wrong not to return what one had been lent. When questioned by the astonished count, he related how the seneschal had lent him a 'buffet' (the pun is the same in English) and he had merely given it back. He could pay it back with interest if so desired. A long roar of laughter followed this explanation as soon as the gist of it was understood and the count cheerfully assigned the reward to the peasant for having caused 'la meillor risée / Seur toz les autres menestrels'. The rich steward picked himself up, furious with anger and covered with confusion. But the poor cowherd went off muttering contentedly: 'qui siet, il seche, qui va, il leche.' So the story ends with the characteristic proverb, 'L'en dit qui bien chace, bien trueve'.

Another 'fabliau' which is justly celebrated for its real literary value is the *Lay du vair palefroi*. The real hero of this poem is the dappled horse which, by taking the wrong road at a crucial moment, carries a beautiful girl to the house of her lover instead of to church, where she was to be married to an old miser. The lover was a valiant, courteous knight, but though he was 'riches de cuer', unfortunately he was 'povres d'avoir'. The intended bride's father was also a worthy prince, but he had, to his detriment, amassed great wealth. He had become 'riche à démesure' and the owner of wide lands. So he agreed to the suggestion of another rich old man who proposed that he should marry his friend's daughter and thus double their possessions. The coming together for discussion of the two avaricious old men is well described. No wonder the girl exclaims:

> 'Fi de viellece, fi d'avoir!
> ... Haïr doi l'avoir qui me part
> De celui-la ou je claim part' (ll. 637 ff.).

A rich young man is bad enough, but an old rich man is worse:

> '... cuers qui gist en la viellece
> Ne pense pas a la jonece
> Ne au voloir de jone eäge:
> Grant difference a el corage
> De viel au jone, ce m'est vis.'

But the contrast is not so great between the old and the young as it is between the rich and the poor. Mercifully the situation was saved by the action of the 'vair palefroi' and the greedy old man who hoped to gain his wish 'por son mueble et por son avoir' is disappointed in the end.

It is no exaggeration to say that this strain of thought runs through nearly all the 'fabliaux'—even the obscene and bawdy ones of which there was a goodly spate in the early years of the thirteenth century. They may be left aside without undue loss, though they evidently enjoyed considerable popularity. They probably answered to a strain of vulgarity which exists in most natures and which can be indulged in with impunity in certain circles and at certain epochs. Perhaps they were no worse than the story contained in the pamphlet (of which Boswell tells us in his *Life of Johnson*, A.D. 1778), written against Sir Robert Walpole, which Lord Orrery had to explain privately to the Duchess of Buckingham lest she should make herself ridiculous by asking the author for his meaning.

The stories directed against women and their guile are tedious. The subject is such a well-worn one that it is difficult to take much interest in this theme. Probably the excessive adulation of women in the courtly literature and the troubadour poetry had its share in producing a reaction against the danger of placing woman on an undesirable pedestal. We may also take into account the perennial French interest in domestic life which would give zest to the enjoyment of a 'fabliau' such as *De Sire Hain et de Dame Anieuse*, in which the race for the trousers ends satisfactorily for the husband. Such a subject would be amusing at all times and certain to raise a laugh except in the most alembicated society. But to treat the 'fabliaux' simply as 'une risée et une gabée', as the tendency has been to do, is to ignore their importance as a social phenomenon and to lessen their value as practical lessons of common sense, or in some cases of morality. The many proverbs strewn amongst them are indications of this latter tendency and the compact and well-expressed form they often take shows by no means illiterate origin. Indeed, great care must sometimes have been put into the composition of these poems, for they were not always meant exclusively for the market-place. The author of *Les trois aveugles* tells us that the wise minstrel should take great pains to compose 'biaus dits et biaus contes':

> C'on dit devant Dus, devant Contes.
> Fablel sont bon a escouter
> Maint duel, maint mal font mesconter.

Even the dilemmatic question is to be found in some of them, as we have seen. They were profitable, moreover, for the author of one with an unspeakable title and subject tells us:

> Flabel sont or molt encorsé,
> Maint denier en ont enborsé
> Cil qui les content et les portent.
> Quar grant confortement raportent
> As anovrez (= désœvrés) et as oiseus . . .

The heyday of tournaments was over and there must have been many 'anovrez' young knights roaming about the land like the hero of the last-mentioned 'fabliau'. These and many other disgruntled types of society would assuredly find 'alegeance et grant confortement' in listening to this witty form of escape literature which circulated among the fairs and the cathedral cities of northern

France, where the penniless 'escolier' loved to give vent to his affected scorn for the rich, prosperous 'bourgeois'.

The 'fabliaux' are often grouped together in a class by themselves, but the boundary lines between the different genres in this mass of popular literature are extremely dim. *Fabliau, dit, conte, exemplum* and even *fable* sometimes seem almost synonymous terms. The two *fables* of Marie de France treating of the peasant and his aggravating wife (*femme felonesse* in one and *femme contrariuse* in the other) might well be classed among the *fabliaux*. In another of Marie's so-called *fables* ('De la femme qui fist pendre sun mari') we recognize a story of woman's heartlessness which forms one of the tales of the *Sept Sages de Rome*. But Marie's attitude is not cynical like that of the authors of the *fabliaux* even though her sympathy is always with the poor and the oppressed as against the rich and the powerful—with the lamb against the wolf and the mouse against the lion. Her moral conclusions are full of common sense but have not the egalitarian, utilitarian outlook of the typical 'esprit bourgeois'. The fact that 'li nunpuissanz a poi amis' must just be accepted as an inevitable but regrettable fact. It is worthy of note that in these overlapping forms of literature—some purely critical, some philosophical or moralistic in tone—the choice and use of proverbs is often indicative of the class whose approbation or edification the author has in mind. There is the neatly-turned proverb of the penniless adventurer, or the peasant weary of his daily task: 'Qui siet, il seche / Qui va il leche' (see supra, p. 149); there is the truly characteristic proverb of the shrewd, commercially-minded man who has to look to his profit (*garder son preu*) and believes in business tactics: 'Tant as, tant valz'; and there is the saying of the blue-blooded aristocrat that birth will out (*nature pert*) to express the advantage of *nature* over *nourriture* (= training, upbringing)—a favourite theme in the court romances. For the utilitarian, materialistic outlook on life we must turn to another group of compositions in which wise sayings are intermingled with examples and criticisms meant for the warning and edification of the man in the street.

The *Disciplina clericalis* of Petrus Alfonsi, the Spanish Jew, has already been mentioned in another connection (see chapter on didactic literature) and will only be introduced here as an example of the opportunist and commercial spirit which was creeping upward during the twelfth century from the prosperous cities of Italy and the culturally more highly developed Jewish and Arab literature of Spain. The French translation (*Chastoiement d'un père à son fils*)

L

probably became widely known towards the end of the century
and we come across the wise sayings of Arab philosophers and
others in most of the 'enseignements' by French, Provençal and
Italian writers of the early thirteenth century. Here the old ideas
of *'lignage'* and *'parage'* and gentility inherent in blue blood received
a severe knock. 'Nobility proceeding from myself is more precious
than that proceeding from my ancestors' one philosopher is quoted as
saying. 'Rosa ex spinis orta nequaquam blasphematur' says another,
which the French translator develops in his doggerel as follows:

> . . . molt povre hom a engendré
> Tel filz ou ot molt de bonté;
> Et apres ce li clers a dit
> A ceux qui l'orent en despit:
> La rose de l'espine naist,
> E neporquant assez vos plaist.

But natural goodness must be accompanied by hard work for there is
no merit in being a poor man. There is no sign of the animosity of the
indigent scholar against the successful merchant here. In the pursuit
of wisdom, as of wealth, a man must give his whole mind to it:

> Encor te covient penser
> En travaillier, en bien pener
> Que ne soies trop encombrez
> Ne ne chiées en povretez.
> Quar l'en dit qu'en petit avoir
> N'a mie granment de savoir.

It was no disgrace, according to the authors of most of the 'fabliaux',
to have a threadbare garment (*tenue mantel*) but, in the *Chastoiement*,
although birth as such is of little account, a tenuous garment was
indicative of a tenuous intelligence—in fact, a lack of ability to get
on in the world. Much practical advice of this sort is given to the
son by his worldly-wise father. It is sometimes said that proverbs
emanate from the 'little man' and are the product of native intelligence. But many of the instructions in this treatise come from the
wise sayings attributed to a great king (Solomon) and others from
those of a much admired philosopher (the pseudo-Cato). A
majority of them reflect a very utilitarian outlook on life. 'Noli
associari rei deficienti, et ne postponas te associari rei crescenti', says
a philosopher, which the French translator renders faithfully:

> Biaux filz, ne pren pas compaignie,
> Se tu croiz chose que je die,
> A la rien qui vait descroissant,
> Mais a cel qui vait amendant.

Here is good advice for the climber—but it must be admitted that it is followed by an admonition to spend well what one has gained. Thus do good morals and shrewd business go hand in hand.

That Petrus Alfonsi was both known and appreciated in England at an early date is evidenced, not only by the number of manuscripts (including the best) of his work in English libraries, but also in the traces of his influence in works which originated on English soil. The Anglo-Norman poem entitled *Enseignements Trebor*, by Robert de Ho about the year 1206 (mentioned for his didactic tendencies in the chapter on that subject) are as much indebted to the *Chastoiement* as they are to the Distichs of Cato (probably in the translation of Élie de Wincestre—a compatriot of the author). Robert de Ho, who gives the impression of being a citizen of good standing—he devotes an interesting though brief section to what appertains to knightly training—is nevertheless imbued with the same opportunist, mercantile approach to the affairs of this life. Here again we find the depressing proverb of the go-getter: 'Tant as, tant vauz, tant t'amerai', followed by the ancient warning that 'riche home a asez d'amis'. More attractive are Robert's sentiments on the subject of true nobility. For him 'gentillece' is not a mere matter of birth for who knows whence true 'gentillece' comes? God is the Author of us all (*de Deus sunt trestuz estraiz*). It comes from the heart he concludes, and not from one's ancestry:

> Ke de cuer vient la gentillece
> Ice sachiez, e la proece,
> Plus que de ceux dunt es venu (ll. 1980-2).

Many a peasant's son who has had to beg his bread has proved by his actions that he ought to be called 'gentil', and again the fact is insisted upon that 'de cuer vient la grant franchise'.

Under the broad umbrella of 'bourgeois' or middle-class literature, some other treatises may find their place here, which not only inculcate good advice but sharply criticize the evil practices of both Church and State from the standpoint of the average man. The *Livre des Manières* of Étienne de Fougères is the first of these critical treatises in the vulgar tongue which have come down to us. The author was a chaplain at the court of Henry II of England and bishop of Rennes from 1168-78. He can be dated roughly, therefore, as having flourished in the third quarter of the twelfth century. The clerical origin of the work is assured as it proceeds from the cultured court of the 'clercs lettrés' with whom Henry surrounded himself. Undoubtedly he had Henry in mind when making his cynical remarks about a king's worst enemies being those who had received most benefits from him; about the hiring of the Brabançons as well-paid mercenaries; about the dangers of a too great love of hunting and too great restlessness in a monarch:

> Ça et la veit, sovent se torne / Ne repose ne ne sejorne,
> Ne repose ne ne sejorne   / Chastiaus abat, chasteaus aorne.

This is a firsthand description of Henry's life and tallies exactly with Wace's description in his *Chronique ascendante* (see p. 198). But he has a high ideal of a king's functions. A king does not live for himself—he belongs to all: 'A toz sera; si n'iert pas son. / Oblier deit tot le son bon / Por le comun, si'l est prodom' (xli, 161 f.). No one escapes Étienne's censure—priests, deacons and the deans with their 'prestresses' are almost as badly treated as they are in the 'fabliaux'. They are worse than heathen. But he has not the same mistrust of riches and power as we find in those poems. He does not encourage sentiments of revolt though he expresses much sympathy with the 'vilain'. After naming the three classes of society—viz. the 'clercs' who are created 'pour prier', the knights 'pour defendre', and the peasants 'pour labourer'—he shows his liberal spirit:

> Molt devon chiers avoir nos homes
> Quar li vilain portent les sommes
> Dont nos vivons quantque nos sommes...

and again:

> Sor le vilain est la bataille
> Quar chevalier et clerc sans faille
> Vivent de ce que il travaillent.

And yet they never taste a 'bon morsel' themselves (cxlvi, 581 f.). These were brave words to use at court. Merchants returning from Spain and Italy should have just weights and measures and not indulge in usury or amass wealth for themselves alone. This cautious Norman, a functionary at court, is not so virulent as some of those who came after him. He does try to be unbiased. His instructions to women are addressed impartially to *dames, damoiselles* or *meschines*. Famous women of the past (e.g. Helen or Delilah), rich merchants' wives of his day, indeed, any wife who deceives her husband or is led astray by Richeut (heroine of the 'fabliau' of that name: see supra, p. 143) and plays the coquette[1] is equally castigated. But the author ends with the comforting thought that good women do exist and he cites as example the duchess of Hereford, a veritable paragon of virtue.

By the end of the twelfth and the beginning of the thirteenth century attacks on the manners of the clergy and the hierarchy of Rome had become bitter and widespread. One of the best-known of these half-satirical, half-serious sermons in verse is the one to which the name of *Bible* was given by its author, Guiot of Provins. If, as we may reasonably suppose, this town was the place of origin of Guiot it is appropriate to recall here the importance of this market town in the twelfth century under a series of good counts. Guiot, who had perhaps been a court minstrel in his younger days, claims to have known an incredible number of great people and to have frequented courts and festivals including that of Frederic Barbarossa at Mainz. By the time he composed his poem he had become an unmitigated 'laudator temporis acti' and one of those uncompromising attackers of the Church who raised their voices against the abuses of Rome throughout the twelfth and thirteenth centuries and amaze us by their freedom of speech. His avowed intention was to open a door on to the state of the 'siècle' in his time which he considered to be 'puant et orible' (l. 1). The world used to be 'biaus et granz' but it will soon shrivel into nothing ('Faudra par amenuisement', l. 289). Indeed, like others of his time who were preoccupied with apocalyptic ideas, he wonders why the end of the world is so long delayed. So he feels obliged to utter his warning note and prayers for God's help:

> Que de lui viennent li bon dit,
> Et tuit li bon enseignement (ll. 24–5).

So here again is a form of 'chastoiement' composed by a man of the world who has tried many things and found them wanting. Guiot begins by saying that though he is going to blame and criticize no one need take this 'commun blasme' to himself. But in the end truth will out:

> Mes la roë du char qui bret
> Ne se puet celer ne covrir.

After giving a list of ancient philosophers grouped together in

[1] His description of the 'dame jolive' is a telling one:
> 'Vers son mari est morne et mue
> Et devant lui tost se remue
> Vers son dru point sa face et mue
> Plus qu'espervier qui eist de mue' (l. 1013 f.).

strange pairs (e.g. Lucans et Diogenes), he regrets the decadence of
France and the fall of the noble houses:

> Haï, France! haï, Borgoigne!
> Certes vos estes avuglées.
> . . . Or plorent les bones mesons.
> Les bons princes, les bons barons
> Qui les granz cors i assembloient
> Et qui les biaus dons i donoient ll. (113–18).

The last line is probably the key to this passage. The princes have
become so mean. Why were they born if they do not love 'joie et
deport' and do not summon the 'conteörs' to their courts? Old and
young are out for money-making. So here we are once more at
the root of bitterness which has caused this impoverished, much
travelled ex-'clerc' and ex-'conteör' to take up his pen:

> Nuz ne bée (= strives) a honor avoir.
> Tant sont angoissous sor avoir (ll. 597–8).

Leaving aside the details of the author's previous life, the interest
of the poem lies in the information we can glean on contemporary
conditions in a commercial centre where patronage and concessions
to both clergy and merchants were in force, where Jews and usurers
flourished in an atmosphere of commerce and intellectual activity.
It is the 'Romans'[1] who inspire Guiot with the greatest bitterness:

> 'Cors de Rome, com estes toute
> plaine de pechiez criminals!' (ll. 710–11).

He begins at the top with 'nostre pere l'Apostoile' but, as is often
the case in these denunciations, the Pope personally is spared and
only admonished. He ought to be like the pole star (*la tresmontaigne*)
which guides the mariner by means of an 'art qui ne puet mentir'
(viz. the use of the compass) on the darkest night. If, however, the
father kills his own children then things are in a bad way indeed:

> . . . 'Ha, Rome, Rome,
> Encore ociras tu maint home.
> . . . Tout est alei tout est perdu
> Qant li chardenal sont venu' (ll. 661–8).

Now the author gets into full swing. The cardinals are burning with
covetousness, full of simony, without faith and without religion.
They have sold God and His mother and are worse than heathen.
Then again he comes back to Rome:

> Rome est *la doiz* de malice (MS. A).
> dont sordent tuit li malvais vice
> c'est un viviers pleins de vermine . . . (ll. 771–3).

---

[1] By 'Romans' Guyot means the whole hierarchy of the Pope and Rome.

and he reflects the opinion of many at that time in wondering why the crusading army of the Marquis of Mont-Ferrat was deflected against the Greeks (*Grifons*) in 1203, instead of attacking more dangerous enemies. Then he proceeds to the bishops who eat too much (*Il sormenjuent, il sorboivent*); the clergy who are obsessed by covetousness and envy. He does admit that there are a few good ones amongst them, but the good ones are very few and at bottom it is 'l'avoir' which is the spring and source of all the evil. Here Guiot's democratic spirit peeps through—every worthy person should have a chance of advancement. The 'prodome de bas lignage' as much as the well-born, for 'tuit li prodome sont gentil' and even a king's son, if he commits a 'vilaine œuvre', is 'vilain' in every sense of the word. From the monks and the clergy he passes to the Orders. He claims to have passed four months at Clairvaux with the white monks, where he witnessed their commercial spirit, their cupidity and their greed at first hand. He knows by hearsay of the meanness and cruelty which goes on at Chartreuse; of the disorders of Grant-Mont where hypocrisy reigns for, though they look so noble,[1] no one knows what goes on behind their closed doors. Moreover, they are ruled by their own 'convers' (lay-brothers) and dare not even begin a service without their permission, for the 'convers' have got hold of the gold and silver and have thus got the whip-hand over the monks and the priests. 'La vait li chars devant les buez.' He has a good word for the Templars. They constitute 'l'ordre de chevalerie' and are much respected in the East. They have 'ordre belle, bone et certainne'; they behave well in church and their members are knights who have tasted and seen much of the world. Moreover, they have everything in common; but, for Guiot, they have one grave defect—they are too fond of fighting; he could not join them because, rather than be killed, he would prefer to be 'cowars et vis'. Perhaps, if he told the truth, as an ex-minstrel, he would not have been received amongst the luxurious Templars of his native town. He has some very hard words, on the other hand, for the 'convers de St. Antoine' and the 'hospital plain de contraiz' which they have founded. They travel wide with their emblems on their breasts and their pigs (St. Antony's legendary accompaniments), making money wherever they go; but both they and their leader—Duranz Chapuis—are the most shameless impostors who have ever existed. If Guiot's hatred

[1] They wash and comb their beards at night and bind them in three portions so as to make a fine show the next day when they come amongst the people.

of fighting was genuine, he should have welcomed the sort of peace-pledge of the 'Capuchonnés' in which Duranz played a conspicuous part.

Guiot does not indulge in the savage diatribes against women that we find in some of his contemporaries. They are more difficult to understand and more unpredictable than the movements of the sun and the moon. So he prefers to let them alone. In a passage, either interpolated, or borrowed from the *Roman de Troie* of Benoît de St. More, he tells us:

> Qant qu'elle ait en set ans amé
> Ont elle en un jor oblié . . . (l. 2120 ff.).

But he frankly admits that there have been good ones amongst them from the days of the Virgin Mary and the Magdalen onwards.

Guiot then turns to the liberal professions, which is unusual in this kind of work. He begins with the 'devins'—the theologians— and, lest the word should not be understood, he describes them as masters in the art which brings forth the highest intelligence in man, and in which dwells unquestionable divinity. But, although theology is the crowning art which produces eloquence and doubles sense and faith, its exponents are not loyal to it. Like so many others 'il ne béent mes qu'à l'avoir' and, however eloquent they are it avails them nothing. For even though they give forth refreshing streams, they themselves are dirty vessels (or channels, gutters) and, though they send forth light, they themselves are consumed like candles in the process. The 'langue bien parlant' is of no avail when accompanied by 'œvres puans', for by our works we shall be judged. Next come the law-students and lawyers. They go off to Bologna to study and there they extract bad learning from the 'fontaine de sapience'. For they practise all kinds of trickery wherewith to deceive the people and they too are dirty vessels in which the clean water of 'bone clergie' is defiled.

Guiot's last section, on the subject of doctors, is amusing and personal. No life is so 'diverse' or so 'perverse' as theirs. They disguise their guile under high-sounding terms. Whether they come back from Montpellier or Salerno, they sell us 'vescies por lanternes' and make people swallow cheap drugs under high-sounding names for which they charge outrageous prices. And yet there are good ones amongst them, as usual, and Guiot qualifies what he has been saying. They do sometimes bring relief to those in distress:

> mainte gent qui se desconforte
> en lor conseil molt se conforte.

As for the author, although he likes them when he is ill, he would pack them off with all their physic in a galley to Salonica as soon as he was well and would never want to see them again.

There ends this lengthy work. It is ably written and its 2,686 lines do not pall too badly. Not much space is given up to the rather foolish allegories and word-plays which were in vogue at the time. Although the author claims familiarity with court life and gives us an imposing list of patrons, his outlook is that of the man in the street, whether he is abusing the clergy, the lay-brothers, the lawyers or the doctors. But it is the outlook of a member of the cultured professional class rather than that of the merchant or the artisan. Guiot's metaphors are bold and striking, as where he speaks of the world having become so small and contemptible that two or even four men could fight out their quarrels in a pot. This 'plaisante hyperbole' was admired by Pasquier for its boldness in his *Recherches de la France* (chapter vi). Pasquier has mixed up the author of this 'longue satyre ou il taxe tous les Estats sous le titre de la *Bible Guiot*', with the author of another work of the same kind— the *Bible* of the Seigneur de Bercy (or Berzé) which we must now briefly examine.

Pasquier's confusion between the respective authors of the two 'Bibles' may have been due to the fact that in one of the manuscripts containing the *Bible Guiot*, this satire is immediately followed by an insipid poem entitled *L'armeüre du chevalier* which begins with the words: 'molt ai alei, molt ai venu', which are practically identical with the opening lines in the *Bible* of the Sire de Berzé in which he gives the reason for inditing his work:

> Cil qui plus voit, plus doit savoir
> Quar por oïr et por veöir
> Set l'on ce que l'on ne savroit
> Qui toz iors en un leu seroit,
> *Tant ai alé tant ai veü.*
> Que j'ai du siecle coneü
> Qu'il ne vaut riens a maintenir
> Fors por l'ame del cors partir (ll. 1–8).

These opening words give the tone to his poem. Like the authors of the Anglo-Norman religious poems of the twelfth century, he simply wallows in the idea of death. He has seen the sad fate of no less than four emperors of Constantinople and noted how inevitable death is. The 'arbaleste' may miss its mark 'mes la mort ne se faudra jà'. Look at Methusaleh, who inquired of God how long he had to live, as he wished to build himself a house. But when God, who loved him greatly, sent back word that he would live another 900 years, Methusaleh—appalled at the thought of dying so soon—remarked that ' . . . jamès ne feroit / Meson por si petite vie' (l. 544). And we cannot be certain of even living a day. Like Guiot, though in a more melancholy strain, he looks back to happier times when the courts were gay with song and laughter and frequent tournaments. But now covetousness, anxiety and pride have killed all that and everyone is out to 'deschevauchier' his neighbour.

Like Étienne de Fougères, the Sire de Berzé then briefly describes the functions of the three 'Estats du Monde' which God has ordained. There are the priests to serve him, the knights to punish the evil-doers, and the labourers. All have failed in their functions—the chastity of the clergy is corrupted and their loyalty turned to falseness; the knights are out to rob 'les menues genz' instead of protecting them; the labourers try each one to enlarge his boundary at the expense of his neighbour. From them he turns to the state of the Church. When the 'loi de Rome' failed, good and holy men took counsel and created the Orders:

> Li uns l'Ordre des moines noirs
> Et l'autre l'Ordre de Cistiaus (ll. 239–40).

Then came the Templars and the Hospitallers. But all have failed. The 'moines noirs' are the worst—'c'est des Ordres la plus faillie'. They are full of deceit and hypocrisy and turn back to front to deceive those they meet. There may be one or two good ones amongst them, but most are quite corrupt. The author puts his finger on the weak spot of each order—The Cistercians are charitable to the needy but all out for land:

> Que s'il puent plain pié de terre
> Sor lor voisins par plet conquerre,
> Cest sanz merci qu'il en auront,
> Ja tort ne droit n'i garderont (l. 291 f.).

But though he gives each of the Orders a bad mark he grants that if anyone kept their rules faithfully and repented sincerely his soul might be saved. Without true repentance even the hermit's life is useless and 'guerpir le siecle' of no avail. We may note here the reaction of the layman against the hermits of whom such a spate appeared in the literature of the turn of the century. But the Sire assures us that a life of 'mesaise' in this life does not necessarily mean a life of ease in the next. A sad, gloomy, solemn man may lose Paradise and the jolly man gain it—provided he repents of his sins. The poet considers himself a good judge in the matter—more worthy of belief than the hermit, for he has plumbed the depths of the world and found that worldly joy is pure nothingness (*fins noienz*). He recalls from experience that when the army ceased to be humble and forgot God, God forgot them. Then, when their 'bone cheänce' failed them, their fall was great, for it was 'De si haut si bas sans respit' (l. 474).

Concerning what the author calls 'un pechié qu'on apele amor', a rather diverting dilemma is raised. The sin consists mainly in the action of calling to mind the fair one after a period of separation, and our author seriously debates whether the merit of repentance is greater if the lady is fair than if she is ugly. He concludes for the latter: 'Quar il lais pechiez est plus noirs.' But he adds rather wistfully:

> Mes li biaus est plus deliteus
> Et plus plesens a remembrer (ll. 754–5).

Like the most critical authors of this period in which the acquisition of wealth played such a large part, the Sire de Berzé is obsessed with the folly of this chase after riches:

> Li povres brait toz iors et crie
> Qu'il ait avoir et manantie,
> Et li riches muert de paör
> Qu'il ne le perde chescun ior' (ll. 367–70).

Perhaps the grapes were sour. The author tells us that he is 'ne clers ne lettré'. Probably in the early part of the thirteenth century, when fighting in the East had somewhat lost its glamour, the landless knights were as penurious as the wandering scholars. But after all, he reflects, the only things that really matter in life are good works and true repentance and they are open to all.

The Sire de Berzé was not the only one to raise the question of values at this period, for the author of the *Poème Moral* (mentioned in a previous chapter for its didactic tendencies and the Life of St. Thaïs it contains), gives a telling example of how God estimates the relative value of a life of retirement from the world and a life lived in the world but redeemed by good actions or abstention from sin. Saint Paphnutius, the hermit by whose intervention the courtesan Thaïs was snatched from a life of sin, growing a little weary of his 'vie d'angle', asked God to direct him to someone equal in sanctity to himself. Soon after setting out he was met by a disreputable 'jogleör'—a former robber who had taken to this 'lait mestier' in his advancing years. When questioned as to his life he related how, on two separate occasions, he had assisted poor women in distress. The hermit had to admit: 'Ne fis ainc si grant bien', and on his return to his cell he prayed and fasted more vigorously than before. After a suitable interval he again besought God to show him 'son per'. This time he was directed to the house of a wealthy landowner who, in the midst of the good things of this world, lived a life of complete charity and purity, untouched by the worldly attractions around him. Once again the hermit metaphorically took off his hat to someone better than himself. A third request, after a further interval, brought him in touch with a wealthy merchant returning from Alexandria who offered him an alms and was obviously a 'saintisme' man. Once more the saint was able to rejoice at God's mercy. Not long after this lesson Paphnutius was on his death-bed and addressed some salutory words to the sorrowing brethren:

> Nus ne cognoist, fait il, les homes, se Deus non,
> . . . Teis a guerpi le siecle, qui ja Deu ne verrat
> Et teils est qui converse al siecle et Deu avrat,
> Teils siet sor son cheval, qui mellor corage at
> Et miels pense a Deu que teils qui a piet vat (ll. 2513 ff.).

This refreshingly liberal view is characteristic of the whole poem (in spite of the author's dislike of the jongleur, see p. 19). He is a man of the people and has 'le commun des hommes' in his mind. God does not care what a man's occupation is as long as he is upright. Many a one indulges in wine and flesh and raiment, who loves God more than a water-drinker (ll. 231–20). A man who knows how to 'garder mesure' on all occasions can live in any surroundings, for the heart, not the place, makes the man.

Moderation marks the work of the author of the *Poème Moral*, but this cannot always be said of the critics of this period—even of those whose choice of subjects was beyond reproach. Here is Gautier de Coincy—the author of so many 'Lives' of saints—who joins in the outcry against the abuses of the Church which had started half a century before his time. In his *Vie de St. Léocadie* we get one of the severest indictments against the corruption and greed of the prelates that has come down to us. It is money again, which the author personifies as 'dant Denier', which is at the root of the trouble. The prelates sell the prebends two or three times over; their faces are always turned towards gain—'Vers l'avoir ont les bés

(= *becs* = faces) tornez'. The cardinals are 'plein de convoitise' and Rome fills her purse:

> Rome nos ret (= *rase*) toutes les mains
> Rome ret tot et plus et mains . . .

The prelates sell the patrimony of the Cross to those 'qui ne sevent lor nes moscher' (l. 952). They have gotten to themselves all the gold and silver. Poor students who burn the midnight oil over their studies, are left penniless. Many of them go off to Bologna where they learn how to cheat the poor and Bologna grows fat while Paris grows thin (*amenuise*). Then there are the hypocrites, the Papelarts who put on the appearance of hermits. God hates them, for they practise a 'vilain mestier'. They are guilty of sodomy—like grammar they join *hic* to *hic* whereas nature would join *hic* and *haec* together. 'Terre, terre', the author exclaims, 'Por qoi n'uevres?' And so the poem proceeds, with many foolish word-plays and much repetition. But the familiar strain runs through it—the disastrous effect of the love of money, the wickedness of hypocrisy and the grievous state of those who make a god of their belly (l. 1598).

We seem to detect the genuine voice of the people in all these works by middle-class authors of varied standing—a protest rising up against the pretensions and extortions of the Church, but equally critical of the disproportionate wealth of many of their own class who had lost all their moderation in the mad lust for gain. We are as far removed in atmosphere from the rarefied air of the courts where knights and high-born ladies discussed their dilemmatic love-questions, as from the mysterious twilight of the forests and enchanted lands where knights wandered to and fro in search of adventures or in pursuing the quest of the Holy Grail. And yet these widely divergent expressions of life were manifesting themselves roughly at the same time, though in different surroundings and in different strata of society. At times a problematic love-question may stray into the framework of a 'fabliau' or a satire on the Church, or, on the other hand, a kindly word for the 'vilain' may creep into a 'roman courtois'. But taken all in all, the outlooks are miles apart and, in fact, one was moribund whereas the other was overflowing with life and energy.

For some time longer the critical spirit continued to express itself freely. It can be followed through Gilles li Muisis, Jean de Meun, and Rutebuef, whose free-lance attacks on Church and university are well known. But its suppression was inevitable when the fear of heresy made the Church less tolerant of abuse. It would have been a dangerous weapon in the hands of the reformers. It is interesting to note that a manuscript beginning 'del siecle puant et terrible' (evidently a copy of Guiot's poem), which was mentioned in a 'procès verbal' of the Albigensian heretics, was confiscated in 1274 by the inquisitors of Toulouse from the library of someone convicted of heresy.[1] This may have been the fate of many other manuscripts besides one of those containing Guiot's *Bible*.

BIBLIOGRAPHY

Les Fabliaux, études de littérature populaire etc. par J. Bédier. 5th ed. Paris 1928.
Richeut, Le Fabliau de, Études romanes dédiées à G. Paris. Contribution by Bédier. 1891.
Fabliaux, Recueil de: Méon et Barbazan, Fabliaux et Contes des poètes français. Paris 1808.
Le Boucher d'Abbeville. Ed. by J. Orr. Edinburgh 1947.
Le Vair Palefroi par Huon le Roi. Ed. par A. Längfors. Paris 1927. (CFMA).
Disciplina clericalis. See chapter on didactic literature.
Chastoiement d'un père à son fils. See Méon et Barbazan, op. cit. Vol. 2.
Enseignements Trebor par Robert de Ho. Ed. M. Young. Paris 1901.
Disticha Catonis. See chapter on didactic literature.
Estienne de Fougieres: *Livre des Manières*. Publ. par J. Kremer. (Ausg. ū Abh. XXXIX.)
Guiot de Provins: *Bible* (1) Barbazan et Méon. Vol. II.
 (2) J. Orr. Les Oeuvres de G. de Provins. Manchester 1915.
Sire de Berzé: *Bible* (1) Barb. et Méon. Vol. II.
 (2) F. Lecoy. La Bible au seigneur de Berzé. Paris 1939.

[1] See Orr's edition of *Guiot de Provins*. Introduction, p. xxxiii.

CHAPTER VII

THE EVOLUTION OF THE *CHANSONS-DE-GESTE*

IN this chapter it is proposed to trace the subtle change of outlook which was taking place during the second half of the twelfth century, and see how it affected the most firmly established form of literature of that period—viz., the epic poem. No account will be given here of the famous three great cycles of epic poetry—the *geste du roi*, the *cycle de Guillaume d'Orange*, and the *cycle des barons révoltés*—as it would merely be reproducing so much that has been written on the subject. But attention will be drawn to the special interest of a cycle of smaller dimensions and less important issues, but of real historic significance for the light it throws on social values. The *Geste des Lorrains* (or *Geste de Pepin*) as it is sometimes misleadingly called has its roots in a part of France where courtly ideas and an artificial state of aristocratic society were relatively neglected, and it belongs to a period when crusading fervour was at a low ebb and the new mercantile spirit almost at high tide. It has to be admitted that these poems are local in character, but this does not alter the fact that they represent ideas which were becoming very widely diffused.

In the earliest epic poems the stress throughout is on nobility of character, which is associated quite naturally with nobility of birth:

> 'Prus fut mes pere et mes ancestre
> et jeo sui mult de bone geste (= *family*)
> e, par meïsme, dei prus estre.'

says young Huelins in *Gormont et Isembart* as he rushes against the heathen king. (See ll. 217-20.) This is the true feudal spirit and it is inherent in the system. Even for Étienne de Fougères, a liberal-minded cleric, there were but three estates in the realm—the 'clercs', the knights, and the tillers of the soil. The merchant barely comes into the picture. Moreover, there was a great cause to fight for—'essaucier la chrétienté'. Loyalty to one's religion, to one's lord and to one's family combined with prowess in battle—these were the ideals of the early Christian knight. Love, wealth or learning have little place in this economy except as accessory advantages. The passages in the *Chanson de Roland* are almost too well known to quote. Roland's last thoughts, before his final confession, are for 'dulce France', 'des humes de sun lign', and for 'Charlemagne, sun seignor ki'l nourit'. They do not fight for themselves but for a sublime cause, and the loss, when they are killed, is a loss for their cause and their country. Guiburc's lament in the *Chanson de Guillaume* when she hears of Vivien's death is on the same lines:

> 'Il (Willame) ad perdu sun noble barné,
> De dulce France la flur et la belté;
> Ocis li unt Vivien l'alosé;
> En paienisme n'en la crestienté
> Mieldre vassal ne pout estre né
> Pur eshalcer la sainte crestienté'

(Chançun de Willame, 1371–6).

The contrast is between treachery and loyalty, cowardice and valour, not between nobility and wealth, *chevalier* and *vilain*, not always even between heathen and Christian. King Louis, in *Gormont et Isembart*, has a sincere admiration for the heathen king:

> 'Ahi,' dist il, 'vers amires,
> tant mare fuste, gentilz ber!
> Si creïssiez en Damne Deu
> hom ne poüst meilleur trover' (ll. 529–33).

He then has Gormont's body carried to the tent, and the author remarks: 'De ceo fist Loöwis que ber' (l. 534 = 'he acted like a nobleman'). Valour and loyalty to one's cause constituted the touchstone of a man's value. His wealth did not consist in the abundance of things he possessed ('avoir') but in the faithfulness of his friends. 'Riches on est qui plenté a d'amis.' The mercantile proverb 'tant as tant vaus', which we meet in later poems, might apply to one's vassals or one's friends, but not to one's wealth. 'Dans Deniers' is not yet the power that rules all.

It may have been noticed that the *Chanson de Guillaume* (or *Chançun de Willame*, as it appears in its Anglo-Norman dress) has been included amongst the earlier epics. This poem, which was greeted with great enthusiasm on its first discovery as a contemporary of the *Chanson de Roland* and so going to the very root of the Guillaume legend, has of late rather fallen from its high estate. Doubts have been expressed as to its antiquity—indeed, its latest editor[1] would place it subsequent to the well-known poems of that cycle (the *Couronnement de Louis*, the *Charroi de Nîmes*, *Aliscans*, and the *Enfances Guillaume*), and describes it as 'la cadette des poèmes qui racontent les événements des Aliscans d'Arles'.[2] The arguments

---

[1] Macmillan: *La Chanson de Guillaume*, I.
[2] Ibid. See Introduction, Vol. II, p. 130.

for the later date are based on considerations of language—always a slender foundation in view of modifications and corruption of the original poet's work. It is justifiable in a poem of this kind, which may have passed through several hands and been listened to by many pairs of ears (possibly of different nationalities), to ask oneself whether it evokes the spirit of any particular age by the sentiments and feelings it expresses. In the case of a composition which, like the *Chançun de Willame*, is not conspicuous for literary merit, this is even more justifiable than when a work of art, which is for all time, is in question. The *Chanson de Guillaume* (or *Chançun de Willame*) can take its place alongside the *Chanson de Roland* as a crusading epic. It is not concerned with fierce passions, it does not even relate the taking of a town (like the *Charroi de Nîmes*) or the winning of a wife (like the *La Prise d'Orange*). The object, as in *Roland*, is to 'essaucier sainte chrestienté'. Vivien and his uncle are out to kill as many heathen as possible, and Vivien's vow never to flee or turn his back on the heathen is like Roland's pride in face of the enemy. 'Kar chascun jur de mort s'abandunet' (l. 390). The true feudal spirit animates both these poems, and we see it in the attitude of the knights towards their 'seignur'. Guillaume, in the *Chançun*, may not admire 'sun dreit seignur' but he would not claim to be his peer even in valour—'encontre lui ne me dei vanter' (l. 1609)—and Vivien's attitude towards Guillaume is precisely that of Guillaume towards the king. Guillaume prides himself on his justice and mercy in his treatment of his vassals. He tells us of his clemency towards the widows and orphans. If the father was killed in his service he would not even exact the retaining fee which was due until the son became of age ('Tote la terre li rendi sanz relief', l. 1579). The same contrast is there—between right and wrong, between the traitor and the loyal knight, between cowardice and valour. In a poem with such a strong Anglo-Norman colouring and which, whatever the language of the original, was probably destined for Anglo-Norman ears, arguments based on versification and infractions of the rules of declensions must inevitably be used with great caution. But the poet was bound to write what would please his contemporaries.

By the time we come to the second half of the twelfth century the glory of Charlemagne and his twelve peers had largely been eclipsed by the renown of Arthur and his Round Table. Epic had been superceded by romance. Collective heroism and outsized magnanimous heroes had been replaced by individual valour and elegant knights. Nevertheless, the old epic spirit still survived, and

M

it is the evolution in this form of poem and the characters it celebrates that will be considered in the following pages.

Already by the time that Chrétien was engaged in composing polished poems at the request of highborn ladies (e.g. the *Roman de la Charette—circ.* 1176) in the artificial courts of Western France, a great change in social conditions was far advanced and a new set of values was in course of being established. The 'three estates' no longer sufficed to cover all the social grades. A crop of merchant adventurers was now disseminated over Europe, gradually working northwards from the Italian cities which the Crusades had made so prosperous. There was opportunity now for the man with enterprise of any rank to rise and attain to the power that money can give. There was an outlet for energy and ability such as had never before been experienced. Even a 'vilain' could become rich, though this would not happen if he was content to stay at home without venturing to look about him. 'Trop puet l'on garder le perier son aiuel',[1] said the *proverb au vilain*, expressing the same idea as the one quoted from the 'fabliau' of *Le Buffet* (cf. p. 149). 'Qui siet, il seche; qui va, il leche.' Now the founder of the family whose adventures fill the poems of the *Geste des Lorrains* was a 'vilain' and the son of a 'vilain', and the exploits of the father, his sons and his grandsons fill out thousands of lines. We must therefore inquire a little more nearly what the term 'vilain' connoted.

It is clear that the word 'vilain' which in Étienne de Fougères denoted the serf, the worker on the land who laboured not for himself but for his lord, underwent a considerable extension of meaning. For, as we have seen in the *fabliaux*, the successful vilain might become the prosperous merchant, or the rich city magnate or the powerful seneschal—thus constituting a real danger to the monopoly of privilege hitherto enjoyed by the blue-blooded knight. The scholar, too, looked upon this climber with an oblique eye, as he himself was generally impecunious. Out of this feeling doubtless developed the 'sens péjoratif' which was attached to the word 'vilain' in most of the literature of the second half-century. This sense was doubtless aggravated by the existence of the non-related word 'vil' which helped the meaning of 'low-down', disloyal, to be added to that of humble origin.

A glance at some of the *Chansons de Geste* enlightens us as to the idea evoked by the word 'vilain'. In the first branch of the *Couronne-*

---

[1] One can cultivate one's garden (or one's ancestor's pear-tree) too long.

ment de Louis Charlemagne warns his son Louis in the coronation scene not to make an advisor of a vilain:'

> 'Que de vilain ne faces consellier,
> Fill a prevost ne de fill a veier:
> Il boisereient (*would deceive*) a petit por loier' (ll. 206–9).

The rather unworthy last line shows the suspicion which attached to a man of ignoble birth who had raised himself to wealth and power by his ability. (We shall hear of the 'fils a prevost' and the 'fils a voyer' again.) But it may have been intended simply as a foil to the noble character of Guillaume, who is generally represented as gaining little reward for his loyalty and who felt his poverty bitterly:

> 'Ensi va d'omme ki chiet en povertés,
> Ja n'iert cheris, servis ne honorés,'

as he says rather pitifully in *Aliscans*. But Guillaume was built on large lines and his liberal spirit often breaks through in spite of his pride of family. Had he not married a heathen woman (whom he had shamelessly snatched from a pagan king) and adopted her uncouth nephew Rainouard as his own? In his rather long prayer in the *Couronnement*, too, he reminded God that at the day of judgment:

> 'Li prestre n'iert plus avant de clerçon,
> Ne l'arcevesque de son petit garçon,
> Li reis del duc ne li cuens del troton' (ll. 1009–12).

Even Charlemagne could ignore lignage on occasions and make new knights of persons of low degree (cf. *Ch. d'Aspremont* in a passage based on an episode in the *Pseudo-Turpin*—one amongst others where a wider tolerance is shown). The 'vilain' Varocher plays a noble part in the Italian-French poem *Macario*. He protects the banished queen and is finally knighted for valour and actually fights a duel with the proud Ogier le Danois. But the prejudice lingered, especially against the 'riche vilain' who is often synonymous with the 'marcheänt'. 'N'ai soin d'avoir, ne sui pas marcheänt,' says Girard de Viane proudly; but the insistence on 'gentillece de cuer' as opposed to wealth tended to become somewhat sententious as time went on. Perhaps, too, a little inverted snobbery set in which would have left Guillaume cold.

In the 'roman courtois' it is not merely, as has sometimes been assumed, a question of the contrast between *vilain* and *courtois*. The confusion between *vilain* and *vil*, *vilainement* and *vilment*, *vilainie* and *viltance* is quite obvious. 'Vilain', of course, still designates a peasant, but sometimes vaguely 'the people', 'the crowd', as in Chretien de Troyes' *Erec*, when the coronation is being described. The church was packed, but:

> Onques n'i pot antrer vilains,
> Se dames non et chevaliers (ll. 6912–3).

But the word has many other connotations and Chrétien's use of it is interesting and characteristic. His ambiguous couplet in *Yvain*— 'Qu'ancor vaut miauz, ce m'est avis, / Uns cortois morz qu'uns vilains vis'—means no more than that a true lover, even after his death, is more worth telling about than an unworthy lover in his lifetime. The preceding lines in the text make this quite clear. Chrétien employs the useful word *vilain* in all its acquired meanings—spiteful, ignoble, cruel, inconsiderate. 'Vilaine mort', with its equivalent 'mort felonesse', is a favourite invocation, as in most writers of the period. Kei's habit of always saying jealous and unpleasant things to the other knights is 'vilain':

> Envieus estes et vilains
> De ramposner vos conpaignons.

Indeed, this is the usual meaning now, and we feel that the contrast is forced when the very tricky conception of 'fin'amor' in *Cligès* is compared with the not 'resnable' love of Tristan and Iseult which 'torna a vilenie' (cf. l. 3152). Often 'vilain' means nothing more than inconsiderate, as when Enide, whose very tactful action in going without escort to comfort a young girl in distress calls forth the remark 'ele n'estoit pas vilaine', which simply means that she was kind and considerate. A similar litotes describes an 'ostel' as being 'sanz vilenie', which is rendered in other manuscripts by 'molt bon' and 'tot aisie' (cf. Eng: not bad).

Towards the 'vilain' as such, Chrétien's real attitude often breaks through. The hideous rustic (see p. 120) who is guarding the beasts in *Yvain*, when questioned by an astonished knight as to who he is, replies with dignity: 'I am a man', and proceeds to give a most intelligent account of the magic fountain and its guardian knight. He is not so appealing as the well-known 'vilain' in *Aucassin et Nicolette*, but he is by no means treated with contumely. Nor do the common people in the *Roman de Perceval* have any reflection cast on them in one of the most vivid scenes from that author's pen. Gauvain ('li preuz, li alosez'), by whom all knighthood is illuminated, is caught flirting shamelessly with the daughter of the man he has killed. One of the townspeople gets wind of his presence in the

palace and the mayor and corporation are warned. There is a sly
dig at these well-fed city magnates whom the messengers find
sitting in conclave: 'Le major et les eschevins, / Et d'autre borjois
a foison, / Qui pas n'avoient pris poison, / Qu'il estoient et gros et
gras' (ll. 5906–11). But they rise with alacrity at the news and are
soon joined by a crowd—'vilains angres', 'trestoz li peuples', 'la
commune—' who snatch up any weapon wherewith to attack the
hated Gauvain. The damsel tucks up her skirts, she swears, she hurls
the pieces of chess at them:

> 'Hu, hu', fet ele, 'vilenaille
> Chien enragiee, pute servaille'.

But the 'vilenaille' are worked up, and in spite of the great chess
pieces which come hurtling down and the armed porter who brains
them as they come up, they press to the attack and are only checked
by the sudden arrival of the king. The people and the 'commune'
come off best in this adventure, for Yvain was rightly hated ('Car il
i est de mort haïz, / Einsi a droit con vos savez') by the king's loyal
subjects. The dedication to Philip of Alsace who died in 1191 proves
that this unfinished poem must have been begun before that date.
It is interesting to note that the first assembly composed entirely of
bourgeois was held in 1186 and that there was a 'Commune' at
Toulouse in 1189; and in 1193 Philippe-Auguste, when he departed
for the Crusade, delegated his power in the towns to the 'prévot'
and the bourgeois. If Chrétien's home and birthplace were really
Troyes (and there seems no reason to doubt it) he must have been
well acquainted with the solid, merchant class, the powerful civic
authorities and the smaller fry who composed the 'commune', for
Troyes shared with Paris and Provins and the other cities of the
north a high reputation for its mercantile importance.[1]

It would be easy to multiply examples of the loose way in which
the word 'vilain' was often used. Its meaning did, indeed, cover a
multitude of sins. Marie de France gives it its rather rare but correct
original meaning of 'belonging to the town' in the fable *De la suriz
de vile et de la suriz de bois*:

> Ci dit d'une suriz vilaine
> Que a une vile proceine
> Voleit aler pur deporter.

MARIE DE FRANCE

---

[1] In considering Chrétien's use of the word 'vilain' we have not mentioned the poem
Guillaume d'Angleterre which is sometimes attributed to Chrétien de Troyes, although the
author does not give him his full name. The references to the 'vilain' in this work are in
such bad taste and so silly that, in spite of much similarity in vocabulary and language (so
easily copied), it is difficult to believe that it is by an author of such wide sympathies as the
author of *Yvain* and *Erec* and the *Conte de Perceval*.

In one sense Marie is less provincial than Chrétien de Troyes. (Was she not *de France*?) But she has much sympathy with the underdog and she does not vilify the 'vilain'. She obviously does not feel drawn to the greedy vilain who wants to get an unduly high price for his horse (*Del vilein e de sin cheval*), but she does justice to his cleverness in getting out of a bargain for which he had pledged his word:

> Li sages hum en grand destreit
> Turne suvent sun tort en dreit.

On the other hand she has no sympathy with the foolish 'vilain' who takes the advice of his wife ('sa vilaine') and tries to kill the serpent which has brought him all his luck. In the use of the word in its moral bearing Marie hovers, like other writers, between the meaning of discourteous or merely irresponsible, and the meaning of 'vilenie' in its modern sense of villainy, hardly distinguishable from 'vilté'.

This rather long discourse on the word 'vilain' and its multiple meanings has been made with a view to ascertaining what light the group of poems we have mentioned (*la Geste des Lorrains*) throws on the gradually changing state of society in the twelfth century. This 'geste' or 'cycle' stands a little aside from the other three 'gestes' on which attention is generally focused, although it naturally has a good deal in common with the cycle of rebellious barons. But the hero is neither an emperor's nephew, nor the king's nephew, nor the son of a great baron. He is a 'vilain' and the son of a 'vilain'. He comes from the town of Metz where trade flourished, and the poems of the cycle all revolve in the orbit of King Pepin (son of Charles Martel and father of Charlemagne), whose family originated from that city. Hence the interest is local if it cannot be said to be historical. The story revolves round Hervi de Metz and his two sons Garin and Bègue. The outstanding poem of this little group (or cycle), both on account of its epic qualities and literary value, is the *Roman de Garin le Loherain*, as its title appears in the manuscripts. It is obviously earlier in date than the other poems of the cycle, all of which dwindle into romance. *Garin le Lorrain* never does this. Its language, style, characters and descriptions of early feudal customs all point to the end of the twelfth century—probably a date not far removed from that of *Raoul de Cambrai* with which it has a good deal in common. It does not give the impression of being homogeneous in character. Certain sections are due to the poet Jean de

Flagy, of whom nothing is known. So it must be judged for its intrinsic value—always the most satisfying mode of approach.

The subject is the rivalry of certain great feudal families, indeed almost of two rival factions which, though both nominally loyal subjects of the king in the first part of the poem, gradually sort themselves out as the true supporters of the king and his interests on one side, and the very doubtful, often intriguing, obstreperous barons on the other. Indeed, the old contrast of loyalty versus treachery lies at the root of the whole poem. As the battle sways to and fro and the rival armies march hither and thither we learn of the havoc caused to the countryside by the foragers (*foreörs*), the burners (*ardeörs*), and the pillagers, so much dreaded by the peasants. The outstanding personalities, amongst a crowd of less worthy ones, are all of one stock—viz. the family of a citizen of Metz, to whom, in order to save his dukedom, Pierre, the improvident and impoverished duke of Metz, had given his daughter in marriage. This rich 'prevost', Thierri by name, himself the son of a rich merchant, possessed all the qualities which the duke lacked. He was rich, virtuous, loyal and wise—but he was a merchant, or 'vilain' in the extended use of the word, and the fact is never forgotten. In spite of this, however, in the early part of *Garin de Lorrain*, Hervi, the son of Thierri, is the mainstay of the kingdom which, under Charles Martel, is threatened by the Vandals (*Wandres*) and in grave danger of foundering. Hervi boldly advises the king, against the wishes of the ecclesiastics, to give back the tithes to the knights to enable them to equip themselves for the war against the heathen. Hervi himself leads the king's armies, attends Charles on his death-bed and defends his heir, the youthful Pepin, against the intrigues of the traitor Hardré. It is obvious that here we have a regional rival to the southern Guillaume d'Orange, whom Hervi resembles in his straight dealing, his plain speaking, and his loyalty. The king loves him dearly, while he depends on him. He is the 'bons dus', the 'palasins', the 'riche prince'—'li gentis et li ber', or simply 'li dus Hervis', whose advice the king always takes. And yet his father was a merchant, a 'prevost' (what would Charlemagne have said?)—in fact, a 'vilain', and his only title to nobility was through his mother, the daughter of the profligate duke of Metz. No disgrace, however, attaches to him in this noble poem, no slighting remark is made concerning Hervi himself or his sons, or his 'filleul', another Hervi or Hervi del Plesseis (son of the 'filleul') and his diverting son Rigaud, all of whom are distinguished at different times by the epithet of 'le vilain'. It is duke Hervi's 'filleul' who is most consistently spoken of as 'le vilain', but he is none the less respected for that. When Bègue, in doubt on one occasion as to what course to pursue, hesitates whether to accept his advice, the whole army exclaims 'li vilains a bien dit'. Another episode, well worth recalling on its own account, illustrates the democratic attitude taken up by the author, or authors, of this interesting poem. Bègue, a great favourite with the king, is besieged by his inveterate enemies, the Bordelais, in his castle of Belin. He wishes to send to King Pepin for help, but does not know whom to send on this dangerous journey through the enemy's lines. Hervi (the 'filleul') suggests a man who knows the country well and who would make a good messenger, but who is to be found in a tavern playing dice with ladies of doubtful reputation. His name is Menuel Galopin and he is 'germains cousins' to Bègue, and so ought not to fail him at need. Menuel, however, in answer to the summons, replied:

> 'Je n'ai mestier de si riche voisin;
> Mieux aims taverne et le soulas de vin,
> Ces demoiseles que vos veez par ci,
> Que je ne fai duchés a maintenir' (Vol. II, p. 100).

He agreed to go, however, when Hervi had paid his bill. After confessing who he is to Bègue and referring somewhat shamefacedly to his downfall, he refuses his cousin's offer to make him a knight and reinstate him in his lands if he will give up his folly. He replies with a laugh, 'Mieus aims taverne et de putains les dis'. But he is willing to go on the embassy. He sets out the next day with letters to King Pepin enclosed in a 'barril' tied round his neck. He is well received everywhere and, on arriving at Orleans, lodges with 'la bele Heloise', who turns out to be another cousin but who is not in the least ashamed of her relative. Galopin, in spite of her pressing, insists on spending the night at a tavern because he prefers the wine and the company he meets there to all the abundance in his hostess's house. The next day he is taken before the emperor and the empress, to whom he presents his missive. He is nearly attacked by the treacherous Bernard de Naisil, a sworn enemy to the family of Hervi de Metz, but the empress rescues him with her own hands and, when insulted by Bernard for doing so, retreats weeping to her room, taking Menuel Galopin with her. Bernard has to slip out by a back way and escape ignominiously across the countryside, riding all night. He at last reached safety, though only with difficulty, and the author remarks 'Ainsi va d'home qui mauves plet bastit'.

This episode, which is told at some length, introduces the more important one of the siege of Bordeaux by the king's troops in which both Garin and Bègue took part. It was a bloody battle. Garin was badly wounded and many others slain. Unfortunately the king's forces had to retire discomfited and great would have been the joy in the enemy's camp had not Bègue, who only arrived with his force toward the end of the battle, somewhat saved the situation. And now follows an interesting sequel to the battle which throws some light on the vexed question of the *tournoi* and the conditions under which it was fought at this period. It was no affair of a 'ronde table' or blunted weapons yet, such as we find in texts of a later date.[1] On the contrary, it turned out to be exceedingly deadly. This was scarcely surprising, with the treacherous Bernard de Naisil and his uncle Fromon in command of the Bordelais and the two indomitable brothers Garin and Bègue the leading spirits among the Lorrains. Some clash between these two rival factions had become inevitable. As soon as the French had retired disconsolate to their camp the foxlike Bernard[2] suggested that Fromont's son, Fromondin, should be knighted and that a *tournoi* should be held in honour of the occasion. This Fromont agreed to after some hesitation. Fromondin duly received the accolade and a challenge was sent to the king of France to 'summon' (*mander*) the tourney for the next day. King Pepin replied that he had had no time to consider it and that his army was tired. The messenger was insolent and scoffed at the king for not accepting the 'defi' of one of his vassals. The situation was saved by Bègue, who leapt forward and not only accepted the challenge, but declared that he would capture Fromondin's horse and present it to his squire Rigaud (the son of Hervi 'le vilain'). Next day the lists were prepared and the rival armies were drawn up in regulation fashion. Young Fromondin led his army gallantly to the attack, followed by a group of leading knights who are enumerated by the author and who were followed by the rank and file with much sounding of horns and trumpets. The king's army advanced in similar fashion, headed by knights of distinguished names. Fromondin soon unhorsed two

[1] See descriptions on pages 185 and 186.
[2] 'Renart resemble qu'en la taisnière est mis' (II, p. 53).

knights and his friends rushed up to guard him from being seized as he got entangled in the press. Then the battle became general:

> Et li tornois fut tot ensemble mis;
> La oïssiez grosses lances croissir,
> Et chevaliers contre terre flatir
> Dont li cheval fuient par le larris (II, 165).

Garin had four horses killed under him, for he had to bear the brunt of the battle—'Trestous li fais en vint desor Garin'—and things were beginning to go badly for the royalists. The king began to get anxious:

> 'Diex', dist le rois, 'aïde, saint Denis!
> Defendez-moi ne soie mors ne pris.
> Oü est dus Bègues qui'a aus s'aati?'

A time-serving knight hinted that Bègue was drunk when he had accepted the challenge, but, in fact, he was still sleeping after having kept watch the night before to prevent a treacherous attack in advance. As soon as he was awakened he sent for his squire (Rigaud) and his horse and rushed to the fray—but not before he had humbly asked a few chosen friends to come to his aid if they saw him in danger of being taken. As was customary in these 'tournois' great importance was attached to the capturing of horses, and the taking prisoner of knights with a view to a high ransom. But this was not a *tournoi* with blunted weapons such as we shall find in later descriptions. Such a combat would not have suited Bègue who, after merely overthrowing one or two knights, drew his sword Floberge when he found himself surrounded by the enemy:

> Entre aus se lance, de bien faire aatis:
> Coupe visages et bras et poins et pis.
> 'Diex'!. dist le rois, 'li dus Bègues est ci!
> Or pert il bien que il n'est endormis.'

But the important combat was still to come. Bègue had, in fact, challenged Fromondin and sworn to have his horse. The duel took place between them and soon Fromondin was stretched on the ground. Bègue could have killed him at once, but it was the horse he wanted and, seeing Hervi 'le vilain' near him, he bade him seize the steed and lead it to the camp. Meanwhile the friends of Fromondin had arrived to rescue him. Arrows flew thick and fast; Bègue's horse was killed and Bègue himself would have been in danger if Garin had not arrived with friends to remount him. Then the battle grew more desperate and two of the chief leaders on the Bordelais side were killed—viz. Guillaume de Poitou and Bauduin de Flandres. When this became known, their case was recognized to be serious and a general retreat was ordered—'Ça retornons; nos sommes desconfis'. Bègue had to be almost dragged from the conflict in which there were many killed and wounded:

> 'Certes', dit Bègues, 'ci out bon ferreïs;
> Sor toutes choses itex gieux m'abelit.'
> '—Diables estes' ce dit li rois Pepins.

Such was the 'tournoi', the 'ludus militaris', at the time when *Garin le Lorrain* was composed.

The victory having been gained by the Lorrains, nothing remained but for Rigaud to be knighted. An amusing, but instructive, scene follows: 'Or vouz alez baignier', says Bègue to his young kinsman, 'Et vous arez et le vair et le gris':

> 'A maleüre'! Rigaus li respondi,
> 'Por vostre vair qu'avez et vostre gris?
> Ne sui cheü en gué ne en larris,
> Je n'ai que faire ne de vair ne de gris;
> Trop de buriaus a mes peres Hervis' (II, 180).

Neither Rigaud nor his father made any secret of the fact that merchandise was their profession and that things should be valued according to their utility. As soon as Rigaud had the regulation knight's cloak thrown around him, he borrowed a knife and cut a good foot and a half off its length: 'Or puis mieus coure et lever et sallir', he coolly remarked. At which the king smiled and said: 'Par mon chef voir as dit', and no further objection was raised. When the 'colée' had been given (which Rigaud much resented) and the sword girded on, the king seated him beside himself at the table and another tournament was announced by Garin for the next day, for honour demanded that Rigaud, now that he was knighted, must joust against Fromondin (l. 182). If Rigaud were overthrown and his horse Baucent captured, Garin would yield up Gascony to the opposing family and their lineage. The challenge was accepted (with some hesitation on the part of Fromont) and the tourney started early next day. Rigaud excelled all the other knights in the bloody mêlée that ensued, and soon achieved his object of capturing not only Fromondin's horse, but also its rider, whom he led back in triumph with ten other captured knights. There were great rejoicings amongst 'nos Roiaus', who all agreed that Rigaud 'de nostre gent en a porté le pris'. After this, the family, or rather regional, feud died down for a time and Bègue, the restless warrior, was obliged to take to that only other knightly occupation—

hunting—to occupy his leisure time. His wife, having noticed how bored he had become, took him to task, reminding him that he had everything heart could desire—'Faucons sor perches assez, et vair et gris, Et murs et mules pale frois et roncins, Et bien avez foulé vos enemis'. But Bègue told 'la belle Biatris' that she had made one bad mistake and the following noble lines are put into his mouth:

> 'N'est pas richoise ne de vair, ne de gris,
> Ne de deniers, de murs ne de roncins,
> Mais est richoise de parens et d'amis:
> Li cuers d'un homme vaut tout l'or d'un païs' (II, 218).

In spite of the warnings and presentiments of his wife, Bègue was determined to hunt a famous boar of gigantic size of which he had heard. Unfortunately this meant entering the territory of his old antagonist, Fromont, whose relations and friends he had slain. Notwithstanding this, the intrepid Bègue set out with Rigaud his cousin, his hunters, 'veneörs sages et bien apris', and ten 'meutes de chiens'. The boar was roused from his covert by the dogs, but instead of standing at bay it left the forest and took flight across the plain—not, however, until it had killed Bègue's best hound and astonished the hunters by the size of its nails and its tusks. It was hotly pursued, but soon all were left behind, including Rigaud. Bègue kept up the pursuit alone with his faithful dogs and was soon lost to sight. And now at last the boar was brought to bay and, rolling its eyes and turning up its snout, it rushed at the dogs and made havoc of them. Bègue, furious, insulted the boar ('fis de truie, etc. . . .') and the animal listened, rolled its eyes, wrinkled its snout again and rushed at the man. But Bègue was ready for it, and with a well-aimed blow from his lance he pierced it through the heart. Then, like Guillaume in *Aliscans*, he uttered a few words of apology to his horse because he had nothing to give it, and the horse replied in the same way as Guillaume's horse by neighing and pawing the ground with its feet. Bègue then recalled his remaining three dogs and gently sounded his ivory horn to recall his men. But alas, though his own men did not hear the horn, it was heard by 'le forestier qui le bois dut garder' who, when he saw the well-equipped knight, did not dare to approach but went straight to Lens to report what he had seen. Fromont was at table, but the keeper whispered his news into the ear of the seneschal and agreed with him that they should share the booty if the knight was taken or killed. The horrid plot succeeded; with six other scoundrels and one other volunteer they set out for the spot where Bègue was resting beneath a tree, with one of his feet resting on the dead boar and his dogs around him. Now an interesting point about this piece of treachery is that the volunteer just mentioned was 'Thiebaus li lerres . . . Frere Estormi de Boorges le fier', so that here the author introduces the two traitors—Esturmi and Tiebaut de Bourges, who deserted Vivien and betrayed the cause so shamelessly in the *Chanson de Guillelme* (see p. 166). This is the more interesting as the *Roman de Garin le Lorrain* shows little conscious knowledge of any of the other 'chansons de geste'. But who can tell what the author, or authors, may have heard in the market-place and vaguely remembered? Thiebaus acts up to his reputation. When Bègue explains that he is a knight and that he would make reparation for his trespass against the forest laws, he declares that Bègue is merely trying to save himself, and tells the others to keep off the dogs and seize their master. When the 'forestier' tried to seize the ivory horn, Bègue hit out and felled the man at a blow. Then the fight began in earnest. Bègue killed three of his would-be captors and the others were about to flee when by chance the keeper's nephew appeared on the scene. When he saw his uncle lying dead he took his bow, fixed in it a large arrow of steel and shot the count straight through the body, severing 'la maistre veine del cuer'. Bègue only had time to utter a short prayer committing his wife and children and his brother Garin to God, and to take three blades of grass between his feet as a symbol of the 'corpus Dei' before he expired. The 'gloutons' then set on his body and plunged their spears into it, thinking they had killed a poacher:

> Non l'ont, par foi, mais un bon chevalier
> Le plus leal et le plus droiturier
> Qui onques fust soz la chape del ciel (II, 240).

The funeral laments (*regrets*) which followed when the event became known are all in the same strain. Even his enemy Fromont calls him:

> Le plus cortois et le mieus ensigné
> Qui portast armes, ne montast en destrier.

Young Fromondin, whose horse he had won for Rigaud, grieved for him 'com la mere son fil':

> Tant mare fustes, frans chevaliers gentis;
> Li miudres princes qui ains beüst de vin ! (II, 248).

The monk who had passed him on the way, not knowing who he was, after reflection calls him to mind:

> Er soir au vespre en passa uns, par ci,
> Gentilhoms fu, que son salut me fist (II, 252).

The barons at his enemy's court are forced to the same conclusion when they saw his noble appearance and the devotion of his dogs which had followed the procession which brought in his body:

> Or l'ont ocis glouton et pautonnier,
> Jamais frans hons ne le voulust touchier;
> Gentis hons fu, moult l'amoient si chien (II, 244).

Garin's lament recalls the description of Roland's character in the *Chanson de Roland*:

> Frans chevaliers, corageus et hardis!
> Fel et angris contre vos anemis,
> Et dols et simples a trestoz vos amis.

But the most touching lament, briefer but far more appealing than the long *regret* uttered by the fiancée of Raoul de Cambrai when his corpse is laid in the church at Cambrai, is uttered by his wife:

> Tant mare fustes frans chevaliers gentis,
> Dous et loiaus, simples et bien apris.
> Lasse, dolente, que porrai devenir . . . ? (II, 267).

On his tomb was inscribed 'Ce fu li mieuldres qui sor destrier seïst'. And this was the grandson of a 'prévost' and the son of 'Hervi le vilain'.

Although tangible proof of acquaintance with other 'chansons de geste' is rare in *Garin le Lorrain*, there must inevitably be a good deal of common ground between this poem and those in which discontented barons were fighting against the king or against each other, for feudal passions reigned in both. There is actually much in common between *Garin* and *Raoul de Cambrai* besides the clash of personalities and the difficulties of serving a feeble king. The references to ancient feudal customs and the expression of very similar sentiments in the two poems justify us in looking upon them as roughly contemporary with each other, and there is the fact that one comes from the north and the other from the north-east of France, where a different spirit flourished from that in the princely courts of the domains of the Plantagenets. Raoul de Cambrai was not of ignoble birth like Hervi de Metz, but the real hero in the poem of that name is Bernier—and he is a bastard, an accident which was continually thrown in his teeth. Hence pride of 'lignage' and

'parage' has to take a subordinate place. Roland was the nephew
of the emperor and Guillaume a proud son of Aimeri de Narbonne.
But Bernier was illegitimate and Garin was the grandson of a
merchant. Hence the importance of friendship rather than family—
'Hervis est riches et enforciés d'amis', says his enemy Hardré when
advising the king not to go to his help. 'Preus fu et sages et ot molt
bons amis', says the mother of Raoul when advising her son not to
make war on Count Herbert; and the author adds: 'Tant buer fu
nez qui plenté a d'amis'. But more important even than having a
large following was to have a sense of God's approval. The author
of *Garin*, relating the escape of Garin from that same Hardré, adds,
'Ja n'iert honis cui Diex vuet bien aidier', and Bernier's mother tells
her son: 'Qui bien sert Dieu, il li mostre sa chere?' The danger of
blasphemy is emphasized in two still more striking passages. When
Isoré (one of the rival Bordelais) is pursuing his enemy Bègue, and
has been baulked of his victim, he swears:

> 'Parmi mes mains le convenra morir,
> *Ne Diex ne hons ne le puet garantir.*'

From that moment Isoré's fate is sealed. He is killed shortly after
by Bègue who tears out his heart and flings it in his cousin's face,
telling him to eat it. 'Hons desloiiaus ne puet longes garir?' The
same danger is even more developed in *Raoul de Cambrai*. Raoul is
pursuing his enemy Ernaut, whom he has already deprived of a leg.
Ernaut turns and begs for mercy, but the implacable Raoul replies:

> '. . . il te convient fenir.
> A cest espee le chief del bu partir.
> Terre ne erbe ne te puet atenir,
> *Ne Diex ne hom ne t'en puet garantir.*'

At this Ernaut breathes a sigh of relief, for he knows that such a
'chien enragié', who denies God and His mercy, is doomed. Raoul
is killed almost immediately by Bernier, aided by 'Diex et drois'.
Although it is somewhat anticipatory, it may be mentioned here
that in *Hervi de Metz* this same phrase with a slight variation (*Ne
dix ne hom ne vous porroit tenser*), when uttered by a robber, actually
had the effect of producing a miracle, for God caused a ray of
sunshine to penetrate through the slits in his helmet right into his
eyes and so to blind him that he missed his stroke and Hervi was
able to strike him dead on the spot. Whereupon the devils carried
him off. Thus, although a common-sense outlook runs through
these poems, and it is a question of individuals fighting for them-

selves rather than an army fighting 'por essaucier seinte þhrestienté', yet there is a moral tendency throughout and a faith in God which relieves even the most gruesome episodes with a conviction that right will triumph in the end. Raoul is born to misfortune because he is such an unregenerate 'démesuré'—the poem is summed up in one well-turned line: 'Hom desreez a molt grant peine dure'—but Garin and Bègue, in spite of the flaw in their pedigree, are 'gentilhome' and recognized by all as such, even by their enemies, their dogs and their horses. In fact, they are 'bien-né' in the best sense of the word.

Garin le Lorrain never degenerates into romance. It remains dignified and reasonable throughout and intensely interesting owing to the vividness of its descriptions and the clever characterization of its 'dramatis personæ'. The noble father, Hervi de Metz, and his two gallant sons Garin and Bègue, must surely have become popular in their own country, for there are at least nine manuscripts (either whole or partial) which contain their story *plus* certain accretions as time went on, for all of which the city of Metz provides a jumping-off ground. The lineal descendants of Garin may be left on one side as being belated subjects of fourth-rate conventional poems, but the poem dealing with the early history of Hervi, the father of the two famous sons, deserves attention for more reasons than one. Here was clearly the case for a national (or, rather, provincial) hero which was too good to miss. The *Roman de Garin*, with its assonances, its archaic customs, its epic character and absence of romance, can be justifiably assigned to the twelfth century. The poem of *Hervi de Metz*, by the very absence of these qualities, must be assigned to a considerably later date—possibly some time before the middle of the thirteenth century—though the temerity of trying to date these poems, written in the literary language of the period and in a form possibly only distantly related to the original, is well known.

The poem *Hervi de Metz* is an excellent example of the effort to carry on a form of literature which had enjoyed great popularity, and at the same time to enhance the popularity of a local hero. The rather nebulous personality of the gallant soldier and wise counsellor of Charles Martel in the early sections of *Garin le Lorrain* is here traced back to its source, and the proper title of the poem should have been *Les Enfances Hervi*, on a par with the 'Enfances' (youthful exploits) of well-known figures such as Guillaume, Vivien or Aimeri. His strange adventures were well worth such a comparison.

Hervi was the son of Thierri, 'prevost de Metz, la mirable cité', himself the son of a very rich 'bourgeois' of the same town: 'N'avoit si rice en la crestienté' (l. 26). Thierri had not kept his talent wrapped up in a napkin. He had traded with it throughout the fairs of all Christendom and had amassed enormous wealth. He carried out his stewardship faithfully, for he was merciful to the poor and despised the overbearing rich, protected the pilgrims from violence and the merchants from robbery. He was 'sage et courtois, por bon conseil doner'. The duke of Metz, his master, was the extreme opposite, for he was an easy-going spendthrift. He was in the hands of the usurers (*les Lombards*) to such an extent in respect of his towns and his strongholds that he was in danger of having to sell his heritage:

> Que ne savoit comment peüst finer,
> Si il ne vent la mirable cité
> Et Loerraine la riche duchee (ll. 19–21).

Reluctantly, but to save the situation, he offered his daughter in marriage to Thierri the 'provost' who, after demurring so modestly that the duke was touched by his loyalty, accepted the proffered bride and the marriage was consummated without delay. The duke then departed for the Holy Land—but before setting out he urged his daughter to be faithful and loyal to her husband in spite of the fact that she was 'bassement mariée'. In due time a son was born to the merchant and his wife. He was christened Hervi and was elegantly brought up and educated in all the arts considered necessary for a young man of the aristocracy. At the age of fifteen there was no better-equipped 'bacheler' in Lorraine. Then the trouble began. Hervi asked his father for arms in view of shortly being made a knight and seeking tournaments in other lands. But Thierri had other ambitions for his son. He was to go forth in search of gain, for even a fortune is soon run through, and had not wealth enabled his father to obtain a duchess for a wife? Hervi protested vigorously that he knew more about falcons and dogs and horses than about costly materials and 'le vair et le gris', but his father was adamant and he was packed off to the fair at Provins under the escort of his uncle and well furnished with money. But he muttered under his breath as he set out:

> 'Par cele crois u le fiz Diu fu mis
> Quant je verrai (*viendrai*) a la foire a Provins
> J'acaterai mon bon et mon devis' (ll. 321–3).

N

And he kept his word, for after having entertained a crowd of merchants lavishly at his hotel and rudely told his uncles not to interfere ('Taisies, vilain . . . Peletier estes, si com il m'est avis'), he spent all the rest of his money on a hawk, two small hounds, a pure white greyhound and a horse which had taken his fancy as he rode round the ramparts of the town. His father's wrath on his return may be imagined, but his mother pleaded for his youth and the affair was passed over. But the following Christmas there was a fair at Lagny which had to be attended, and once more Hervi was anxiously entrusted to his uncles and furnished with an even larger sum of money to purchase 'des dras de Flandres . . . Qui tuit venront a la foire a Lagni'. This time his father warns him:

> 'Se pers l'avoir, con fesis a Provins
> En mon ostel ne te lairai jesir
> Mengier ne boire ne aler ne venir' (ll. 597–9).

Once again the protesting son set out, but with the firm intention of spending the money just as he liked. This time he brought back a young lady.

From this point the *chanson* develops into a rather conventional *roman d'aventure*, but its interest from a sociological point of view does not diminish. The maiden purchased by Hervi was actually the daughter of the king of 'Tir' and Constantinople and sister to Floire the king of Hungary. She had been captured by some irresponsible young men when her parents were away from home, whilst she was enjoying some day-dreams alone in a garden. Not knowing what to do with her, her captors were taking her to Paris to sell her at a fair. Hervi, who had come across the party in a wood near Lagny, had felt such pity for the maiden and was so struck with her beauty that he paid all the money wherewith he had been entrusted to free her and then mounted her on a mule and took her back with him to Metz. This was too much for Thierri. In spite of the beauty of Beatrice which, according to the author, was so great that the guests at a feast 'le mangier laissent por la dame esgarder', he believed her to be a 'pute', and refused to have anything further to do with Hervi, whom he proposed to banish from his domain. He was only induced not to do so by his son-in-law Baudri, who reminded him that Hervi was heir to the duchy and that the 'prevost' would only injure himself by such an ill-advised act:

> 'Cis a sa face, prevos, desfiguré,
> De son viaire qui son nes a copé' (ll. 2106–7).

Even a wolf spares its own flesh and devours that of another. This good advice is successful so far that in the end Hervi and Beatrice are allowed to take up their abode with their brother-in-law (a good bourgeois if ever there was one), who paid for his kindness in the end by being completely ruined by Hervi's extravagance. Shortly after this the couple were married and their two sons Garin and Bègue were born in due course. Here it must be recalled that the account of Hervi's marriage in *Garin le Lorrain* is quite different. Whether the author of *Hervi* had forgotten what he had heard, or whether he purposely ignored it, must remain a matter of conjecture —possibly the latter, as the story of the purchase of the maiden and the mystery of her identity is the whole pivot on which the later poem turns.

Hervi and his wife lived in solitude and obscurity, for his father, whom disappointment in his son had rendered unreasonable and hard, had forbidden anyone in the town to have anything to do with the young couple. Not unnaturally, Hervi soon became bored with his inactivity and, financed again by his obliging brother-in-law, he set out in search of adventure—which meant, in his case, pastimes such as 'tournois' and 'rondes-tables' (l. 2779). He entered heart and soul into a tourney of this kind, and we have a valuable description of what took place. Hervi, having heard from a young man who was passing through Metz that a tourney, having been 'crié' at Chartres, was to take place at Senlis in a week's time, hastened to the spot and arrived the day before it was to take place. All the available 'ostel' in the town had been taken, but Hervi and his young squire Gerard managed to find accommodation in a 'rue forainne' at the house of a rich citizen. Next day, 'devant la tierce' in order to avoid the hottest part of the day, the herald went around the city calling the combatants to arms. Hervi learns that it is the conte de Bar who has 'pledged and sworn' this tourney against the conte de Flandres, and that it is going to be a fine one, for the count of Bar has Loherencs, Bourgignons and Champenois on his side, and the count of Flanders has Flamencs et Hainuiers on his. Moreover, both the counts have mutually pledged each other that whichever of them is 'vaincus ne matés' will lose a thousand marks of pure gold to his victor. So they were fighting, or rather playing, for high stakes. Hervi went to church that morning and heard Mass, and then came back to his hostel, where he armed himself with a

hauberk, a helmet (or *bacin*) and a truncheon (or *baston quarré*) three
and a half feet long. The tourney took place between a wood and
a meadow. Flemings and Barrois rushed at each other 'les frains
abandonnés', and each leader of his troop engaged with a leader of
an opposing troop in a confused mêlée. There was such a clashing
of swords and lances that one could barely have heard God thun-
dering. The 'conte de Bar' was hard beset and in grave danger of
being taken when Hervi, seeing how matters stood, rushed into the
fray and saved the situation. For he laid about him so hard with his
blunt-headed weapon that heads and arms and shoulders suffered
badly. Now the count of Bar was remounted and Hervi made
straight for the count of Flanders. He forced his way through the
ranks, making good use of his truncheon, seized the count, dragged
him off his horse, and rode on, carrying the conquered knight across
his saddle. He was surrounded by enemies, but now the count of
Bar rushed to his aid and rescued him by main force. By this time
the tourney was practically over. Hervi had, in fact, decided the
result; the Flemish had lost horses, palfreys and pack animals, and
the honest count of Flanders had to pay his ransom in due course.
There was much rough horse-play, but no lives were lost and the
young man enjoyed it so much that he wandered about the country
in search of more:

> Juant s'en va li enfes contreval le païs (l. 2777).
> ... Desor s'en va Hervis par estranger regnés
> Querre tables reöndes et sovent ajoster
> Maint cheval gaagna, si les a tous donés.
> Seignour, tant demora, que il ot aloué
> Trestot l'or et l'argent que il en ot porté (XXIX, 2778–84).

More and more the poem degenerates into a romance of adventure
with all its artificial features. This brings about a change of tone,
and the reproaches against Hervi on account of his birth make their
appearance and are constantly brought up against him by his
enemies, like the charge of bastardy against Bernier in *Raoul de
Cambrai*. The character of the good 'prevost' himself, too, has
undergone a complete change. He has become mean, implacable
and servile in turn. It is pitiable the way in which, after all his
harshness, he truckles to his son when the latter at last comes back
fabulously rich. Hervi, it is true, must have been an exasperating
son for a well-to-do conventional bourgeois, and the hard side of

his character shows itself in the way he repulses his father's advances, throwing at him the hateful name of 'vilain':

> A vois escrie: 'Vilains, que sus estez! (= 'stand off')
> Moi renoiastes por ma grant poverté.
> ... Per Deu, prevos, je n'ai mesoblié,
> Putain ma femme avez II fois clamé,
> Mais vos mantistes con vilains esprovez' (ll. 4869–76).

The provost had to go on bended knees to Beatrice to obtain her intervention, and it was some time before Hervi relented—'car li prevos est vilains naturez, il m'a failli en ma grant povreté'. However, peace reigned at last and Hervi was knighted in due course. The second half of the poem relates the feudal dispute between Anseis, king of Cologne (a title which had been resurrected by the author of *Garin le Lorrain*), and the prince of Brabant. Hervi had by now been formally 'fiefé' by his grandfather with 'Mes la mirable cité, Et Loheraine', and having received the homage of the citizens of Metz, he set out for the battlefield. Once again his prowess is acclaimed on all sides, but the king of Cologne refers scornfully to his birth:

> Fix de vilain certes ne doit tenir
> Tel ducée; car n'afiert pas a lui (ll. 6376–7).

A gigantic Frisian, too, challenges him as 'fix de vilain', but he is soon laid low for his impertinence. At last, worsted in the battle, Anseis flees back to Cologne. The queen, who has heard rumours of Hervi's valour, asks her husband:

> 'De quel lignage et de quel parenté
> Est li duc, sire, dont je vos oi parler
> Qui tant est fiers, cremus et redoutes?' (ll. 6908 f.).

The king replies that he is grandson to the late duke on his mother's side:

> 'Mais de vilain a esté engendrés
> Fix d'un prevost est il, si m'aït De' (ll. 6916–7).

The queen is comforted by the thought that at least Hervi was of noble birth on his mother's side and his own people were not in the least perturbed about his title to the duchy, for had he not a duchess for his mother—'La fille au duc de Metz la fort cité?' It was only his enemies, as remarked before, who cast his birth in his teeth. The father and brother of his wife never ceased to be grieved at the thought of her sad fate:

> 'C'est grans damages, grans duels et grans pité,
> Fix de vilain jut aine a son costé' (ll. 2821–2).

By the end of the poem, however, Hervi has won universal admiration, the Lorrains are regarded as 'molt a redouter', and the city of
Metz is more glorious than ever.

There is much that is of interest in this lengthy poem, part epic
and part romance. The author's attitude towards the provost, that
'bons et loyals bourgeois ... qui tant ot de bonté', and towards the
'bourgeois seignoris' who rank with the 'princes', the 'chevaliers'
and the 'soldoiers de pris' (l. 6475), is evidence of the recognition
of the class of merchant nobles which had long existed in the big
towns of Italy. True, the good 'prevost' showed a regrettable
tendency to 'goulouser' wealth wherever he saw it, but Guillaume
d'Orange used to 'goulouser' every fine horse he saw and shunned
no cruel action to obtain it. So it was but a different set of values.
The fairs at Lagny, Provins and Bar, with their crowds of merchants
from all parts, mixed with scholars from Chartres, Orleans and
Paris, come vividly before us—Provins, famous for its costly materials and its horses; Paris for its precious metal-work ('joiaus ...
hanaps et coupes', etc.), and Metz, of course', the queen of them all—
'la mirable cité'. Other sections of the poem recall the earlier, more
warlike epics. There is a series of 'laisses similaires' beginning: 'Fiers
fut li caples et li estors mortels', and it is full of phrases such as 'Cui il
ataint molt a courte duree' (with its many variations), which might
have come out of any older epic. The author certainly knew
Raoul de Cambrai, as we have seen before and, curiously enough,
several lines seem actually to have been borrowed from that poem.
In *Raoul* we find:

> Bertolais dist que chanson en fera
> Jamais jongleres tele ne chantera

which our poem reproduces as follows:

> Uns clers a dit que canchon en fera
> Et il si fist, moult bien le devisa.
> Jamais jongleres millor ne cantera (ll. 6637 f.).

There are echoes, too, of some of the poems of the Guillaume cycle,
and the broad outlook and generous, though somewhat coarse,
features of the characters are often reminiscent of the very human
Guillaume d'Orange. And this brings us to a poem of that group
which links up in a curious way with the one we have been
examining.

It has already been mentioned that in the early part of *Garin le
Lorrain* Hervi de Metz plays a very similar part to that of Guillaume

in several of the poems of that hero's cycle. He is the supporter of a weak king against the intrigues of traitors by whom he is surrounded, and whose battles he fights without much reward for his pains. Now Hervi has two sons who uphold the traditions of the family and whose feuds and fortunes fill the rest of the poem. But Guillaume's union with the heathen Orable (later the Christian Guibourg) does not seem to have been blessed with a family. Guillaume, however, had plenty of nephews, as he had five, or possibly six, brothers, and the relation of uncle and nephew was a very intimate one in the earlier chansons. Moreover, a connection somewhat similar to that between Charlemagne and Roland was indicated. So Guillaume was provided with a special nephew who should act as a foil for his uncle and draw out his paternal feelings. The youthful Vivien, known from the *Chançun de Willame* and the nearly related *Aliscans*, was probably created to fulfil this function. He is of rather uncertain parentage from the start. In the *Willame* he was the 'fiz Boeve Cornebut al marchis, / Nez de la fille al bon cunte Aimeris' (l. 297). Thus his father, and that of his younger brother Gui, was the brother-in-law of his uncle Guillaume. In other poems, however, he is the son of Garin d'Anseüne, one of Guillaume's brothers (see *Chevalerie Vivien*, etc.). There are many complications, too, about the youthful years of Vivien and the upbringing of himself and his younger brother Gui. It would look as though the earlier version was that contained in the *Chançun de Willame*, where his upbringing by his uncle and aunt is stressed, and that this was either unknown to, or ignored by, the authors of the later poems in order to weave a romantic story round Vivien's youth. This story is to be found in the poem which goes by the name of *Les Enfances Vivien*, which must have had a considerable vogue, if we may judge from the ten extant manuscripts of the work. The supplying of a hero with a history and with a genealogy (either ascending or descending) was a well-known proceeding of the 'jongleurs'. Vivien had but a short life, so that, besides the *Enfances*, there was really no room for another poem. The *Chevalerie Vivien* was a quite unnecessary addition and is correspondingly feeble, as it merely reproduces what is found in other poems. This is not the case, however, with the *Enfances*, which has a definite value of its own. In this version of Vivien's youth he has been given Ustace, the daughter of duke Naime, for a mother, and Garin d'Anseüne, one of Aimeri's family of sons, for a father. When the story opens, Garin has already been a captive for seven years in the

hands of the Saracens in the Spanish town of Maldrane. The heathen
will accept no ransom for Garin except the person of his son Vivien
whom they hate because his mother is the daughter of duke Naime.
When the exchange was first mooted Garin indignantly refused,
but seven years in a Saracen prison had weakened his power of
resistance, and at last he gave way, and a messenger was sent with
the cruel alternative to Vivien's mother. Vivien, a mere boy,
declared his willingness to go to Spain in exchange for his father,
and Dame Ustace must choose between husband and son. A council
was held amongst the boy's relatives at which his uncle Guillaume,
'li marchis au cort nes', was present. Guillaume, who, the author
tells us, was a noble and upright man (ll. 321–2), spoke uncondition-
ally—husband and wife should stick together and their children
should care for them:

> 'Mal soit de l'arbre qu'el vergier est planté
> Ki son seigneur ne done ombre en esté' (ll. 335–6).

Poor Ustace knew not what to reply. She felt like the sheep that
deserts her lamb when it sees the wolf coming (l. 405). But
Guillaume's word was law and Vivien went. He was on the point
of being put to death by the heathen when the town Maldrane was
attacked by a hostile army and sacked. Vivien's execution was
stayed, he was released and carried away as prisoner to the coast.
Here the army ran into a band of merchants and a kindly woman
bought the good-looking boy:

> De Portingale i fu dame Mabile,
> Marcheände est, s'estoit prous et nobile.

This is something new in the Guillaume cycle, when we remember
Guillaume's scornful words in the *Charroi de Nimes*: 'Tant m'avez
hui escharni et gabé, / Et marcheänt et vilain apelé, / Ge ne sui mie
marcheänt par verté' (*Charroi*, ll. 1361–3)—on being addressed as
'marcheänt' by the heathen. Every kindness is shown to Vivien by
his mother by adoption and all the advantages of a merchant's life
are put before him:

> 'Enfes Vivien', dist la marchande, 'or voies
> Con suy bien faite, avenant et cortoise,
> Bien m'entremech de marchés et de foires' (ll. 949–52).

These are followed by a description of the miseries of a soldier's
life—how he dies in battle without priest, or confession, or holy
water. But Vivien is not impressed: 'Tot cois se tint li enfes'. The

next appeal is made by the merchant who believes the boy is his own, for he has only just returned from years of trading in foreign lands. If Vivien will go to the fairs and buy and sell 'ces bons dras', learn about hay and corn, weights and measures, and the management of money, the merchant will make him rich and leave him everything when he dies. But alas, Vivien replies:

> . . . 'de folie parler.
> de marchandise ne donroie un denier
> mais .i. destrier me faites amener
> et .ii. brakes me faites delivrer
> i. espervier me faites aporter
> par ces montaignes me irai deporter,
> prendrai de quailles et de perdrix assez' (ll. 353–60).

Here, too, each time the father is exasperated the mother makes peace (how true to life!). Once again Vivien is given all he wants and he goes out into the fields looking 'courtois et acesmé' in all his expensive clothes. But though he starts out cheerfully, the song of the birds makes him sad and he begins to weep as he thinks of his real parents. Other merchants who observe him say he was never the son of a merchant, but his foster-father ('Godefrois li senés') makes one more effort to bring him to a right state of mind. He calls Vivien and gives him 100 francs to trade with, saying that he himself had started with only seven deniers. But he had multiplied them many times and exhorts his son to do the same. 'De gaäignier pensez', is his final instruction. In order not to grieve the honest merchant Vivien replies aloud, 'biax peres, volontiers', but under his breath (*entre ses denx*) he adds 'de ces deniers n'irez mes gaäignier'. It is all rather pathetic and is told more dramatically than the corresponding episode in *Hervi de Metz*. This second attempt to turn the boy into a merchant is no more successful than the first. Vivien sees a young squire with a 'palefroi' which takes his fancy. He offers the delighted squire his 100 francs for it. The bargain is struck and each of the boys hastens away lest the other should look round and repent his bargain. Once again Godefroy is angry when he sees what a poor deal Vivien has made with his money, and again his wife pleads with him on account of the boy's youth and inexperience.

As time goes on Vivien becomes more and more unhappy. All he wants is to be a 'bons chevaliers armés', and he asks awkward questions about 'Surie . . . et des batailles devers Constantinople'.

But, says Godefroy, merchants too run great risks and go to Italy and Spain in search of trade:

> 'Por chou sont riche, assasé et manant,
> et marcheänt sont il bon et vaillant.
> Faites ensi, biax fils.'

And so the conflict goes on and things go from bad to worse. At last, however, at another fair to which he is unwillingly taken, Vivien has a stroke of luck. With the help of some young companions he manages to rout a band of hostile heathen merchants and get possession of their wealth. With this he repairs to Godefroy, and at last he meets with his approval. Shortly after this he is taken prisoner by some Saracens and carried back to Maldrane. His devoted foster-mother goes to court to beg the king to send a rescue party. The king hesitates, in keeping with his character. So Dame Mabile finds the boy's real father, Garin d'Anseüne, and makes a clean breast of her foster son's story, how she bought him, then adopted him and brought him up, and how they failed to make a merchant of him. Here the interest of the story ends from the point of view of our study of the bourgeois element and its intrusion into that family of aristocrats to whom 'parage' and 'lignage' meant so much. For Vivien belongs to that family, of whom the worst thing that could be said about any member of it was: 'N'est mie de ma geste.' It is true that in the end the author rather weakly invents a noble origin for the kind-hearted 'bourgeoise'. But this does not detract from the value of the attractive portrait of the worthy merchant and his wife. It is true that the love of a good bargain is as deep-seated in the character of the merchant Godefroy as it is in the rich 'prevost' in *Hervi de Metz*, but the bad effect of it is more marked in the latter case and the relations between father and son are not so delicately handled. The *Enfances Vivien* is remarkable for its insight into child psychology and, indeed, into other characters which are introduced to give more dramatic effect—such as those of the weak king and the bluff Guillaume d'Orange. The greater skill in this respect may point to a later date for the *Enfances* than for the cruder though equally romantic features of *Hervi de Metz*, but it is exceedingly difficult to find an adequate reason for assuming which was borrowed from the other.

In the final act of the *Chanson de Roland*, Charlemagne had handed over the unfortunate hostages of Pinabel to a functionary of undefined status ('un soen *veier* Basbrun') to be hung on a Judas tree. The 'veier', with the assistance of 100 servants under him, had

carried out the emperor's orders. Charlemagne might use function-
aries but he did not trust them. His injunction to his son in the
Couronnement de Louis will be remembered—viz. never to receive
advice from 'fill a prevost né de fill / a veier', because they would
soon deceive him for gain. He little thought that legend would
make him owe his very existence to the fundamental goodness of
a 'veier'.

The brother of 'la bele Beatriz' in *Hervi de Metz* was Floire, king
of Hungary. This is how the author introduces him:

> Freres la dame fu Floires li gentis
> Qui Hongerie avoit a maintenir.
> Icis fu pere Bertain o le cler vis
> Que prist a femme li riches roys Pepins
> Dont issi Karles li rois poesteïs . . . (ll. 620–4).

Thus the ill-starred 'Berte au grand pied' in the poem of that name
was the niece of Hervi de Metz and his wife Beatrice. The subject
of *Berte au grand pied* is well known—how 'Pepin le bref', in the
orbit of whose reign all the poems of this cycle move, sent to the
king of Hungary for his daughter whom he wished to marry; how
a maidservant was substituted for the princess in the royal bed, and
the real, intended wife was left to perish miserably in a forest, and
how she was discovered dying of cold and hunger by a kind-hearted
'voyer' whose wife and daughters took her in and made her one of
the family for seven years. When she was at last recognized by the
inequality in the size of her feet she became the wife of the un-
deceived king who, unable to wait till they got back to his palace,
consummated the marriage in a large 'char' which was conveniently
at hand in the forest, and to commemorate the occasion named the
son who was born to him in due time 'Char-le-magne'. The story,
which is quite entertaining for its own sake, is humorously told.
But the point we wish to stress here is that quite the noblest character
in the poem is that of Simon le Voyer, the good, comfortably-off
citizen who, with his wife and daughters, saved the poor lost girl
from almost certain death without any thought of gain and not
knowing in the least who she was. Yet Simon is a 'veier'—a term
which at this date was probably not far removed in meaning from
the title 'prevost'—the very type of person which Charlemagne had
told his son Pepin not to trust. A great change of outlook had taken
place during the lapse of time which separates the *Couronnement* from
these varied poems of the thirteenth century.

BIBLIOGRAPHY

Gormont et Isembart: Texte critique, éd. par A. Bayot. (CFMA).

La Chanson de Roland, publiée d'après le manuscrit d'Oxford ... par J. Bédier. Vol. I, Text; Vol. II, Commentaire. Other editions too numerous to cite.

La Chançun de Guillelme: hgg. von, H. Suchier Halle 1911. (Bibl. Norm. VIII.)

La Chançun de Willame. Ed. by E. Tyler. New York 1919.

La Chanson de Guillaume. Publ. par D. McMillan. 2 vol. Paris 1949–50.

Le Couronnement de Louis. Ch. de Geste du XIIᵉs., éd. par E. Langlois. Paris 1938. (CFMA).

Le Charroi de Nîmes. Éd. par J. Perrier. Paris 1931. (CFMA).

Aliscans. Kritischer Text von Wienbeck, Hartnacke ū Rasch. Halle 1903.

Les Enfances Guillaume. Ch. de Geste du XIIIᵉs. publiée par P. Henry. Paris 1935. (SATF).

La Chanson d'Aspremont. Ch. de Geste du XIIᵉs. éd. par L. Brandin. 2 vol. Paris 1923–4. (CFMA).

Macario. Macaire, ch. de g. publié d'après le ms. unique de Venise par F. Guessard. Paris 1866. (Anc. Poètes. 9.)

Garin le Loherain, Li Romans de, publié par Paulin Paris. Paris 1833.

Hervis de Mes (Metz), herausgeg. von E. Stengel. Dresden 1903. (*Gesellschaft f. rom. Lit. I.*)

Les Enfances Vivien. Éd. par A.-L. Terracher. Paris 1923.

Berte aus grans pies par Adenet le Roi, éd. par U. Holmes. Chapel Hill 1946.

Berte au grand pied. Adaptation d'après 2 mss., par L. Brandin. Paris 1924.

CHAPTER VIII

CHRONICLERS AND HISTORIANS

IF the second half of the twelfth century is, as we have seen, remark‑ able for the non‑religious character of its romances and the worldly trend in its literary output—which is not merely 'courtly' (*courtois*) but actually 'court' literature—an equally noticeable change may be detected in the historical output which has survived from this fruitful period. The historical records from the first half of the century onwards break away from the trammels of dry Church annals and the historian, like his more literary brother (the story‑ teller), moves from the monastery to the court. Hence the change from the collective to the individual, from the anonymity of the pious monks and writers of saints' lives to the almost obtrusive self‑assertion of the court poet. For the writer (be he poet or historian) must live, and—being no longer supported by a com‑ munity—must make himself and his work agreeable in order to gain a favourable hearing and a material reward. The age of patrons has arrived. The authors of the *chansons‑de‑geste* appealed to a larger, more mixed audience and their 'oyez, seignors' might be heard in the castles, the fairs, or along the pilgrimage routes. But in the courts an individual approach was necessary, and many a pathetic appeal provides evidence of a real anxiety on the poet's behalf concerning the wherewithal to make a living. It was, perhaps, easier for the chronicler, for kings and great men not unnaturally wish their deeds and conquests to be handed down to posterity and for this they would be willing to pay. In the recently conquered Britain a group of notable chroniclers sprang up to whom we owe a knowledge of this period which gives an invaluable background for the 'floraison littéraire' which marks it. For the moment the scene moves over to England as it was from the confines of England and Wales, where Norman nobles had been provided with available land and had frequently intermarried with their Celtic neighbours that a new race of chroniclers sprang. William of Malmesbury, of Norman and Saxon birth, although a monk, heralded this new school of nonmonastic literature in his *Gesta Regum Anglorum* into which, discarding the old annalistic arrangement, he introduced romantic stories, quaint legends and court scandal—for he was no student-recluse and had many contacts with the court. He portrays Henry I probably from the life. He had discussions, moreover, with Earl Robert of Gloucester, the king's son—the same Earl Robert to whom Geoffroy of Monmouth dedicated his work. To William of Malmesbury we owe the account of Henry I's upbringing (*egregie educatus*); of his being so impregnated with the love of letters that no tumults of war or cares of state could banish them from his mind; of how, even as a child, in the presence of his father he would quote the saying 'Rex illiteratus asinus coronatus'.[1] We hear, too, of the liberality of his first wife, the Scottish princess Matilda, who was so generous that 'scholastici tum cantibus tum versibus famosi' flocked in crowds to her court and 'he who could soothe the ears of his lady by the novelty of his song thought himself a happy man'. She was particularly generous to foreigners and thus her fame was spread far and wide. Henry I's second wife, Aalis de Louvain, was also known as a patroness of letters. It is uncertain which of these two ladies commissioned the poet Benoît to produce a vernacular version of the *Voyage de Saint Brendan*, as the dedication in one manuscript (C) is to Dame Mahaut, in the others to Donna Aalis. The words of the prologue would point rather to the earlier in date,[2] but, in fact, it matters little to which lady the author owed his inspiration. The point is that already the court was becoming a centre of literary activity and the feminine influence was beginning to make itself felt in the first decades of the twelfth century. To 'Donna Aaliz le reine' Philipe de Thaün dedicated his *Bestiaire*, and it is interesting to recall the fact (recorded by William of Malmesbury) that Henry I kept a menagerie of wild beasts at Woodstock, including lions, leopards, camels, lynxes and other strange beasts from foreign lands. Even more interesting is the information given by Gaimar in his *Estoire des Engleis*—the first rhymed chronicle in the vernacular—that the 'raine de Luvain' (that same Aaliz, wife of Henry I) had commissioned a poet, David, to write her husband's 'Life', which Dame Custance (Gaimar's patroness) often read in her bed-chamber. He mentions Robert 'li quens de Gloucestre' who lent his translation of Welsh books to Walter l'Espec who, in his turn, lent them to the husband of Dame Custance. The interchange of books and ideas was thus proceeding vigorously in the reign of Henry I and the themes of romance were already taking shape.

[1] Wm. of Malmesbury: *Gesta reg. angl.*, ch. v. Cf. Gir. Cambrensis—who tells us his court was 'schola virtutum et sapientiae ante meridiem, post comitatis et reverendae laetitiae.' Dist V, ch. v.

[2] See Ritchie in *Med. Aev.* Vol. XIX, 1950.

The popularity of the chronicles need surprise no one for the pills of history are coated with the sugar of romance. Gaimar in his *Estoire des Engleis* recounts the story of Haveloc the Dane (see chap. V, p. 135), and gives a somewhat garbled account of Hereward the Wake from which we can obtain a glimpse into the unsettled state of those times when 'Des utlaghes *(outlaws)* mulz i aveit' (l. 5467). Unfortunately Gaimar's chronicle only extends to the end of the reign of William Rufus whose death in the New Forest he describes with some interesting details. It is regrettable that his account of the colourful side of Henry I's court (omitted apparently by David) either remained a pious intention or was buried in oblivion. Amongst the mass of Anglo-Norman literature which has perished must be included also Gaimar's translation of Geoffroy of Monmouth's *Historia* which his patroness had procured from him when Robert of Gloucester lent it to her husband. Its neglect, or loss, may be due to the fact that it was eclipsed by the famous translation of Wace, the Norman poet, native of Jersey, whose work had such an influence on subsequent literature. For it was Geoffroy of Monmouth's *Historia* which, though sometimes despised by sober critics, contained the spark which set all literary Europe aflame for many a decade. Geoffroy's early life corresponded roughly with the reign of Henry I of England, at whose cheerful post-prandial gatherings (see *Note*, p. 196) poets and learned men were welcome. After the first fifty years of Norman rule, continental culture had begun to permeate and act as a stimulus to the dormant literary life in England. It was a stroke of genius on the part of Geoffroy to constitute Arthur, about whom, as well as the enchanter Merlin, legends were already in existence, the central figure of a characteristically Norman court where courteous wit and competing valour were the order of the day. Knighthood was not yet deflected from loyalty by the love of woman—rather did 'dames wax chaste and knights the nobler for their love'. Arthur was still an active warrior as well as the dispenser of gifts, and the knights, when not engaged in fighting, kept themselves fit by competition in games and sports. Gaimar, as we have seen, was acquainted with Geoffroy's work, but it was not till nearly twenty years after its publication in 1139, that Wace's work in the vernacular was launched into the literary world. The *Brut*, as Wace's poem was called after the eponymous founder of Britain (celebrated at some length by Geoffroy), was not a mere translation of the original. Many details were added from various sources, such as the well-

known one of the 'reönde table / Dont Breton dient mainte fable'.
But it was based on the *Historia*, and for a better example of Wace's
own history-writing we must go to his history of the dukes of
Normandy composed some years later. The *Roman de Rou*, as this
is called after the first Rollo, was composed partly in alexandrines,
partly (the major part) in the customary octosyllabic verse. He
begins pleasantly about the duty of recording in writing the deeds
of the ancients as otherwise they would be lost in oblivion:

> Pur remembrer des ancesurs
> Les faiz e les diz e les murs
> Doit l'un les livres e les gestes
> E les estoires lire as festes,
> ... Pur ceo firent bien e saueir
> E grant pris durent cil aueir,
> Ki escristrent premierement. ...

And again, after the fashion of the pious Anglo-Norman moral
poets he reminds us of the shortness of human life ('Tute rien turne
en declin / Tut chiet, tut muert, tut vait a fin ...', 65 f.) as compared
with the record which is put in a book by a 'clerc'. All this is, of
course, propaganda. Wace has been called the first professional
writer, for he was employed by Henry II to write up the lives of his
ancestors—the dukes of Normandy. His language is excellent and
his style good (he had been a scholar in Paris); but he was superseded,
greatly to his indignation, by another protégé of Henry who
commissioned Benoît de Ste. More to take over the work just when
Wace had arrived at the period which would interest us most—so
that the latter's work was rather eclipsed. A short history of the
dukes of Normandy, working backwards and hence sometimes
called the 'Chronique ascendante', constitutes a kind of prologue to
his work and forms an interesting part of the poem for us. Starting
from the date at which it was undertaken—1160—the author begins
with a panegyric of King Henry II and his wife Eleanor, who had
'assuaged him with gifts' and then goes on to state his intention of
recounting the 'geste ... de Rou et des Normanz'. The dislike of
the Norman for the French comes out when he castigates them for
being *forslignié, fals, suduiant, cuveitus* and—what counted heavily for
a court poet—*de duner eschars*. He gives us an idea of the rapidity
with which king Henry moved from one place to another. He
almost seemed to fly:

> Treis iurnees u plus en un sul iur errer,
> Ceo quidoent sa gent que il deüst voler.

His love of hunting is remarked on, the justice that he meted out to 'feluns humes' and his love of women which made him suffer 'maint freit et main chalt' (l. 141). Working backwards, he tells of the Empress Matilda's escape in her shift from Oxford to Wallingford on a winter's day. But, though interesting in details, his poem is mainly a work of translation from the wealth of Latin chronicles which marked this epoch. Wace is not in the least ashamed of saying that he writes for 'la riche gent / Ki unt les rentes e le argent / Kar pur eus sunt li livre fait / E bon dit fait e bien retrait'. His highest praise is reserved for Henry II and his 'largesce' in spite of the fact that he was thrown over for another author at the end. Though the histories were undertaken with a somewhat more worthy object in view than were the romances—viz. to perpetuate the memory of their patrons rather than simply to entertain them— the mode of flattering dedication was practically the same owing to their common object—the obtaining of material reward.

The important part played by Normans and Anglo-Normans will have been noted in these chronicles written in the French tongue but almost simultaneous with this later work of the Norman Wace, another very different work made its appearance and the contrast in treatment·and attitude is extremely interesting. The *Vie de St. Thomas*, which has been already included amongst the group of saints' lives (in effect it partakes both of the saint's 'life' and a work of history) comes from France proper, for Garnier (or more correctly, Guernes) tells us he was born at Pont-Sainte-Maxence situated in the north of the Île de France. The Frenchman's attitude towards Henry II is, unlike that of Wace, consistently hostile. His work as we have seen (cf. p. 30) is largely based on a Latin source, a fact which detracts from its historical value. But it is in good French and events are so graphically described as to make it surprising that an event, which had such repercussions all over Western Europe, should have found so little echo in the literature of the court circles with which it was contemporaneous. For Becket's death was in 1170—the very year in which Wace was writing his *Rou* and Chrétien de Troyes is generally supposed to have been at the height of his activity. But the new school of literature, represented by the imaginative Norman-Welsh chroniclers and the Normans of the English kings' continental domains was for the time being carrying everything before it. It is amazing that the restless Henry II, harassed by troubles and hostilities from every side—from Scotland, Wales, the French king and even his own family, could still be the 'bon roi', praised for his 'largesse' by scholars and poets alike in so many dedications. And yet how empty and superficial these dedications often were. Giraldus Cambrensis, in his *Topographica Hibernica*, written in 1188, actually dedicated his work to Henry II, whom he describes as 'vir affabilis, vir flexibilis et facetus . . . et, quod his temporibus conspicuum est, literis eruditus', vaunting elsewhere his innate liberality; and yet his invectives against the Angevin kings, when he had nothing to gain, were monstrous and unfair. He is, however, honest enough in the preface to his works to bewail the profitless dedications of the earlier ones and state that henceforth he writes for posterity alone. Meanwhile in France the same mercenary practice was being pursued at the French courts as we have seen when discussing the works of Marie de France, Gautier d'Arras and Chrétien de Troyes. There can be no doubt that the effect of patronage on individuals was demoralizing, though it may have been a necessary evil and productive of good results.

Other rhymed chronicles of the period must be set aside with a mere mention—for example, the poem of Jourdain Fantosme on Henry II's war against Scotland in 1173-4—and we must pass on to the most considerable and perhaps the most impressive of these long works written to order and probably for gain. This was the life of Guillaume le Maréchal, who had been regent of England during the minority of Henry III and had lived through the reigns of Henry I, Stephen, Henry II and John. *La Vie de Guillaume le Maréchal* was one of the last considerable rhymed chronicles written to command and, considering that it runs to some 19,000 lines, it was time that verse gave place to more succinct prose, as indeed it was about to do. Guillaume died in 1217 and the account of his life was written at the behest of his son—the facts being supplied by Guillaume's loyal friend, Jean d'Erley, who plays a considerable part in the poem. It is written in excellent French; the writer was probably a native of one of the continental domains of the English king. The marshal is portrayed as a 'chevalier sans peur et sans reproche', scrupulously loyal in his dealings both with the English and the French king. One realizes how disturbing those divided loyalties must have been —how, in fact, it was difficult to be loyal at the same time to one's king and one's overlord and not to incur on occasions the blame of being a traitor—a contingency which did actually occur in the life of Guillaume. But whether some casuistry was necessary in such an eventuality or not, the author is full of praise for his hero whose life he portrays from early boyhood to death. It must be remembered that the account is written by one of those 'qui de trover volt vivre'.

The marshal's long life was eventful and the scene shifts continually from England to France, or to Ireland as the case may be. Like his royal masters, Guillaume may be described as 'rarissime sedentem' for he had little chance of taking root anywhere. For a considerable time he was moving about Normandy, taking part in every tournament in which there was a chance of gaining honour and reward. A description of one of these tournaments (which the author tells us took place almost every 'quinzaine'), though wearisome in the telling, throws much light, not only on the character of this knightly occupation, but also on the social importance of Normandy as the scene and centre of this form of sport. It played, indeed, a large part in the life of a knight, for not only fame, but great material rewards lay in store for the victorious combatant. Moreover, there was an element of danger, for the right place for 'les proz' was under the horse's feet (l. 6092). The Church did not altogether approve of tournaments, but there was little ecclesiastical bias in the aspirations of a knight in these unsettled times. It is worth while to recall the description of one such tournament in which the marshal took part with much glory. It was in the reign of king Richard (about 1180) and took place 'en un lieu delitos et bel' outside the castle of Joigni. The countess, accompanied by her ladies, all beautifully dressed, came out to watch the sport. The knights leapt forward to meet them, for they knew their valour would be enhanced 'por la sorvenue des dames'. Before the tournament began someone called out '... Kar carolomes / Dementiers que ci atendomes' and all took hands to dance. Then the cry was raised: 'Qui chantera por nos?'—whereupon the marshal, who was a good singer ('though he never boasted of it'), began in a clear, sweet voice to sing a familiar song and they all joined in. When this was finished a young herald—a mere boy—intoned a new song ending with the refrain: '... Mareschal / Kar me donez un boen cheval'. Whereupon the marshal broke from the ranks of the dance (*la karole*), rode straight at a knight, unhorsed him and handed over the horse to the youth. Then the tournament began in earnest and even the timid took courage from the presence of the ladies. Great was the booty won by the victors and all agreed that the marshal 'out le pris'. We might be reading *Ipomedon* or any of the romances of adventure. But in spite of the colourful accounts of jousts and tournaments, we are always conscious when reading the poem of

the unhappy state of the English king's domains—constantly ravaged
by hostile armies and never enjoying any settled peace or prosperity.

The author of the *Vie de Guillaume* is frankly hostile to the 'cort
de Rome':

> Quer toz diz convient que l'om oingne
> A la cort de Rome les paumes:
> N'i estuet chanter autres psaumes (ll. 11362–5).

He then proceeds to inform his hearers that the cardinal who was
sent to King Philip had been well taught how to 'turn back to front'
and deceive his victim. His sympathies are with the English in the
long struggles which devastated the domains and reduced them to
a state that recalls the grim descriptions of the 'land of Logres' under
a spell in the prose versions of the grail story:

> . . . la tres cruel guere
> Dunt essilie esteit la tere,
> E la gent morte et confondue
> E tote joie esteit fondue . . .
> Quer kant povre gent n'ont que prendre
> Ne n'ont de quei lor rentes rendre
> Si lor estuet laissier la tere
> E aillors, aillors lor pain querre (ll. 659 f.).

He does less than justice to the French king when he accuses him
of having caused the death of Henry II and all his four sons by his
trickery. He relates the story of the 'elm of Gisors' which the French
cut down to 'shew their prowess'—but he does add that the French
king blamed his men severely and said it would be told to the shame
of France that his expedition had achieved nothing 'fors de cel
arbre découper'. It is a little group of French knights, however,
who, envious of the Englishman's popularity, hatch the plot against
the marshal and get hold of someone they believe to be the 'amicus
auricularis' of the English king in the hopes that he will insinuate
into Henry's ear the unpleasant stories they have concocted. The
author was clearly familiar with court intrigues but, before mentioning some of the characteristics of the fashionable court poetry
which are to be found in the poem, two incidents in the marshal's
life, one at the beginning, the other at the end, are too well-told to
be passed over unnoticed.

As a small boy William had been handed over as a hostage to the
king (Stephen) by his father as a pledge of good faith. But the
father broke his word and the little hostage was due to die. Again
the flatterers (*losengiers*) of the king got busy and told the king that

the boy must be hanged. On the way to the gallows, along a street lined with spectators, William, who had no idea of his destiny, seeing a knight with a fine 'javelot' in his hand, said, with the simplicity of a young Perceval, 'Sire, donez moi cel bozon' (l. 530). The king (whose heart was full of 'douceur') was so touched that for all the wealth of France he would not have allowed the child to be hanged. Another day William was happily playing in the fields whilst the king was sitting in his tent. The boy picked a bunch of 'chevaliers' (thin-spiked plants with a head of small flowers) and ran up to the king:

> Si dist al rei 'Beau sire chiers
> Volez joïr as chevaliers?[1]
> —Oïl, fait il, beau duz amis'.
> ... Puis dist 'Liquels ferra avant?
> —Vos', fet li reis, 'beaus amis chiers ...' (ll. 607 f.).

So they played and the king's flower lost its head first, much to the child's delight. There was no more talk of Guillaume's death. The whole episode shows a pleasing side of King Stephen's character besides giving us a sketch of child-life rare in medieval French literature.

The other episode that stands out is at the end of William's long life. He is on his death-bed. Quite suddenly he said to those around him: 'I have not had such a longing to sing for the last three years as I have had the last three days.'—'Sing, then, Sire,' replied his faithful friend, Jean d'Erley, 'it might strengthen your inner man ('nature dedans vos') and give you an appetite.' But Guillaume refused as he thought his friends would laugh at him. Then someone suggested he might like to hear his daughters sing. So they were fetched—but they did not feel much like singing when their father was dying:

> 'Chantez, Maheut, premierement.'
> Dist il, mes el n'en ot talent. ...

She sang some lines of a song, however, and then the next daughter was summoned:

> 'Joane, chantez, con qu'il prenge' (l. 1857).

So Joane sang a verse of a 'rotruenge', but she sang so nervously (*cremeitosement*) that the duke stopped her and showed how it ought to be sung.

Guillaume's spirit never failed him. To a monk who wanted him

---

[1] A game still known as 'soldiers' in some parts of England.

to leave some of his booty to the Church for complete 'quittance' he replied angrily:

> 'Taisez, malves!' (ce dist li cuens);
> 'Unques vostre cuers ne fu boens'... (ll. 18695–6).

The Church might look with disfavour on the treasure and booty he had acquired by his prowess, but he was not going to let his knights be deprived of the last perquisite he could give them. Finally, before dying, he gave orders for a length of silk (which he had kept for the purpose) to be fetched in which his corpse was to be wrapped and some grey felt to cover it if the day of his burial should prove to be wet or snowy. Perhaps he remembered the sad state in which his master's (Henry II's) corpse was left by his attendants after his death.

A few brief words must be said about this amalgamation of court poem and chronicle. All the stock forms of rhetoric are to be found in its long length. Apostrophes to death (which is the *arc-qui-ne-faut*—l. 6922), little excurses on Fortune and her wheel; allegorical personifications of *envie, largesce, oubliance, remembrance, gentillesce*, etc. Sometimes they are silly, as when we are told that Guillaume had married *largesce* with most satisfactory results. But they were in the taste of the time and his allusions to Arthur, Merlin, Kei, etc., to 'renommee qui tost vole', to 'nature creatrice' and other favourite rhetorical devices show that he was familiar with the romantic literature of his day. His love of proverbs, particularly those of a rather robust kind—e.g. *de bien fait col frait, plus dure hunte que soufraite* and the somewhat unusual one '*grant chose a en "faire l'estuet"*' (= need's must)—together with his references to the older epic heroes and the allusions to 'companionnage' show that he was familiar also with the 'chansons-de-geste'.

The *Vie de Guillaume le Maréchal* shows all the advantages and disadvantages of the rhymed chronicle. It is much too long and encumbered by details—some true, some false. As the writer of the prologue to a lost prose chronicle on Philippe-Auguste says:

> Quer enviz puet estre rimee
> Estoire ou n'ait ajoustee
> Mançonge por fere la rime (see *Romania* VI, 494 ff.).

On the other hand the anecdotes and details introduced to enliven the narration often throw an interesting light—not only on individual characters but on the customs and manners of the times which we should look for in vain in a serious prose chronicle.

This is eminently true of one of the last of the rhymed chronicles, viz. the *Chronique rimée* of Philipp Mousket which was composed about the middle of the thirteenth century. The author, a native of Tournai, sets out to give us a history of the kings of France. He, too, must have been well-versed both in the quasi-historical and the purely romantic history of his time. His sources are hard to determine with certainty, for some of his stories of epic heroes differ from those we find in the *Chansons-de-geste*, as in the case of the Gormont and Isembart legend. The same is true of his historical facts. In any case he could tell a story well—whether it be that of Richard I being captured in Austria on his way back from the crusade, or the equally popular legend of the Faux-Baudouin—the hermit who claimed to be Baudouin, the emperor of Constantinople who had mysteriously disappeared. To this episode Mousket devoted 1,000 out of his 30,000 lines. The story would make a strong local appeal for the hermit first appeared in the wooded country round Tournai, and the writer may well have gleaned details as to his demasquing after a brief triumph and his horrid end from local gossip.[1] The story was well known, however, and is found in various collections of anecdotes in the second half of the thirteenth century. In the work known as the *Récits d'un ménestrel de Reims*, in which history figures as a mere accessory to fiction, it is related with a few details added—such as the fact that when the hermit's shoes were taken off he was found to have no toes to his feet. The author of the *Récits*, though he sets out to write a kind of universal history, passing lightly from one country to another, was obviously out to please a heterogeneous audience. His work, though in prose, was destined for recital as we can gather from the constant appeals to his hearers: 'or vos lairons ci ester du conte'; 'si revenrous au roi Philippe'; 'si com vos l'orrez par en avant', etc. His skill as a story-teller belongs to another chapter.

So far the histories we have mentioned have been mainly concerned with the history of France. Universal history did not flourish in France as much as it did in Germany. But classical history was not altogether neglected. It is represented by a little group of works based on the writings of Caesar, Sallust, Lucan and Suetonius respectively. Jean de Tuin, about the year 1240, composed his *Hystoire de Julius César*. It was in prose and largely based on Lucan's *Pharsalia*—as the author tells us: 'de latin en roumans mis selonc les

---

[1] See J. Jaques: 'The "Faux Baudouin" episode in the *Chronique Rimée* of Ph. Mousket.' *French Studies*, III, 3. July 1949.

X livres de Lucan'. This was translated into alexandrine 'laisses' in
the second half of the century by Jacot de Forest. Drawn from the
same authors, under the name of *Li Faits des Romains*, stories about
their Roman ancestors were diffused in France and certain characters
achieved a considerable amount of popularity. Cato of Utica, so
much admired by Lucan, was quoted as a model of virtue, and
sometimes mixed up with the Pseudo-Cato, author of the distichs
(see chap. II). Lucan's noble words about Cato could not be
without their effect:

> ... *Servare modum* finemque tenere
> naturam sequi *patriaeque impendere vitam*
> nec sibi sed toti genitum se credere mundo (Bk. II, ll. 380 f.).

'Modum', 'mesure', 'mâze'—the word runs all through the literature
of the Middle Ages and the willingness to lay down one's life for
one's country or one's lord was the inspiration of the earliest epics.
But it is interesting that in the French works the character of Caesar
has been completely transformed. Instead of the violent man of
blood, the 'démesuré' that we find in Lucan, Caesar appears as a
generous conqueror whose 'gentillece, francisse et pitiés et miséri-
corde l'ont a çou amenet k'il pardoinst son maltalent a cascun'.
Mysterious groves, poisonous serpents, powerful Thessalian witches
are introduced into many of the later romances, for Lucan 'represents the transition from the high realm of poetry to that of
romance'.[1] Though intended to give the history of the first twelve
emperors, Jean de Tuin's work does not get beyond the death of
Julius Caesar. So many popular contemporary features were
introduced (funeral regrets, descriptions of feminine beauty, of
battles (in which the horses took part) resembling medieval tournaments, etc.) that the going was slow. But Lucan's fame as a historian
was firmly established.

CHRONICLES OF THE CRUSADES

In this brief survey of works written to order and largely eman-
ating from the court, we have left on one side a great source of
inspiration which was flowing strongly through all this eventful
century—viz. the holy war against the infidel. Nothing could be
more different in tone and character than the stream of chronicles
which, from its source on the borders of Wales, was carried on by

---

[1] See the author's *Lucan in the Middle Ages. Mod. Lang. Review*, Vol. XXV, No. 1. January
1930.

the Norman-Welsh court chroniclers of the first half of the twelfth century and the parallel stream of writing inspired by the religious fervour and self-sacrificing spirit which animated both chroniclers and poets who wrote and sang about the crusades. In the absence of actual chronicles in the vulgar tongue relating the events of the First Crusade, we may point to the *Chanson de Roland* as being a crusading epic in all but name. There is the religious fervour—the zeal for a cause (not just for personal glory), the longing for martyrdom in a good cause, the faith in a future life and a personal God (not just fate or 'fortune')—which is conspicuously absent from the court chronicles and romances we have been studying. Actually there is little in the vulgar tongue about the first crusade. Prose had not yet established itself and contemporary accounts which have survived are mostly in an easily readable Latin. The *Gesta Francorum et aliorum Hierosolymitanorum*, by an anonymous author, is a good example of this—but it makes us wish that the French and Provençal accounts, to which allusions in contemporary documents occur, had survived. The author of the *Gesta* refers at the outset to the 'mighty stirring' (*motio valida*) amongst the peoples which worked up to the crusade; he gives a vivid description of the hardships born by the rank and file who had no lure of personal aggrandisement to draw them on, and of the gradual disillusionment which overtook them. The description of the siege of Antioch is a good example of this method of history-writing. There is a mystical and romantic character about it, strongly reminiscent of the early *chansons-de-geste*. At a moment of discouragement in the course of the battle, a mysterious army with white standards and on white steeds, led by the three warrior saints in person (St. George, St. Mercury and St. Demetrius) was seen descending from the mountains to the aid of the Christians. And this must be true, says the author 'quia plures ex nostris viderunt'. They recognized them straightway as 'adiutorium Christi'. In like manner did not 'Li ber Gilie por qui Deus fait vertuz' appear on the battlefield in the *Chanson de Roland*, and three warrior saints—St. Denise, St. Meurisse and St. Jorge—throw the Saracens out of their tents in the early and oldest part of the *Roman de Garin le Loherain*? On this occasion, too, their presence was authenticated for 'moult furent bien et veü et choisi'.[1] In fact, throughout the whole work we find the same combination of Christian devotion and brutality, of the highest and lowest characteristics of the epoch, which marks the *chansons-de-geste* of the

---

[1] Ed. P. Paris, Vol. I, p. 108.

earlier period. The author of the *Gesta* was probably a Norman of southern Italy—one result of the crusades was to bring together inhabitants of different regions of Europe and mingle their traditions. For the Norman of southern Italy, as for the more northern author of the *Chanson de Roland*, the heathen were idolators whom it was a service rendered to God to kill. But he is just to the fighting qualities of the Turks and he, too, admits that—had they been Christians none could have been more valiant men or more skilful in war. It would be pleasant to linger longer over this fascinating and largely authentic account of the First Crusade, but it only enters into the consideration of French literature by reason of its spirit and tone which connect it so intimately with the Old French crusading epic as we know it.

It was impossible but that the *Gesta* should leave its mark on contemporary and later literature. Even the *Chanson d'Antioche et de Jerusalem*, though not based primarily on it, probably owes something to its vivid descriptions. The author delights in romantic episodes culled from various sources, such as that of Kerboga playing chess when the messenger arrived to say that the French were attacking—a preview of Drake and his game of bowls. In the *Chanson* an extra warrior saint is added to the three we read of in the *Gesta* and the fate of the poor man who found the holy lance was even more gruesome for, after his ordeal by fire, not only his garments but his hair was torn from him in the rush for relics:

> Les chevels li desrompent et ses dras li deschirent
> Des vestemens qu'il porte voelent faire reliques.

It was not surprising that he only lived five days after such a double ordeal. Even the shroud of the respected archbishop of Le Puy was torn to shreds by the relic-hunters. Undoubtedly the hardships undergone by the 'menue gent' (for whom most of the chronicles show great sympathy) produced a fruitful soil for superstition and portents. And there is naturally a stronger religious bias in the *Chanson d'Antioche* (which is written in 'laisses' of assonancing alexandrines) than in the epic proper, but there are many reminiscences of the *chansons de geste*. The author delights in the single combat in which the magnificent Turk is hurled from his saddle in the familiar words: 'Tant com hanste li dure, l'abat mort en l'erbage'. Strange-looking heathen 'as mustels rostis et plantes creves' are led into battle by the King Tafur inspiring terror as they go. The sufferings of the poor pilgrims are graphically described;

on one occasion they are actually reduced to eating dead Turks. Fortunately red crosses (*vermeilles comme sang*) appeared on the corpses of Christians so any mistake was avoided. The original part of this poem, dealing with the capture of Antioch, was the work of a Flemish pilgrim (Richard le pèlerin) and was composed in assonances, as we have seen, in 1130. It was revised later in the century and a continuation dealing with the conquest of Jerusalem was added by Graindor de Douai, who replaced the assonances by rhymes. It is in the early section that the part played by the common people is emphasized and its value from this point of view is greater than the continuations and interpolations which were added later.

The descriptions of the sufferings of the pilgrims could not be without their effect on men's minds and many a *chanson de croisade* was written to encourage the unwilling to set out again. Composed for the Second Crusade about 1140 was the poem opening with the words 'Chevalier, mult estes guariz / Quant Deus a vus fait sa clamur'[1] and encouraging the knights to follow the example of King Louis who had so much more to lose and yet had abandoned 'e vair e gris / Chastels e viles e citez' in order to fight in the tournament 'entre enfer e pareïs'. Another such poem of later date (written for the Third Crusade)[2] uses stronger words: 'Cil doit bien estre forjugies / Ki a besoin son seignor lait. . . .' It was hard for the multitude to believe that death could be 'douce et saveureuse' even if one conquered the 'resne presieus' thereby. And even the knight of noble birth (Conon de Béthune) who spoke these words would gladly have been spared from going, especially as the disputes and tyrannies of the 'haus barons' were becoming a by-word.[3] There is, in fact, little in French literature to commemorate the Second Crusade. The entertaining story of that 'diable' Eleanor of Aquitaine and her intrigue with Sultan Saladin related in the next century by the Ménestrel de Reims must be completely discounted owing to the author's disregard of chronology. But the 'jongleur' knew what his audience would enjoy. Queen Eleanor, he tells us, was caught when she was already 'd'un pié en la galie', and brought ignominiously back to her shocked husband (Louis VII). The 'ménestrel' has some equally unauthenticated stories to tell of Henry II, of Saladin and of Richard Cœur-de-Lion—good examples of the legends about well-known heroes which were current nearly a century after the events. The different versions contained in the

[1] P. Meyer: *Recueil* I, 39, p. 366.   [2] Ibid., No. 42, p. 369.
[3] Cf. Conon de Béthune. Nos. IV and V.

individual manuscripts show how they could be varied to suit the audience at any particular time or place.[1]

The Third Crusade called forth one of the most interesting documents in the vulgar tongue which have come down to us—*L'Estoire de la Guerre Sainte* by an author who calls himself Ambroise and about whom we know nothing more than that he was probably a Norman by birth and certainly a follower and admirer of the English King Richard. The 'Estoire' is the first example of a rhymed chronicle of contemporary events in French. It is the work of a professional writer—in fact, the nearest approach that we have to the account of a war correspondent who writes of what he sees, but knows nothing of the inner workings of diplomacy or councils of war. The greater part of his account is an actual report of an eye-witness and is thus of real historical interest. It was destined to be recited and in a remarkable passage Ambroise tells us what is the object of his work. The passage is worth quoting for the light it throws on the jongleur's stock-in-trade (ll. 4179–4202):

Seigneur, de la mort Alixandre,
De la cui mort fut grand esclandre,
Ne del message de Balan,
Ne des aventures Tristran,
Ne de Paris ne de Heleine
Qui por amor orent tel peine,
Ne des faiz Hartur de Bretaine
Ne de sa hardie compaine,
Ne de Charlon ne de Pepin
D'Agoland ne de Guiteclin,
Ne de vielles chançons de geste
Dont jugleür font si grant feste
Ne vos sai mentir ne veir dire
Ne afermer ne contredire,
. . . Mais de ço que tantes genz virent
E qu'il meïsme le soffrirent,
Cil de l'ost d'Acre, les meschiefs
Qu'il orent es cuers e es chiefs,
Des granz chalors, des granz freidures
Des enfermetez, des injures,
Ço vos puis jo por veir conter
Et il feit bien a escolter.

It is, indeed, an unvarnished tale that Ambroise tells, not written up for a patron, pedestrian in style and often tedious owing to the exigencies of rhymed verse. There are no dramatic invocations to Death, or Fortune; no allegorical personifications—but rather a

[1] See Introduction to Natalis de Wailly's Editior, p. xxv.

superabundance of pious tags. Some of his similes are, however, striking. The negroes with their red headgear seen bobbing about in a mass remind him of a ripe cherry tree. The Turkish method of fighting, which is to flee at one moment and return more fiercely to the attack the next, is like that of an angry fly:

> Si a la custume a la mosche
> Enuiose e pleine d'entusche;
> Toz iors chasciez e il fuira
> Retornez e il ensivra (ll. 5659 f.)

He achieves a somewhat dramatic effect at times by a sort of epic repetition. When telling of the defection of the French 'marchis Conrad de Montferrat' (of whom he has no good to say) he concludes each enumeration of the sufferings of the army in ten successive 'laisses' with the words: 'Lor maldisoient del marchis / Par qui il erent si aquis'. It was this same 'marchis' who was responsible for one of those evil marriages contracted with a view to obtaining a kingdom. Conrad already had two wives and insisted on marrying a third—the wife of Rainfrei de Thoron who was heiress to the kingdom of Jerusalem. The words are worth quoting as Ambroise comes nearer to a touch of humour here than in most of his descriptive passages:

> Quant li marchis ot esposee
> Cele qu'ot longtens golosee
> Ses noces fist et ses convives.
> Ore en ot il treis totes vives,
> Une en sa terre et l'autre en ost,
> E encor la tierce en repost (= cold storage !) (ll. 4145 f.).

But the Church disapproved of the marriage and God was not present at the ceremony (l. 4144).

The poem gives us a vivid picture of the sufferings of the pilgrims —particularly of the 'menue gent' on their forced marches. Sometimes these were due to lack of food caused by the holding up of convoys by the merchants. But many died of heat and thirst, of the heavy rains in winter and (especially 'la gent peoniere' or footsloggers) were tormented by reptiles and stinging insects which could only be driven off by making a fiendish noise each night with kettle-drums, trumpets, etc. Even worse were the tiny flies along the river banks ('muschetes / Que si esteient petitettes / e si sutils cum estinceles'—l. 9529 f.) which bit them so badly that they looked like lepers and had to wear 'visieres' to protect their faces and necks, though already they were overburdened with their equipment and harassed by enemy darts. The presence of women in the army was found to be so disturbing that, after the capture of Acre, only very old women were allowed to follow as 'lavenderes':

> Qui lavaient chiefs e dras linges
> E d'espucer valeient singes (ll. 5690-1).

We read of Cornishmen and Welshmen in the army (ll. 5680-1) but the chief source of disputes (next to the enmity between the French and English kings) was the presence of contingents from the different domains of the two kingdoms. Sadly the author regrets the good old days of Charlemagne as depicted in the *chansons de geste*, when they could all be lumped together, as 'Francs' (l. 8509). He treats the enemy simply as heathen idolators, 'chiennaille'—only made to be exterminated, but he concludes with an interesting conversation between the bishop of Salisbury and Saladin. The pilgrims were permitted by the Sultan to visit the sacred shrine even though they had not captured the town. Saladin paid great respect to the bishop and asked him about King Richard whom all his men feared almost immoderately. The bishop replied discreetly that if the qualities of the English king and the sultan could be mixed ('vos teches mises / Ovec les sues e assises') there would not be two princes in the whole wide world 'si vaillanz ne si esprovez'. The sultan reflected on the bishop's words and then replied sagely that Richard, in spite of his prowess, was too foolhardy and that for himself, however great he was, he would prefer:

> Largesce e sens *o tot* mesure (= together with)
> Que hardement e desmesure (ll. 12151-2).

Oliver himself could not have spoken more wisely to Roland. It is difficult to stop quoting from this chronicle—it is such a mine of wealth for information and interest. Ambroise is a biased writer, but he is not often unfair. The chief impression he leaves with us is one of admiration for the heroism of the rank and file who, though obliged at times to walk backwards to avoid their heels being trodden on, though worn out by strange maladies that made even their teeth drop out, scratched by prickly plants and covered with venomous bites, scorched by heat and tormented by thirst—yet, in spite of moments of discouragement, never lost their eagerness to reach their goal and bitterly resented it when 'li reis e li halt home' decided it was more prudent to give up the final attack and make a truce. There was much weeping when Richard departed finally for

England. They feared the future not only for him but for future pilgrims and they grieved for the land they were leaving behind:

> E disoient: 'Haï! Sulie,
> Cum hui remanez sans aïe!' . . .
> Lors veïssiez mult gent plorer.
>
> (ll. 12279–80; l. 12285.)

And now the turn of the century had come. Richard was dead and Jerusalem was still in the hands of the infidel. The king of France was once again engaged in warfare with the king of England. The poets had lost their faith in dedications (cf. supra, p. 200); the patrons themselves were ready for fresh adventures for, with the decay of the Angevin kings of England, some of the colour had gone out of their lives and Normandy was no longer the arena for glamorous tournaments. But there were still rich conquests and abundant treasure to be had in the East, and the recovering of the holy sepulchre was a good pretext for leaving wife and children and going out to seek adventure. In the year of the Incarnation 1203 (or 1204 as one chronicler tells us) 'maistre Foukes de Nuelli'—a parish in the bishopric of Paris—a good and learned man, went about preaching the cross and many followed him on account of his goodness and the miracles God performed by him. He collected much money for the expedition and many enthusiasts,[1] both high and low, took the cross. The kings did not go this time, nor were the English much affected by this fourth crusade. But nobles from the different regions of France enrolled themselves, and there were poets among them—Conon de Béthune (who played an important part as ambassador), Thibaut de Champagne, and the Châtelain de Couci. We are fortunate in the fact that two eye-witness accounts in French prose, one by a member of the aristocracy, the other by one of the rank and file, have come down to us—the chronicles of Geoffroi de Villehardouin and Robert de Clari respectively. So much has been written about Villehardouin and his curious attitude towards the objective of the crusade that small space need be given to him here. But the importance of his work as being one of the first examples of good French prose, following as it does the long rhymed chronicles, and to a certain extent replacing them, cannot be overlooked. It is not a very colourful prose—he has not many similes or phrases that remain in the memory—his highest flight of imagination consists in a remark such as that on an occasion of a

---

[1] Lists of names will be found both in Villehardouin, Robert de Clari, and the Anonyme de Béthune.

clash of the two armies it was as if 'terre et mer fondist ensemble'. But his language, though without embellishment, is clear, as is also his presentation of cause and effect. Villehardouin knew what was going on behind the scenes. He went on ticklish, even dangerous embassies. But as regards the great question of the deflecting of the expedition from Jerusalem to Constantinople we cannot be quite sure that he was sincere in his constant accusation against those who were of a different opinion from his own, namely, that they wanted to 'dépécier l'ost'—a phrase he repeats to satiety. Villehardouin was, so to speak, a member of the inner cabinet and could hardly be free from the intrigues and aspirations of the 'hauts hommes' who decided on the plan of campaign. He was an adherent of the ambitious Boniface de Montferrat, whose equally ambitious brother Conrad had become a 'triple adultère' (as Ambroise has already told us) in order to obtain a kingdom. The humbler chronicler, Robert de Clari, tells us much about the marquis' aims and intrigues and his disappointment when he did not succeed in becoming Emperor of Constantinople. Perhaps those not so near the throne had a clearer vision than those in its immediate entourage. Villehardouin, however, gives us a very clear idea of the plan of campaign and describes battle-scenes as well as missions. He does not write for effect and yet gives a pleasant impression reminiscent of the older epic with his 'la veïssiez meinte lerme plourer' or 'or pourrez oïr estrange prouece'. His frequent repetition of 'or pouez saveir, seigneur' and 'or sachiez' prove clearly that his work was meant for recitation or reading aloud and his own prominent part in it all must have made it very impressive.

Robert de Clari played a much less exalted role. He was at best one of the 'pauvres chevaliers' not far removed from the rank and file on foot. He begins his chronicle in the same way as Villehardouin with a list of the barons and important persons who took part. But when he comes to enumerating those who distinguished themselves by acts of prowess he does not confine himself to the 'riches homes' but includes the 'povres'—giving a special mention to his own brother Aleaumes de Clari en Aminois, 'li clers . . . qui molt y fist de hardiment et de proesces'. This is characteristic of the whole work and marks a most interesting change in public feeling. It is not 'lignage' that counts now, but solid achievement. Robert is indignant when the 'haut home' seize all the best 'ostels' and keep to themselves the priceless treasure they found in Constantinople. He mentions the fact that, when starting on an expedition, the bulk of the army were not even told where they were going (*mes tout chil de l'ost ne seurent mie chest consel fors li plus haut homme*). And yet he can give in some detail an account of the negotiations with the Venetians, and describes graphically the discussion as to what the objective of the army should be: 'Ba! que ferons nous en Constantinople?' said some. 'Nos avons no pelerinage a faire. . . .' But the others replied: 'Que ferons nos en Babyloine ne en Alexandre, quant nos n'avons viande ne avoir par quoi nos puissons y aler?' And so it goes on and Robert adds shrewdly 'et li marchis de Monferras y metoit plus paine que nus qui y fust d'aler en Constantinople, pour che qu'il se voloit vengier d'un mesfait que li empereres de C. qui l'empire tenoit, li avoit fait' (chap. xxxiii). This rings truer somehow than Villehardouin's strictures on those 'qui vouloient dépecier l'ost'. He makes us realize, too, that the majority of the army, unlike the ambitious leaders, were not without a conscience as to fighting fellow Christians. After a rather bad reverse at the hands of the Greeks even some of the barons were 'molt abaubi' and began to doubt the rightness of their cause. Then 'li vesque et li clerc' put their heads together and judged that the battle was 'droituriere' because the Greeks had been 'inobedient à la loi de Rome' (chap. lxxii). So they were no better than dogs, worse than Jews, and enemies of God, and it was 'grans aumosne' to kill them, just as it was to kill the heathen in the crusading epics. It will have been noted that Robert's style is effective, if not elegant. Even the conversations between princes might have taken place between the shepherds in *Aucassin et Nicolete*. 'Ba!' said the emperor when asked by the marquis why he had betrayed him—'ensi est ore'. 'Or, de par dieu', replied the marquis, and so the conversation ended—but not the marquis' anger.

Robert's language may not be elegant but his narrative style is clear and concise—not unlike that of the 'Ménestrel de Reims' whom he somewhat resembles also in his art of story-telling. He is much more credible, however, and we may speak justly of his work as a chronicle, though he will pause in his record of events to bring in a good story even though it breaks up the unity of his work. The account of the traitor Andromes, who seduced a queen, strangled an emperor, tried to murder three young men of royal lineage but was himself dethroned by one of them, had to take to flight and hide (still dressed in his imperial robes) behind the vats in a wine cellar, was dislodged by a 'haut homme . . . cui pere il avoit destruit', was brought to trial and condemned to a most disgusting death, may

P

be true or may not. But it is brought in and related in seven long chapters inserted into the history of the pilgrims with the definite object of accounting for certain facts in the past. The other traitor—Morchofle—comes in more in the course of the narrative. He is shown as a boastful, deceitful (even if courageous) character always displaying himself and 'faisant grant beubant' (repeated three times). But he, too, had to flee ignominiously, leaving his banner and a very precious eikon (*ansconne*) behind on the battlefield. He was seen later riding along in style with a large retinue including 'dames et demiseles'. But he was captured and thrown to his death at the doge's suggestion from the top of a hermit's pillar. 'De haut home . . . haute justiche', said the duke. In each of these descriptions Robert has shown his grasp of the connection between cause and effect, for in each case the character of the traitor's end corresponded to the tenor of his life. It may be that a little of this was mere coincidence, or that some of the details were added by the author, who was certainly not without imagination, for besides stories of traitors and Nubian Christians and an occasional miracle, Robert revels in descriptions of any striking scene or object. He waxes lyrical over the starting off of the fleet when it looked as though the sea was 'toute embrasee de nes' or the brave show made by the army as it marched, which filled the Greek 'dames et demiseles' with such admiration as they watched them that they said amongst themselves 'que che sanbloit . . . que che fussent angles', so splendid was the equipment both of the knights and their horses (chap. xlvii). But it is in the description of marvellous objects that Robert perhaps excels. He is thrilled by the splendour and skilled workmanship that marked the buildings of Constantinople. There were the many-roomed palaces with their floors of gilded mosaic and the churches with their gorgeous interiors, especially the Church of Sainte Sophie. But what struck most this man of ordinary tastes was the wealth of mechanical devices—the contest between two teams of mechanized figures in the stadium which went by the name of 'The Emperor's Games' and on the result of which the emperor and empress had bets. Then there is the horrible instrument (*buhotiax*) which, if placed in the mouth of a sick man, gripped him till it sucked all the poison out of his system, and many other marvels. But, as a pilgrim, it was, perhaps, the relics which impressed him most, and the number of the churches, the abbots, the nuns and the priests (30,000), all of which made him remark, like St. John the evangelist, that 'nus hons terriens . . . ne le vos porroit nombrer ne aconter, que qui vos en conteroit le chentisme part de la riqueche, ne de la biauté, ne de la nobleche, etc., en la vile ... ne cresries vos mie'.

Rather in the nature of an annal than of a chronicle is the so-called *Chronique de l'Anonyme de Béthune*. The author was in all probability attached to the 'maison de Béthune'—possibly in the capacity of a minstrel. Much of this record of events is based on historical or quasi-historical, or even legendary documents (e.g. the *Chronicle of Turpin*), but Part IV contains in annalistic form an account of the reign of Philippe-Auguste from about 1185 to 1216, between which dates the Third and Fourth Crusades took place. The author is really much more interested in the quarrels between the French and English kings than in the crusades against the infidels. Very briefly he announces that 'en l'an de l'incarnation Jhesu Christ mil ans et cent et quatre vins et set ... se croisierent grant partie des haus homes devers Occident', and he gives a list of some of those who went. Then, passing briefly over the years in between, he tells us how, in Richard's reign, moved by the sermons of 'un saint home, un precheör qui ert apéles maistres Folques de Nuellie, se croisierent maint haut home el regne de France por aler reconquerre la sainte cité de Jerusalem que Safadin tenoit, li frere Salehadin qui ja est mors'. Then follows another detailed list of the great men who set out in 1202. He barely mentions the vexed question of the change in plan which led the army to Constantinople instead of to Jerusalem, merely remarking, without comment, that, under pressure from the son of the banished emperor, the army turned aside and delivered the city of Constantinople. But he does add that the young emperor they had reinstated betrayed them later on. Again, in annalistic fashion, he mentions that 'en cel tans vint uns pardons en France d'aler sor cels d'Abigois qui mescreant estoient' and gives the names of the 'haut home del regne de France' (including Simon de Montfort, li cuens de Leicestre), who took part in the crusade against the heretics.

But his chief interest lies in the struggle going on in his own country and amongst his own kith and kin. He describes at some length the Battle of Bouvines, interspersing his description with the usual favourite exclamations such as 'Qui lor veïst les preudons de France ...' or 'che estoient beles proeces et parans', etc. He is naturally on the side of the French, and tells with relish what a 'molt bone risée' the Frenchmen had when the English (who were being entertained by the French king at Fontainebleau) drank all the bad wines and did not touch the good ones He cannot resist indulging in a personal comment at times as, when recording the marriage of the king's sister, he adds 'une molt laide dame'; or when reporting the despatch of a French knight to look after the dauphin's conquered territory at Nicole (Lincoln) he adds: 'Cel chastel de Nicole ot a garder une dame que on apeloit Madame Nicole qui molt est engigneuse et mal-querant et vighereuse vielle.'

And so, in the annals of the Anonyme de Béthune, as in the chronicles in rhyme or prose, we have fact and fiction, authentic reports and mere hearsay enlivened by personal remarks, all mixed up in such a way that it is difficult to sort out the different ingredients or draw a hard and fast line between fact and fiction, narrative and history in this story-loving age. Consequently no apology is offered if there is a certain amount of overlapping between this chapter and those which have gone before.

BIBLIOGRAPHY

Gaimar (Geoffroi): *L'Estorie des Engles*: (1) Ed. T. Wright. London 1850. (Caxton Society.)
    (2) Ed. Duffus-Hardy and Trice Martin. 2 vol. London 1888–9. (Rolls Series.)
Geoffrey of Monmouth. See Bibl., ch. v.
Wace. *Le Roman de Brut de Wace*. (1) Éd. I. Arnold. 2 vol. 1938–40. (SATF).
    (2) Leroux de Lincy. Rouen 1836. 2 vol.
    Le Roman de Rou et des ducs de Normandie: éd. par H. Andresen. 2 vol. Heilbronn 1877.
La Vie de Saint Thomas. See Bibl., ch. ii.
Jordan Fantosme. See Chronicles of the reigns of Stephen, Henry II and Richard I. Tom III. Ed. R. Howlett. London 1886. (Rolls Series.)
L'Histoire de Guillaume le Maréchal, publ. pour la Société de l'Histoire de France par Paul Meyer. Paris 1891–1901. 3 vol.
Anonymi *Gesta Francorum et aliorum Hierosolymitanorum.*
    Ed. (1) H. Hagenmeyer. Heidelberg 1890.
        (2) B. A. Lees. Oxford 1924.
        (3) Bréhier. Paris (*Cl. de l'Hist. de France*).
La Chanson d'Antioche, par le pèlerin Richard. Publ. par Paulin Paris. 2 vol. Paris 1848. (Rom. des XII Pairs XI–XII.)
'Chevalier, mult estes guariz...'⎫ See Paul Meyer: *Recueil d'anciens textes*, I, 39
'Cil doit bien estre forjugiés...'⎭ and 42.
Conon de Béthune. Éd. A. Wallensköld. Nos. IV and V. Paris 1921. (CFMA).
Ambroise: *L'Estoire de la Guerre Sainte.* Éd. par G. Paris. Paris 1897.
Villehardouin: *La Conqueste de Constantinople.* Éd. par E. Faral. Paris 1938.
Robert de Clari: *La Conquête de Constantinople.* Éd. par P. Lauer. Paris 1924.
L'anonyme de Béthune. Extraits d'une chronique française des rois de France, publ. par M. Léopold DeLisle. (*Recueil des historiens des Gaules etc.*, Tome 24.) Paris 1904.

CHAPTER IX

THE GROWTH OF DRAMA IN THE TWELFTH CENTURY

I. *RELIGIOUS DRAMA*
II. *SECULAR DRAMA*

I. RELIGIOUS DRAMA

The history of the rebirth of the drama in medieval times is in reality an international one and it matters little at what exact spot the first signs of life appeared, for its germ lay hidden in a rich soil which gradually extended over all the countries of Western Europe. The spread of Christian culture followed the spread of Christianity itself from East to West (though the direction was reversed in the sixth century) and one of the main preoccupations of the Church was the development of a liturgical tradition which should unite all its component parts. It has been said that 'during the centuries which followed the fall of the empire in the West, all these ages possessed of poetry, music and art found expression in the liturgy'[1] and it is an accepted fact that it was there that the medieval drama was conceived and brought to fruition.

While the decline of the Roman Empire was in progress the classical drama died a natural death. The average public no longer delighted in the delicacy of thought and language which seemed so indispensable to a Cicero or a Horace. Terence tells us in the prologue to one of his plays that people preferred the saltimbanks and the gladiators to his piece. People wanted to be visually entertained —by the eye rather than by the ear—hence the 'spectacles' gained ground and the writers of good style lost it. Mimes and dancers (both male and female) were preferred. Terence and the other classical authors survived in the monasteries—perhaps even in the deserts—but the classical theatre no longer existed for the people. Christianity gave it it's 'coup-de-grâce'. The 'mimi' and 'histriones' had not escaped censure in Rome, but naturally Christian writers held a much stronger view as to their undesirability. The fulminations of Tertullian in his *De Spectaculis* where he joins theatre, circus

---

[1] See C. Dawson: *Religion and the Rise of Western Culture*, p. 37.

and amphitheatre in a threefold condemnation are well known. Chrysostom in the East and his great contemporaries Augustine and Jerome in the West are at one in their condemnation of the evils of the public stage: 'a spectaculis removeamus oculos, arenae, circi, theatri'. (See Jerome: *In Ezechiel*.) As time went on the 'mimi' were competing with the jugglers and the beast-tamers. The code of Theodosius, which did not actually suppress the 'spectacula' but limited their performances, admits that the government must make some provision for the amusement of the people lest too many restrictions should depress them: 'ludicras artes concedimus agitari, *ne eximia restrictione tristitia generetur*',[1] which was probably a very wise concession. Many more examples could be adduced, but it would be a work of super-erogation to go over work which has been so excellently done.[2] Suffice it to say that, with variation in the intensity, these amusements of the uneducated[3] were deprecated by serious-minded people though the necessity of some form of both ocular and oral amusement must be admitted. As learning decreased during the troubled times of the heathen invasions, this necessity became ever greater. Church services and saints' *Lives* were in Latin or Greek, and even when the Latin was that of Gregory of Tours it was hardly likely to be understood by the mixed populations of those days. The Church, however, was not oblivious of this state of things and a new form of spectacle was evolving which would have great results in course of time. The impulse came from the East, and from those centres where most of what these centuries possessed of art and poetry went into the liturgy. In that most interesting document by a Spanish nun generally known as the *Peregrinatio Sctae. Silviae ad loca sancta* we have a description of what was happening in the fourth century in the religious world of the East. Sancta Silvia (or more correctly Sancta Etheria) undertook a pilgrimage to the Holy Land, and we cannot but be impressed by the description she gives of the effect produced on the crowds in Jerusalem by the reading of appropriate passages at a church festival accompanied by hymn-singing and antiphonal chants. The processions were elaborate and exacting—but all, including children in arms, took part in these solemn progressions, and the writer speaks

---

[1] See Code Th. xv, 6.2 (399). Quoted by Chambers: *Medieval Stage* I, 34.
[2] Ibid., Vol. I.
[3] Nor was it only the uneducated. The Christian writer Salvian V.c. relates with horror that, while the Barbarians were fighting outside the city walls and corpses were lying around 'the handful of nobility who had escaped death demanded circuses of the emperors as a supreme remedy for the destruction of the city'. Quoted by N. K. Chadwick, *Poetry and Letters in Early Christian Gaul*. Publ. Bowes & Bowes, Cambridge 1955.

constantly of the 'mugitus et rugitus' and the weeping which could be heard for miles at certain moving moments. The good nun is rather repetitive in her descriptions, but the details are instructive and the zeal of the crowds illuminating. They would start at dawn, 'as soon as one man could begin to recognize another' ('id est prope luce, ante tamen quam lux fiat') and continue in slow motion the whole day. There is actually a touch of drama (or one of its ingredients, viz., illusion) when the bishop is led from the Mount of Olives to the city: 'Sic deducetur episcopus *in eo typo* quo Dominus deductus est' and all the people proceed before him 'cum ymnis vel antiphonis respondentes semper: Benedictus, qui venit in nomine Dei'. The words of the appropriate passages were translated into Syriac, Greek and Latin, respectively, so that all might participate in the emotions of the moment and the whole thing gives the impression of a sacred spectacle enacted both for the people and by the people.

Activities such as this may have persisted in the Church during the Dark Ages though they were probably checked by the migrations of the peoples, but amidst the confusion of tongues and the general state of ignorance outside the Church there could be little hope of many survivals in any vernacular. With the eighth century, however, comes a welcome promise of new things. We are told by Eginhard that Charlemagne tried to collect 'carmina rustica' and we may take that to prove a certain leniency towards popular forms of poetry and public amusements. But his son Louis the Pious took up a different attitude and would not laugh or even show his white teeth in a smile if jests or comic features were in progress so that there evidently had to be some selection and adjustment to the kind of audience. Curiously enough, the 'Comedies' of Terence never completely lost their popularity during all the confused period of the early Middle Ages. They were copied and enjoyed by those who could appreciate the language and the style. So much did his influence seem a dangerous one to a young nun of the tenth century that she tried to replace them by something more wholesome. Hroswitha, Abbess of Gandersheim in the second half of the tenth century, had written six plays in her youth as a kind of Anti-Terence, for she feared lest her companions, enticed by the sweetness of his language (*dulcedine sermonis*), might become corrupted by the contents of his works and so she decided to imitate him, not merely to read him—'Unde ego, clamor validus Gandesheimensis, non recusavi illum imitari dictando, dum alii colunt legendo'. The subjects were strangely chosen for Hroswitha seemed to feel she must pick her heroes and heroines from the same sort of 'milieu' as that which so often supplied 'low' comedy. One might even accuse her of a certain lack of good taste in spite of her spiritual profession. But if this was a concession to the taste of her time the introduction of tedious discourses on the universe was not likely to make her plays popular, and it has to be admitted that, even if she received kind encouragement from some of her patrons (*fautores*) they failed to produce any link between classical and medieval drama. Nor was the popularity of Terence affected by this effort to 'replace' him—in fact, it is rather ironical that it was largely on account of his 'moral sentences' that he was appreciated right up to the sixteenth century.

Though, however, Hroswitha's voice in the wilderness was wafted away by the end of the tenth century, other things—big with consequences—were happening elsewhere. By this time important religious centres of intellectual and musical acitvity had sprung up in various parts of Europe. A notable influence came from Ireland and northern England, which spread to the Continent. The monastery of St. Gallen had been founded in 700 (*circ.*) and had prospered. Winchester in England and Limoges in France were important ecclesiastical centres. The liturgy was becoming the centre of Christian culture in the West, and its importance in the intellectual life of the time cannot be exaggerated. It had a strong dramatic tendency which, as we have seen, was early developed in the East and was intensified by the great prevalence of anti-phonal singing. Many of the Church ceremonies would speak for themselves as, for instance, the action of the devil fleeing from the building at the dedication of a church, when the doors were opened and those impressive words of scripture 'Quis est ipse Rex Gloriae' were spoken, and the reply which makes us realize how dramatic much of the Bible is.

There is no need to tell over again the well-known story of how words began to be adapted to the musical notes following the chant (generally the *alleluia*) in the church service. How these added words were hailed with joy as a sort of 'aide-mémoire' by the monks of St. Gallen when the idea was brought to them by a monk of St. Jumièges in the ninth century, and how little interpolations, which went by the name of *tropes* were introduced about the same time into the liturgy to enliven it and spin it out at a time when the Church with its many festivals was a 'rendez-vous' for all sections of the population. The story has been told by Gautier, by Chambers, by Creizenach and by Young, and all that we have to regret is that such an interesting document as the *Casus Scti. Galli* (which tells the delightful story of the three monks—the *tres inseparabiles*) does not exist for other continental monasteries of the period. For this was a European movement and the earliest dramatic 'tropes', which soon developed into little 'versicles' (*versiculi*), are to be found in many religious centres—at Winchester, at Limoges, at St. Gallen and elsewhere. There must have been considerable activity in this development in the early years of the tenth century. But it is to the monk Tutilo—one of the 'inseparables'—that we may probably attribute some of the earliest known tropes, including the Easter version *Quem quaeritis in sepulchro*, which became so widely diffused. Henceforward it is found in innumerable more or less elaborated forms in France, in Germany and in Italy (in Ravenna, Bobbio and Vercelli, though not in Rome itself), and in rare cases accompanied by primitive stage-directions as to where the speakers should stand. The popularity of the Easter ceremony is proved by the number of manuscripts all over Europe, but perhaps the most elaborate version of the *Visitatio* is that included in the *Regularis Concordia* of St. Etholwold, prepared at Winchester about the middle of the tenth century. The details of the ceremony which accompanied the celebration of this part of the Mass (destined for the use of the Benedictine monasteries in England) are most interesting. They are intensely dramatic in character. Of the four 'actors' (*fratres*) one would be dressed in an 'alb' (*ācsi ad aliud agendum*), the three others were to be enveloped in 'cappis' to impersonate the three Marys, and were to approach the tomb 'pedetemptim'—like people looking for something. Their voices were to be tempered to the part they played, for the instruction was 'mediocri voce dulcisono cantare'. Then the fourth brother who had taken his seat at the head of the improvised grave would pronounce the well-known words: 'Quem quaeritis in sepulchro, O christicole'; and the three Marys would reply in unison: 'Jesum Christum, etc.' in gentle, modulated tones.

Thus the little drama was complete, with illusion, action and dialogue. It is interesting to note the intention of this sort of play-acting which we learn from the same document. In the instructions for the *depositio* of the body of Christ which preceded the *Visitatio*, the author explains that the ceremony was ordered in this wise for the 'strengthening of the faith of the unlearned multitude and the neophytes' (*ad fidem indocti vulgi ac neofitorum corroborandum*). The services were still completely in Latin, but the actions would greatly help the unlearned to grasp what was going on.

Thus the seed of the drama was sown in good soil and its growth was widespread if not rapid. For this simple Easter play was full of possibilities. The number of personages could be increased almost at will—to the three Marys and the angel could be added the merchants selling spices, the pilgrims going to Emmaus, the disciples (chiefly Peter and John in their race to the sepulchre), Joseph of Arimathea, Nicodemus, Pilate, and the soldiers of the watch. Moreover, the simple words of the 'trope': *Quem quaeritis in sepulchro*, could be easily altered to adapt the dialogue to another church festival. It was only necessary to substitute the word *praesepio* for *sepulchro* and the three magi (or kings) for the three Marys and the play was converted into a Christmas play at once. This again, like the Easter play, could be much developed—the star was, of course, introduced, the 'dua animalia' from Habakkuk's prophecy became the ox and the ass which pleasantly added to the spectacle, Herod with his comic potentialities of getting into a rage, etc.—all these elements could be introduced into the church service which soon found its way over all Western Europe, for inter-borrowing must have been rife among all the main ecclesiastical centres. But the Easter play seems to have remained the more popular, especially after it was extended to introduce the Virgin Mary and the Passion itself. It was not until the cult of the Virgin was at its full height that it became necessary to adjust the roles of the women in the Easter plays in such a way that the three Marys did not fill the whole picture, for their laments would pale naturally before those of the Virgin at the foot of the cross. These laments (or 'planctus') brought in a more subjective and lyrical element which is not so prominent in the earliest plays. Even in the *Passion du Christ*, the narrative poem in a mixed dialect which was possibly composed before the year 1000,[1] the grief of the Virgin is expressed only in a few lines and is not expanded into a 'planctus'. Unfortunately we have no really early example of the simplest form of dramatic effort in the vernacular in spite of its widespread popularity as an ingredient of the Church services.

The earliest known play in which the vulgar tongue breaks through is not strictly liturgical in character although it could easily be adapted to either of the important festivals. The *Sponsus* or

[1] This suggestion is due to the reference in the last stanza to the end of the world which was popularly expected in the year 1000. See ch. I, p. 4.

Mystère de l'Époux is connected with the second coming of Christ and is in the nature of a solemn warning. The subject is the parable of the seven wise and seven foolish virgins. To these principal actors are added the person of Christ himself (as the 'Sponsus'), the angel Gabriel, the merchants, and last, but not least, the devils who hurl the foolish virgins ruthlessly into hell. It is a harsh little play, but the second advent loomed rather large in people's minds in those days and it inculcates the dangers of negligent folly. The merchants are as adamant as the wise virgins, and Christ himself, after the first solemn words to the foolish virgins in Latin which fall like hammer strokes (*Amen, Amen, vos ignosco*, etc.), addresses them in French and tells them they are doomed to eternal punishment: 'a tot iors mais vos so(n) penas livrees / en enfern ore serez meneies'. And this happened immediately for, as the rubric informs us: 'modo accipient eas demones, praecipientque in infernum'. The additions to the biblical text and the sorrowful refrains in the vernacular (*dolentas chaitivas*, etc.) were presumably destined to add to the dramatic intensity of the play and make it more comprehensible to the unlettered.

The next play to be considered on account of its contribution to literature wholly or partially in the vulgar tongue also falls some-what outside the field of liturgical drama, although it is drawn from an episode in the life of Christ. We are fortunate in being able to date this play (or 'jeu') as it was composed by a certain Hilarius—probably an Englishman and a pupil of Abelard—about the year 1130. Little is known about brother Hilarius except that he was the author of three extant plays and some rather ribald little poems. The *Suscitatio Lazari* deals with the story contained in the gospel and concludes with the *Te Deum laudamus* or the *Magnificat*, according to the hour at which it was performed. So a certain connection with the Church service is still to be observed, and the word 'ludus' of the rubric ('Ad quem ludum iste persone sunt necessarie') is merely a synonym here for 'repraesentatio'. Christ himself appears in this polymetric little play as do the unbelieving Jews and Lazarus after his resurrection. But the most important roles are naturally those of Martha and Mary, and it is they who drop into French at emo-tional moments, even when they begin in somewhat conventional Latin: 'O sors tristis, O sors dura' . . . sings Maria before bursting into simple French 'Hor ai dolor, hor est mis frere morz; por que gei plor', and Martha, after the conventional tirade against death: 'Mors execrabilis, mors detestabilis', etc., and a lament something like that of the foolish virgins in French (*Lase chaitive*, etc.) reproaches Christ for not having come sooner in a kind of mixed language:

> Si venisses primitus / *dol en ai,*
> Non esset hic gemitus / *bais frere, perdu vos ais.*

For the sake of chronology we will cast a glance here at the other plays of Hilarius although they are somewhat different in character. A very similar method of composition to that of the *Ludus Lazari* is to be found in the *Ludus super Iconia Sancti Nicolai* which celebrates a miracle of that most popular saint. There is the same variety of metre and an increased number of characters: 'Persona Barbari qui commisit ei tesaurum, Persona Iconie (the image of the saint), Personae IIII vel VI Latronum, Persona Sancti Nicolai'. The strophes, part Latin, part French, present the same hybrid appearance as the *Lazarus*. 'Barbarus' expresses his feelings by singing:

> 'Gravis sors et dura
> Hic reliqui plura,
> Sed sub mala cura—
> *Des! quel damage!*
> *Qui pert la sue chose, pur que n'enrage?*'

Why not, indeed? And he straightway takes up a cudgel and, turning to the image of St. Nicolas, exclaims:

> '*Hore ten ci!*' (= 'Now take that!')
> '*Quar ne me rens ma chose que gei mis ci?*'

A certain comic intention of this little drama is obvious, although the barbarian is duly converted in the end. But it does not end with the *Te Deum*.

It is interesting to compare this play, composed *circ.* 1140, partly in Latin, partly in French, with the 'miracle' wholly in the vulgar tongue composed about half a century later by Jean Bodel. Both plays represent the same miracle of St. Nicolas (well known in Latin versions) of the restoration by the saint of a stolen treasure, and both end with the conversion of the sceptical heathen. But in contrast with the earlier play where only two characters actually speak, in Bodel's *Saint Nicolas* there is so much talking that the characters actually fall over one another (e.g. the two *crieur de vin*). Much extraneous matter is introduced, and the tavern scene, so beloved of the citizens of Arras, in which the time-serving landlord entices the king's messenger (the *courlieu* Auberon) to break his journey, is much developed. Other scenes and characters which have nothing to do with the original legend (e.g. the crusading scene and the character of the heathen kings), but which furnish evidence of an author familiar with travel stories from the East, are introduced and the god Tervagant, an old friend from earlier *chansons*, whose role is to foretell the future (by weeping or laughing as the case may be), comes to his usual horrid end of being hurled to his death. It is unnecessary to dwell on the interest of this well-known 'miracle' (or *essemple* as the author calls it in his prologue)[1] as the object here is merely to point out the contrast to the former play on the same subject and to demonstrate the development in dramatic treatment which has taken place in the years intervening between the two plays. What Bodel's *Jeu de Saint Nicolas* loses in unity and simplicity, it gains in variety and interest, and the introduction of the pious 'preudom' and the inspired crusaders adds considerably to the religious character of the play, which concludes with the words:

> A Dieu dont devons nous canter
> Huimais: *Te Deum laudamus.*

We must return now to the activity of Hilarius in view of a third play of which he was either sole or part-author. At any rate, it is under his name that a *Historia de Daniele Representanda* has come down to us. This Old Testament play does not come strictly into a study of the French drama as it is entirely in Latin. It is more elaborate than the other plays of Hilarius—there is a larger number of 'dramatis personæ' and a good deal of choral singing by the soldiers ('Cantabunt milites . . . hanc prosam: Resonant unanimes,' etc.). To the canonical story from the Bible it adds the dramatic apocryphal story of Habakkuk being fetched by an angel and led by the hair of his head to take food to Daniel in the lion's den. The play ends with King Darius starting up the *Te Deum laudamus* or the *Magnificat* according to whether it was performed at Matins or Vespers. A very similar play in which French alternates with Latin was composed probably about the same date and on the same subject by the students of Beauvais, and it is hard to say which may have been the model for the other. Both were the work of students and show much skill in versification—especially the Beauvais play which even introduces 'Cythariste' amongst its many actors. The king and Daniel, however, are always introduced as *speaking* their parts and it was probably into the spoken parts that the French words

---

[1] For a discussion and analysis of Bodel's play (with full bibliography) we may refer the reader to the edition by F. J. Warne—Blackwell French Texts, 1951.

were introduced without any apparent reason. Three times over, when Daniel is apprehended by the chiefs or the attendants, the Latin strophe ends with the words: *Cestui manda li Rois par nos,* and the two languages are again mixed when he is found and brought before the king:

> Vir propheta Dei, Daniel, *vien al Roi*
> Veni, desiderat *parler a toi*
> Pauet et turbatur, *Daniel, vien al Roi*
> Vellet quod nos latet *savoir par toi*
> Te ditabit donis, Daniel, *vien al Roi*
> Si scripta poterit *savoir par toi.*

Both these plays, of which Daniel is the the hero, have intrinsic merit, but they are important from another point of view too, in the history of the religious drama in France. The subject is taken from the Old Testament and yet it is obvious that they are linked with Christian festivals and thus loosely attached to the liturgy. In both of them the last few lines contain prophetic utterances about the coming of Christ, and the rescue of Daniel from the lions' den has the same significance as the miracle of the three young men in the fiery furnace in the story of Nebuchadnezzar. It is these prophetic utterances and the role of prophet assigned to Daniel which form a connecting link with another group of plays which we must now consider.

The story of Daniel was spectacular enough in itself to provide the subject for a play—but when, added to that dramatic episode, there were utterances announcing the end of a dispensation, the subject became a gift in a period of symbolic interpretation and hidden meaning (*significatio*). Once again we must send the reader to the well-known works for a full account of that portion of the liturgy entitled: *Sermo de Symbolo contra Judaeos Paganos et Arianos,* and merely sum it up in a few words. This sermon (probably of the sixth century), which was commonly attributed to St. Augustine in the Middle Ages, is of a very dramatic character. The preacher calls upon the worthies of the Old and New Testaments, together with one or two pagan writers, to come and testify to the coming of Christ. Like the Seven Sages in the little play by Ausonius (fourth century), they come forward in turn and each says his bit before giving place to the next one. The *Sermo* was pronounced from the pulpit (*Lectio Sexta*) and the speaker introduced the prophetic witnesses as follows: Dic Ysaya, testimonium Christo. 'Ecce' inquit, 'virgo in utero concipiet', etc.' Then Isaiah retires and the next one is introduced: Dic et tu, Iheremia, testimonium Christo. 'Hic est', inquit. 'Deus noster,' etc. And so it proceeds. Daniel is rather singled out as 'iuvenis quidem etate, senior vero scientia et mansuetudine', then these first three are followed by 'Moyses, legislator', 'David testis fidelis' and 'Abacuch propheta'. These six prophets from the Old Testament are followed by three from the New: 'Johannis, Zacharias et Elisabeth, iuvenes steriles, in senectute fecundi', and these again by three 'ex gentibus' for the truth could not be hidden even though pronounced by enemy tongues. The three 'gentiles' chosen are 'Virgilius ille poeta facundissimus' (for his fourth eclogue), 'Nabuc odonosor regem scilicet Babilonis', and Sibylla, well known in the Middle Ages for her prophetic utterances. Had there not been too many witnesses from the Old Testament Jews we should have been reminded of 'les neuf preuz', those nine valiant men who were selected for their valour from much the same three groups. The Sybil is expressly brought in so that Jews and Pagans should have their heads broken by the same stone ('ex uno lapide'), like Golias who was decapitated by his own sword. It is a remarkable sermon and we have given some space to it because under the title of *Ordo Prophetarum* it was widely used as a liturgical 'lectio' for the Christmas season in the twelfth and thirteenth centuries. Its dramatic possibilities were felt and utilized to the full. In a Latin verse-version from St. Martial at Limoges there are only slight changes in the personnel. The prophecies mostly coincide with those in the *Ordo*, though the passage chosen from Isaiah is the equally prophetic one (chap. xi, 1–2), 'Et egreditur virga de radice Jesse', which caused such mirth amongst the Jews in later versions. There are no rubrics in the Limoges version; it is in verse and was evidently intended to be sung, and each prophet would come forward in turn as the 'cantor' called him forth. Further developments followed—a version from the Cathedral of Laon (thirteenth century) gives elaborate descriptions of each prophetic speaker. Daniel, as remarked above, always a favourite, is an 'adolescens, ueste splendida indutus', and here is the addition of Balaam, 'super asinam, curvus, barbatus, palmam tenens, calcaribus urgens'. Thus Balaam is already quite the cavalryman, with his slightly bent figure, his spurs and his quick temper when he addresses his ass:

> 'Quid moraris, asina,
> obstinata bestia?
> Jam scindent calcaria
> Costas et precordia.'

To which a newly-introduced personage—'puer sub asina'—replies:

> 'Angelus cum gladio
> quem adstare video
> prohibet ne transeam;
> timeo ne peream.'

There is much in common between this and the Limoges version, but the advance in dramatic possibilities is obvious—also the fact that the personages have now become somewhat stereotyped in character. We cannot follow the further developments of these interesting spectacles here nor enter into the controversy as to whether individual scenes (such as that of Daniel), having grown in size (by *amplificatio*), were detached after a time from the whole (by *disintegratio*) and became little separate self-sufficient plays (Sepet's theory); or whether the plays in question had their own separate origin and independent growth from the start (E. Meyer). But their importance cannot be overlooked as a source of inspiration for the first play wholly in French (except for the rubrics) which has come down to us, and which is a great advance on the Latin-French attempts which preceded it.

The *Mystère d'Adam* was probably composed by a (Norman) Frenchman about the middle of the twelfth century. The date 1150-60 has been suggested, and this would mean that it was roughly contemporary with the first (known) 'fabliau', Wace's translation of Geoffroy of Monmouth, the courtly fashion of love-poetry and sentimental romance at the Angevin courts, and the reforming zeal that marked the third quarter of that century. Nor had the *chansons-de-geste* yet reached their decline, and it is noticeable that a feudal outlook runs through the first two little dramas of 'Adam and Eve' and 'Cain and Abel' which form two parts of the trilogy of which the play consists. There are frequent references to loyalty and faith, help and counsel, and the proper attitude of the 'serf' towards his lord in these two sections. But added to this, there is more than a hint at the lover's attitude towards his mistress in the flattering words of the devil: 'Tu es fieblette e tendre chose / E es plus fresche que n'est rose / Tu es plus blanche que cristal / Que neif que chiet sor glace en val', etc., (l. 229 ff.), and his desire that she should not give him away (*Celeras mei?* l. 215). Eve's admission, too, that her husband perhaps is not quite good enough for her: 'un pou est durs' (l. 222) exhibits her at once as a potential example of the 'mal mariée' of the popular love-songs. And yet the episodes are shot through all the time by the gloomy, heavy outlook so characteristic

of the Anglo-Norman poems of the first half of the century—that
man has wasted all the possibilities of enjoyment for himself and his
posterity for the sake of a miserable apple:

> Por une pome soffri si grant damage
> Qu'en paine met et mei e mon lignage . . . (ll. 462–3).

The lamentations, too, have a familiar ring with their frequent
apostrophes to death: 'Mort, car me prend,' etc. (l. 573); to Paradise:
'Oi, paradis!' (l. 523), and to the unfaithful wife who had caused
all the mischief: 'Oi, male femme, pleine de traïson!' etc., for she
had robbed the man of those two essential qualities of manhood—
'sens et raison'. And so, as in the early visual representations of the
story, God points an accusing finger at Adam. Adam in turn points
to his wife—but Eve, to her credit be it said, does not point to the
serpent already reduced to crawling on his belly on the ground but
—except for a few words—takes all the blame upon herself:

> 'Jo peccheriz, jo lasse, jo chaitive!
> Por mon forfet sui vers deu si eschive,' etc.

It is when she is at her lowest point, lamenting the disaster she has
brought on herself and her descendants, that a ray of hope gleams
through and, in spite of the gloom, Eve, too, takes her place amongst
the prophets:

> 'Mais neporquant en Deu est ma sperance;
> D'icest mesfait car tot iert acordance;
> Deus me rendra sa grace et sa mustrance,
> Jeter nus voldra d'enfer par puissance' (ll. 587–90).

The next little play in the trilogy of Cain and Abel is psycho-
logically interesting but could hardly in the nature of things be used
as a pointer to the coming of Christ—unless Abel's reflection just
before his death contains a glimmer of hope of a better era coming:

> Diex est verais; qui a lui sert
> Tres bien l'empleie pas nel pert (ll. 715–6).

But neither this nor the final words of Eve could be interpreted as
very explicit prophecies of Christ's coming, so we may look upon
these short, but effective little plays as forming a kind of introduction to the performance that was to follow, viz. the procession of
prophets in their significant role of witnesses.

For this 'lectio' the actors (for doubtless gestures accompanied the
speaking) were already drawn up in a spot hidden from the audience.
Hence, after the well-known words of the *Sermo*: 'Vos, inquam,

Q

convenio, O Judei', the prophets issue forth one by one, headed by Abraham who introduces himself quite simply: 'Abraham sui, eissi ai non.' When he has uttered his prophecy he is led back to hell by the devils (for the 'harrowing of hell' is still far in the future) and Moses comes forward. We need not go through the list of speakers, beyond mentioning that Balaam is included amongst the Old Testament worthies, as in the Laon play, and pronounces his prophecy sitting on his ass like a knight (*eques*). The fact that the New Testament witnesses are not introduced and that of the three heathen prophecies we have only a portion of that of Nebuchadnezzar, is probably due to the unfinished state in which the play has come down to us in the solitary manuscript we possess. As in the Latin versions of the *Ordo Prophetarum*, the author of the French play has put a different prophecy into the mouth of Isaiah from that chosen in the 'Sermo' although he had introduced the original passage ('Ecce virgo concipiet') as well. The dramatic versions of Limoges, of Laon and our author are all based on Isaiah's words in the passage: 'Egreditur virga de radice Jesse . . .' and this prophecy has been made the occasion in our play of a rather quaint scene with a recalcitrant Jew (*quidam de sinagoga*) who rises up and disputes with Isaiah, addressing him boldly in spite of the prophet's august appearance:

> 'Or me respond, sire Ysaïe
> Est ço fable u prophecie?
> Quë est iço que tu as dit?
> Truvas la tu u est escrit?
> Tu as dormi, tu le sonjas?
> Est ço a certes u a gas?'

He then asks the prophet to read his fortune in his hand and to divine whether a dry stick is a *verge* or a *baston* and whether it will bear fruit according to his prophecy. He is silenced, of course, by Isaiah, who assures him that he has been taught of God and that all that he says will certainly be accomplished. Isaiah is then followed by Nebuchadnezzar in the middle of whose account of what he saw in the fiery furnace the manuscript unfortunately breaks off and we are deprived of a French version of Virgil's and the Sybil's prophecies and probably of some interesting stage directions at the end of the play. For the stage directions, which are in Latin, form an integral and valuable part of the *Mystère d'Adam*. They include inflexions of voice, movements and attitudes of players—symbolic and otherwise; descriptions of persons and of how effects are to be produced. Although we do not find here the 'puer sub asina' or the little boy hidden beneath the 'secretum' from which Abel's blood cries out, yet we have the 'ollam coopertam pannis suis' on which Cain was to strike his blow and the saucepans and frying pans (*caldaria et lebetes*) on which the devils were to accompany their infernal joy. Colours have their conventional symbolism—Cain is in red and Abel in white—and Adam, after taking his bite from the apple and realizing what he has done, stoops behind the hangings of paradise so as not to be seen, puts off his 'sollempnes vestes' (the symbolical *stolam immortalitatis*) and dons 'pauperes vestes consutas foliis ficus'. What Eve does is discreetly not mentioned. There can be no two opinions as to the skill in the composition of this play with its psychological acumen, its solemnity relieved by light touches, its clever achievement of effect both in the text itself and in the detailed didascalia—which make us realize the distance the semi-liturgical drama had travelled by the middle of the twelfth century and how soon it would be in a position to break away from the liturgy altogether and stand on its own feet.

Side by side, however, with all these plays based directly or indirectly on the liturgical service another important growth was developing out of the same soil, though rather more slowly. A certain hesitation about representing the actual Passion of Christ may possibly have restrained the pious authors of 'tropes' and sequences who amplified the liturgy. But as the movement grew and the three Marys of the Easter versions came into such prominence, it was almost inevitable that the feeling should arise that the Virgin Mary, whose cult was at its height in the twelfth century, was not being given her rightful place. There was no reference in the Gospel narratives of the resurrection to the Virgin's part, but at the scene of the crucifixion her presence is recorded, though not accompanied by a single utterance. Her role was necessarily a passive one, and it is therefore not surprising that a subjective, lyrical side should mark any scene into which her figure could be introduced. Latin hymns were, of course, in existence and feeling references to the Virgin's grief, from the time of St. Augustine onwards. Moreover, touching prayers were addressed to the Virgin at a period when the Trinity was obscured by doctrinal discussion. But now the Virgin herself began to be vocal, and as soon as the Easter play was enlarged to include what happened immediately before the resurrection, and the story of the crucifixion itself began to be dramatized, it was natural that attention should be focused on the mother of our Lord as she stood weeping at the foot of the cross. Moreover, the presence of a 'plainte' or 'regret funèbre' was already a well-known feature of epic poetry and obviously popular from its frequent use. As early as the *Vie de St. Alexis* we have the moving lament of a mother over her son—indeed, the triple lament of father, mother, and deserted spouse. It is interesting to note that these laments had gradually become almost stereotyped in character as time went on. The 'plainte' put into the mouth of the mother of God in a little poem of the twelfth century (in the decasyllabic metre) might well have been uttered by the sorrowing mother or spouse of St. Alexis in the eleventh:

> Beau dous cher fis, simple vis, bele bouche,
> La vostre mort, beau fis, au cuer me touche,
> Des ore mais viverai come une souche,
> Sans nul confort.[1]

Cf. *St. Alexis*, Str. xcvii.

> O bele buce, bel vis, bele faiture
> cum est mudede vostre bele figure
> plus vus amai que nule creature.
> Si grant dolur or m'est apareude
> . . . Ore vivrai en guise de turturele (l. 149).

Examples could be multiplied. The 'motif' of a 'plainte' was a favourite one and it is just possible that the drama of the 'Passion' grew up around this central theme. In the earliest known epic poem in the vernacular[2] (a kind of Franco-Provençal) the *Jesu Christi Passion*, contained in the same manuscript as the *Vie de St. Leger*, there is but a brief mention of the Virgin's grief limited to the prophetic words of Symeon in St. Luke's gospel. But it is noteworthy that already she is enrolled amongst the band of prophets by her faith in his resurrection—'I know for certain He will rise again: *el resurdra cho sab per veir*' (l. 336).

There were, of course, many short lamentations in existence, both of Rachel (weeping for her children) in the Christmas plays, and of the three Marys in the Resurrection Plays—particularly of Mary Magdalene, who had the honour of being the first to see Christ after His resurrection and to take the glad news to His disciples. But the role of the Virgin increased rapidly and was soon much in evidence in all European centres. It was enhanced, too, by the Latin 'Life' of the Virgin (*Vita Beatae Virginis Mariae*), which gives a realistic account of Mary's inconsolable grief as she stands by the

---

[1] See Paul Meyer, *Recueil* I, 46.
[2] See ch. i, pp. 4 f.

cross (cf. Bk. III, *De planctu et dolore Marie Virginis*) and makes
the daring statement 'quod Jesus primo apparuit matri suae Marie
Virgini' which would help to redress the balance between the
Magdalena and the mother of Christ. The touching words of the
prophet Isaiah, 'Non est dolor similis dolore meo visus', which were
variously applied in the Middle Ages, were here put into the mouth
of the Virgin, as they were in the Provençal Passion Play of the
thirteenth century:

> Aiyhat, baros que passat per la via
> S'en hes dolor tan gran con es la mia
> Del mien car filh, mon conort e ma via—
> ... Mort, car no'm prens? ... (cf. ll. 1495-7).

The Latin *Vita* undoubtedly had a wide circulation, but the Passion
play, even in Latin, was slow to establish itself. It had not such
dramatic possibilities as the Resurrection play. A glance at the
Anglo-Norman Resurrection play,[1] a fragment of which in octosyllabic metre has come down to us from the end of the twelfth or
the beginning of the thirteenth century, with its stage directions
and rubrics in narrative form and its number of characters, shows
a possibility for action and invention which the other does not
possess. Moreover, the very poignancy of the scene at the cross
gradually led to a realistic treatment of Christ's sufferings which, as
time went on, tended to become somewhat repellant.[2] This,
however, was not present in the earlier plays although a good many
details were added to the scriptural narrative. The Provençal play
already mentioned does not go so far as the *Vita* in stating that
Christ appeared first to His mother after the resurrection. But it
introduces her skilfully into the conventional scene of the three
Marys at the empty tomb, by making them take the shroud in
which Christ's body had been wrapped (and which the angel
presented to them) to His mother and then introducing a short scene
in which all the four Marys take part. After the appearance of
Christ as the gardener (*ortola*) to Mary Magdalene we have one
more last appearance of 'la maire de Dieu' in which she blesses the
shroud and, addressing her son, rejoices in the thought that 'Salvatz
avetz los peccadors / A mal grat dels Juzeus trachors', ll. 975-6.
We are fortunate in possessing, in the play known as *La Passion du
Palatinus*, an early example from the north of France of those long

---

[1] Edited in Koschwitz ü Förster: *Altfr. Uebungsbuch*, pp. 214 f.
[2] This was especially the case in Germany, cf. the Traktat of the fifteenth century entitled
Christi Leiden in einer vision geschaut' herausgegeb. Robert Priebsch, Heidelberg 1936.

'mystères de la Passion' which enjoyed such popularity as the years went on—an ancestor, in fact, of the elaborate *Passion* of Arnoul Greban in the fifteenth century. It has been shown[1] to be a composite kind of work based on the narrative *Passion* which formed part of the repertoire of 'jongleurs' round about the turn of the twelfth century in France. It is composed in a great variety of metres which are adapted to the different speakers and introduces some popular elements, such as the discussion between the carpenter (*li fevre*) commissioned to make the cross and his vicious wife; the conversation of the devils in hell and the crying of his wares by the merchant (*épicier*). But, for the rest, the framework is conventional; the Virgin utters a 'plainte' at the foot of the cross (after which she does not appear again); the apostle John comforts her and the three Marys speak their usual laments. Mary Magdalene alone strikes a personal and new note in such lines as: 'Vous estiez plains de si grant courtoisie'—'Sire, souvant mi faites coleur muer', contained in a lament beginning in the usual way: 'Lasse moy, dolente, chetive!' There is no disguising the effort to extend and popularize the original theme.

It has been suggested that the whole literary phenomenon of the 'laments' of the Virgin, as of the Passion plays themselves, can be characterized as a wholly 'popular' (*volkstümlich*) one[2]—a kind of popularization of the liturgy for the behoof of the people. It developed on realistic lines, and certainly the 'laments' of the Virgin became very popular in the romance-speaking countries. They were much cultivated in Italy, especially by the followers of St. Francis. They formed a regular ingredient of the repertory of the 'flagellantes' and undoubtedly did much to popularize this form of the worship of the Virgin. But the roots of this worship go much further back even than the flowering of the cult in St. Bernard's time. The influence of the East cannot be overlooked in this field. The apocryphal 'Gospel of Nicodemus'—especially the Greek version which contained the 'plainte de la vierge'—became widely known in the West. It would go beyond the scope of the present work to discuss this question at length, or do much more than direct attention to that intriguing composition entitled *Christos Paschôn* or *Christus Patiens*, which is the only known Christian drama to have sprung from Greek soil. This story of the crucifixion in dramatic form was long attributed to St. Gregory of Nazianzen

---

[1] See edition of Grace Frank (CFMA), Paris 1922. Preface.
[2] See *Die romanischen Marienklagen*, E. Wechssler. Halle 1893.

(A.D. 330–90), whose interest in the subject of the Virgin and of virgins generally is well known. It was translated into Italian under his name in the sixteenth century (*Tragedia di San Gregorio Nazienzeno intitolata: Christus patiens*, etc.). More critical examination of the play, however, has rendered this unlikely, and Krumbacher[1] hesitates to date it earlier than the eleventh century—so difficult is the matter of dating with any precision when the language has no marked characteristics. The interesting thing for us is that it is a 'plainte de la Vierge' on a large scale composed in the classical style. The Virgin Mary appears as Hecate, Cassandra, Andromache and Medea on the stage and a large proportion of the lines are 'centos' culled from the Greek tragedians. It is, in fact, a mass of heterogeneous elements. The chorus echoes the laments of the Virgin with so many reiterated exclamations of grief that sometimes the effect is almost comic (e.g. 'ὀττοτοτοῖ', 'ἰώ μοι ἰω,' etc.). But several points of interest may be noted. The play opens with the Virgin waiting for news of her son on the receipt of which she indulges in a long fulmination against Judas. From then onwards the bulk of the talking is monopolized by the one figure, who is indeed bearing up against 'a sea of troubles' (κακῶν Πέλαϧος). Christ addresses His mother from the cross and a great point is made of the fact that He addresses her first after the resurrection. The role of prophet, moreover, is conspicuous in the Virgin for she has a firm hope, even in the midst of her grief, that He will rise again and ascend to heaven. She pleads earnestly for the forgiveness of Peter because he acted out of fear, and there is much repetition of the two words 'and Peter' as in most of the liturgical plays. An almost monotonous refrain as to the sad destiny of women in general is also repeated to satiety:

> mulier enim et ad lachrymas nata
> „   „   „   „   „   proclivis
> „   „   „   „   „   promptior[2]

Indeed, of things that have life, women are the most miserable plant of all.

The whole play (which can hardly have been meant for the stage) is practically one lament on a grand scale. It would scarcely be a compliment to assign it to Gregory of Nazianzen, but its quasi-classic character does seem to prove that this type of play had a literary rather than a popular origin. Some influence from the East,

---

[1] See Krumbacher: *Geschichte der byzantinischen Literatur.*
[2] See Latin translation: Gregory of Nazianzen: *Migne Patrology*, Vol. 137.

moreover, is distinctly traceable from another source. Philippe de Mézières 'Picardiae miles vitiosus', as he calls himself, but nevertheless a friend of prelates and kings, has told us how he was instrumental in introducing to the West the *festum* of the *Visitatio* which had been celebrated 'in partibus orientalibus' from ancient times ('temporibus namque antiquis et, ut creditur, in primitia ecclesia'), and how, after slight hesitation on the part of the pope the version he had translated from the Greek was performed at Avignon in 1373 in the presence of a large and distinguished congregation, both clerical and lay, 'after the manner in which it had been performed in Venice and other parts of Italy *for many years*'. The 'fête' of the *Visitatio* of the Virgin, which was borrowed from the Greeks, became widely known. It was adopted and rendered universal by the action of successive popes and many indulgences were promised to those who celebrated it. It was suppressed in 1926 as having no scriptural foundation.[1]

The later development of the Passion Play and the subsequent enlargement of the framework of the mystery until it covered the whole life of Christ and His mother, lie beyond the scope of this present work. There is, moreover, a regrettable dearth of documents which would give any continuity to a trustworthy account of the gradual growth from the earlier concise and dramatic story of the death and resurrection of our Lord, to the expanded and inflated versions which later formed a kind of 'Geste de Jesu Christ'.

II. THE SECULAR DRAMA

Difference of opinion has always existed as to whether the 'profane theatre' in France sprang from the same roots as the religious drama or whether it was a descendant of the late Latin decadent amusements represented by the 'mimi et histriones' against whom Tertullian and others raised their voices. A lack of written documents in the early development of this form of entertainment again makes it difficult to dogmatize on the question. The secular drama was undoubtedly influenced by both sources. There were plenty of scenes in the semi-liturgical drama which must have raised a laugh in the most devout. There was Balaam on his ass (the comic effect of which produced considerable effects in later 'festa'); there was the impotent, irascible Herod, the two apostles racing to the tomb in rather unseemly rivalry, the scenes with recalcitrant and

---

[1] See N. Jorga: *Philippe de Mézières*. Paris 1898, pp. 411 ff.

noisy Jews, and, last but not least, the scenes in which the devils play a conspicuous part—whether in their 'parloir' or running about the stage. On the other hand it is more the spirit of the 'fabliau' which probably infused the 'risqué' repertory of the 'mimi et histriones' of which we do not possess many documents for the simple reason that most of the productions of these strolling players were probably never written down. But of the fact that they existed in considerable numbers we have plenty of evidence. John of Salisbury, amongst others in the twelfth century, warns solemnly against them: 'At nostra aetas prolapsa ad fabulas et quaevis inania non modo aures et cor prostituit vanitate, sed *oculorum et aurium* voluptate, suam mulcet desidiam, luxuriam accendit, conquirens undique fomenta vitiorum.'[1] The author of the *Poème Moral* (cf. supra, p. 19) has some hard words to say about those who encourage such people with gifts, for they become soiled just as one would by rubbing against a sow which had been wallowing in the mire. The church would provide much (as we have seen) for both eyes and ears of the more serious kind, but something was obviously needed for the completely illiterate, and even into church music some ingenious spirit might introduce a little light variation. Here is the little sequence (or *cantilena*) contained in a Cambridge manuscript and known as the *Modus Liebinc*, which tells in humorous vein (the words following the rhythmical scheme) the story of the unfaithful wife who, at a loss to account for the presence of a son when her husband returns from his prolonged travels, in her fear invents the story that one day to quench her thirst she swallowed a snowflake and that from this elusive matter a son was conceived. The husband made no remark at the time, but after a lapse of five years or so took the boy with him on a voyage, sold him for a goodly sum to a merchant, came back rich and informed his wife that on a day of torrid heat his son had melted in the sun. Thus fraud was defeated by fraud (*sic fraus fraudem vicerat*), for what snow had conceived the sun had naturally melted. This same story forms the subject of a well-known *fabliau* entitled *De l'enfant qui fu remis au soleil*, which concludes with the same moral in more popular language:

> Bien l'en avint qu'avenir dut
> Qu'elle brassa ce qu'ele but.[2]

The 'mimus' (or *tumbere*, as a Latin-French glossary of the twelfth century translates him) and the 'joculator' were undoubtedly popular

---

[1] See Polycraticus: ch. viii, *De Histrionibus, mimis et prestigitatibus*.
[2] *Fabliaux et Contes*. Éd. Barbazan et Méon III, p. 215 ff.

figures amongst the less-cultivated members of society and more especially in those towns where fairs and markets attracted a heterogeneous population. It was a 'joculator' who was reciting the holy death of St. Alexius one Sunday at Lyons which so greatly moved the merchant Petrus Valdus.[1] For their performances were not always of a ribald character. It was possibly a 'mimus' who declaimed the semi-religious poem of *Courtois d'Arras* which is based on the story of the prodigal son. It is composed in dialogue form and is by no means exclusively religious in tone. Short rubrics are incorporated into the narrative to enable the listener to follow the speaker's change of role—e.g. 'Atant est revenus Cortois', or 'Atant ez un preudom venu, Qui de par Dieu li rend salu: 'Diva, vallet, que te doulouse? . . . ' A similar form of representation has been suggested for *Aucassin et Nicolete* where more than two persons are never introduced as speaking at the same time, and we have called attention to the same mixture of the narrative and the dramatic in the *Mystère de la resurrection* (see p. 235). The effect produced must have been something like that of a broadcast 'feature programme' on the radio.

Courtois d'Arras is in some respects a sort of transition play. Though it treats of a biblical, symbolic subject, it probably owed any popularity it possessed to its tavern-scene which was a favourite element in these compositions hailing from the busy city of Arras. It is not so long drawn-out (fortunately) as in the *Jeu de St. Nicolas* of Jean Bodel (see supra), but the lure of the tavern, with its personnel of doubtful characters of both sexes, is the cause of the complete downfall of the poor simple prodigal. The little drama has preserved the polymetric character of earlier plays and the lament of Courtois in duodecasyllabic verse reminds us of the young knight's chant in the crusader scene of Jean Bodel, without, however, reproducing its appeal, for it is heavy and conventional as so many of the laments had become. The only biblical character who here becomes vocal for the first time is the citizen (*preudom*) who offers Courtois the job of keeping his pigs and encourages him by saying that his luck will change:

> 'Uns ans ne dure mie ades:
> uns ans est pere, autres parastre;
> Si chieus-chi vous tient por fillastre,
> Soies si preus et si gentis
> Que a l'autre an soies ses fis' (ll. 460–64).

[1] Quoted: Koschwitz ü Förster: *Altfr. Uebungsbuch*, p. 207.

The end of the play proves that, as in the Bible narrative, the step-fatherly year did not last for ever.

These 'mimed' productions could, of course, easily be expanded by a clever vocalist. In one of the manuscripts of *Courtois* a rather feeble scene has been introduced in which the prodigal's sister pleads for him. Unfortunately we do not possess many examples of these productions from which to draw conclusions. We can only note that the secular drama by the middle of the thirteenth century had made good growth, particularly in the north-east of France. For two interesting dramatic productions have come down to us from the same region due to the pen of Adam de la Halle, a citizen of Arras from about 1235 to 1287. From a curious prologue to one of his plays entitled the *Jeu du Pèlerin*, by which the author was introduced to his audience, we learn that 'Adam le Bochus' or 'Adam d'Arras', a 'clerc' much loved and honoured in his native city, accompanied the 'conte d'Artois' to Italy towards the end of his life and died there in his service. This prologue to *Li Jeus de Robin et de Marion* fills out what we can learn from other sources largely from his own pen, for he was quite a considerable poet. In his first known play, *Li Jus Adam* or *Le Jeu de la Feuillée* as it is generally called, he tells us how he was seized with a desire to leave Arras and go to Paris to continue his studies, even though it meant parting from his recently-married wife. It is a curious play—too full of topical allusions to be of great interest to us now, but probably a great cause of mirth to those who understood them. Adam brings himself into the play and his avaricious father Henri and many of their acquaintances. For the student, Arras, with its avaricious mercantile outlook, is no place: 'Onques d'Arras boins clers n'issi.' Adam is warned by his father of the sin of abandoning his wife and told that he will get no money out of him towards his expenses. But Adam excuses himself by alleging the spring-time folly which had led him astray and the havoc wrought by time in his wife's appearance even after a brief spell of marriage. The stereotyped description of the wife's original beauty is a reproduction of those contained in so many 'romans courtois' with which Adam was evidently familiar. But we are soon back again in the much-loved tavern, with its grasping landlord and the 'vin d'Auxerre' and the herrings which must be paid for even if the monk has to leave his cassock behind. There is much that is reminiscent both of Jean Bodel and of *Courtois d'Arras*, but the play is enlivened by additions which demonstrate the author's knowledge of the conventional literature of his times. We have the fairy king, Hellequin with his 'mainie', the gay, irresponsible messenger (*courlieu*) corresponding to Auberée in Bodel's play *St. Nicolas*, and Fortune's wheel—all popular features of the period. In addition to these there is the fairy Morgue of whom the king Hellequin wishes to be the 'amis fins', whereas she has 'turned her heart' to a 'demoisel de cette ville' (doubtless a well-known local character) who had taken her fancy:

> Qui set d'armes et de keval,
> Pour mi jouste amont et aval
> Par le païs a taule ronde.

Like all participators in this form of mock tournament (see p. 186), he was suffering from many a blow in his chest and arms and shoulders. But he was 'peu parliers et cois et c(h)elans' (see l. 744), which were indispensable attributes of a 'fin amant'. Thus in spite of the 'bourgeois' character of the play and its provincial origin there is a hint of gentle satire against the artificial character of the court literature which had not yet completely lost its vogue.

The same is true of Adam's other play, the *Jeu de Robin et de Marion*—a 'pastourelle dramatisée' in which the aristocratic knight is parodied and the popular pair of lovers, Robin and Marion, come together after various amusing little adventures. The latter were, of course, stock characters from a lyrico-epic form of poetry cultivated chiefly in the north of France and of a kind of mock simplicity. For, although the heroes and heroines were shepherds and shepherdesses, it was obviously cultivated to tickle the fancy of members of the upper classes. It is skilfully dramatized by Adam—both characters and style are in keeping with the original models. It is altogether a pleasant little play with a profusion of actors (there could be no question of 'miming' here). Well-known refrains are introduced, and the singing is interspersed with games and rustic dancing which could not have shocked the most delicate eyes and ears. Robin was an adept at leading the dance (*mener la treske*) and as he tripped off the scene, hand-in-hand with Marion and singing his final song 'Venes apres moi, venez la sentele / La sentele, la sentele, lés le bos', probably the actors themselves and many of the audience, too, tripped off after him on the green sward.

Both these plays of Adam de la Halle are in the usual octosyllabic lines—except for a few introductory lines in the *Feuillée* and the songs in *Robin et Marion*. The latter play is the more objective of the two—possibly because it was composed while Adam was in Italy in the service of the count and not amongst his friends and acquaintances at Arras, where he was well known (and perhaps feared) for his shorter poems—*motets, rondeaux* and *'congés'* of a somewhat personal character. But there is nothing spiteful in these plays. The wily priest, the fat monk, the rich vilain are not held up to ridicule as they are in the *fabliau*. They are just little comedies containing neither ruse nor malice. For the personification of these particular vices we must turn to the animals.

BIBLIOGRAPHY

For a general survey of the rise of the drama in the Middle Ages any of the following can be studied with profit:

Gautier (Léon): *Histoire de la poésie liturgique au m.â. Les Tropes*. Paris 1887.
Sepet (Marius): *Le drame religieux au moyen-âge*. Paris 1901.
Chambers (E. K.): *The Mediaeval Stage*. 2 vols. Oxford 1903.
Creizenach: *Geschichte des neueren Dramas*. 3 vols. Halle. 3rd ed. 1920.
Young (K.): *The drama of the Mediaeval Church*. 2 vol. Oxford 1933.
    With special reference to France:
Faral (E.): *Les jongleurs en France au moyen-âge*. Paris 1910.
Frank (Grace): *The medieval French Drama*. Oxf. Univ. Press 1954.
    Editions of texts cited:
Silviae vel potius Aetheriae *Peregrinatio ad loca sancta*. Herausg. W. Heraeus. Sammlung vulgärlat. Text. Heft I.
Roswitha: *Theâtre de Hroswitha*. Ed. Ch. Magnin. Paris 1845.
Sponsus, or *Mystère de l'Époux*: Koschwitz ü Förster: Altfr. Uebungsbuch. 4th ed. 1911.
Hilarius: *Versus et ludi*. J. J. Champollion-Figeac. 1838.
    Suscitatio Lazari. S. Gaselee, Oxford book of medieval Latin verse, No. 58. Oxford 1937.
Jean Bodel: *Le Jeu de Saint Nicolas*.
    (1) A. Jeanroy. Paris 1925. (CFMA).
    (2) F. J. Warne. Blackwell French Texts. Oxford 1951.
Le Mystère d'Adam. (1) K. Grass: *Das Adamspiel*. Halle 1907.
    (2) P. Studer. Manchester Univ. Press 1918.
Plainte de la Vierge: P. Meyer. Recueil d'anciens textes français.
    See *Die romanischen Marien Klagen*. E. Wechssler. Halle 1893.
Christus patiens. Ed. A. Ellissen. Leipzig 1835.
    Latin translation under Gregory of Nazianzen, Migne: Patrology 137.
La Passion du Palatinus. G. Frank. Paris 1922. (CFMA).
La Passion provençale. W. P. Shepard. Paris 1928. (SATF).
Courtois d'Arras. E. Faral. 2nd ed. 1922, Paris. (CFMA).
Adam de la Halle. *Œuvres complètes du trouvère...poésies et musique*. Éd. par Coussemaker. Paris 1872.
    Le Jeu de la Feuillée. E. Langlois. Paris 1917. (CFMA).
    Le Jeu de Robin et de Marion. E. Langlois. Paris 1928. (CFMA).

CHAPTER X

ANIMAL LITERATURE

I. *THE BESTIARIES*

WESTERN-EUROPEAN literature owes so much to the creative spirit of France in the Middle Ages that we are sometimes tempted to assume that all forms of modern literature had their birth in France. The narrative literature of the north of France, the lyric of the south, actually did between them constitute the beginnings of literature for the whole of Europe and dominated the scene for centuries to come. But there were certain themes which were not peculiar to one country or one period—which were not even pan-European, but which belonged to all times and all peoples. These themes concerned phenomena with which all human beings were familiar and which, in the nature of things, would be objects of interest and observation, of attraction or fear to all around them. Of such phenomena animals and their habits would be among the first to attract attention. The interest in animals is indeed of hoary antiquity as we may learn from mural cave-decorations or legendary history.

Now this was a theme which lay within the range of the average intelligence and consequently a subject of perennial interest; but it lent itself to metaphorical example and homely simile—the battle-loving horse, the far-seeing eagle which renews its strength, the deaf adder which stoppeth up its ear, the wolf in sheep's clothing, these were illustrations which could be understood by all. It is not surprising, therefore, that, with examples such as these in the sacred text, a collection of other symbolic animals should have been made in the early days of Christianity in order to spread its influence among those as yet unacquainted with its doctrines. Treatises on natural history were already in existence, but in the second century A.D. we have the first known example of a collection of this nature which was destined to be a kind of text-book for the diffusion of Christian truth. This work, known under the title of *Physiologus*, was composed in the Greek tongue and must have supplied a felt need for its popularity was very great. It found its way into other lands and was translated, not only into most of the European languages, but, outside Europe, into Ethiopian, Syriac, Arabic and

Slav. Naturally, modifications occurred in the course of its trans-
plantations. It received additions, alterations and explanatory details.
Latin translations are attested from the fifth century onwards, and,
as time advanced, moral interpretations began to be added to the
allegorical ones, so that, during the Middle Ages it exercised,
through its possibilities both oral and pictorial, an influence almost
as great as that of the Bible. It is not surprising, therefore, that it
became the task of a serious-minded, educated Norman, Philippe de
Thaün, to make a translation from the Latin into French for a queen
who was something of a patroness of learning, viz., Aalis, the
second wife of Henry I of England. We thus have an early example
of French poetry (coloured by the Anglo-Norman characteristics
which are common to the French documents written in England)
in the form of a 'bestiary' in six-syllable rhyming verse, probably
the first of its kind. Philippe had already shown his knowledge of
Latin treatises in his *Comput*, a sort of ecclesiastical calendar written,
rather surprisingly, in French for the use of 'clercs'. He now turned
his attention to something more colourful and at the same time more
edifying, for his *Bestiaire* is really a kind of diffuse sermon in verse.
As in the Latin moralizations of that period every scripture had its
threefold interpretation, viz., the literal, the symbolical, and the
moral, so too the beasts and birds could be utilized for edifying
purposes and in a language which could be understood by the
uneducated. Little is known of the author. He was probably a
Norman living in England, perhaps at the court of the English
King Henry Beauclerc, where letters were cultivated, authors
encouraged, and patrons sought. If the queen had commissioned
this work it is interesting to note her taste for, not only did the
author of the *Voyage de St. Brendan* dedicate his work to her, but
she was the patroness also of the chronicler Geoffroi Gaimar.

Philippe's *Bestiaire* is a translation, or perhaps more accurately, an
adaptation 'en franceise raisun' of a Latin version of the *Physiologus*
to which additions and emendations have been made from other
sources. No two bestiaries are exactly alike, but Philippe is not
guilty of much originality—though it is tempting to ascribe to him
numerous short moralizations which have not yet been accounted
for. His style is poor—six-syllable doggerel for the most part—but,
after l. 2890, he changes to the octosyllabic metre 'pur ma raisun
mielz ordener'. His show of learning and the sources he quotes are
illusory as he obviously merely cites them from the 'livre' he is
translating. The tendency to amplify the moralizing side of his

subject often makes him repetitive and tedious. Like all the authors of bestiaries, he begins with the lion:

> Ce qu'en griu est *leün*
> En franceis *rei* at num
> Leüns en mainte guise
> Multes bestes justise
> Pur ceo est reis leüns . . .

This sounds simple enough for a child to understand. Nevertheless, as remarked above, Philippe knows the approved method of homily-composition well and, some fifty years before the finished sermons of Maurice de Sully were delivered, he reproduces faithfully the threefold interpretation of his text. The size of the animal matters nothing. He lets himself go on the ant just as much as he does on the lion. Each has its three natures to be allegorized. The ant knows the difference between wheat and barley—woe to the usurers who give 'orge' for 'froment':

> Ço est signefiance:
> Par orge entendum
> D'erites (= heritics) la raisun
> . . . E par orge boisdie (= deceit)
> Pechié e eresie . . .
> Furmis n'a d'orge cure;
> Grant chose signefie,
> Oëz l'allegorie . . . (ll. 1021 f.).

Everything 'signifies' something and then, having explained the meaning, every man ('li om') is exhorted to take example from this and look to his ways:

> Li om meïsmement
> En deit prendre esperment

just as in more elegant French prose we find later: 'Bone gent, ice prenons essemple de bien', following the same kind of interpretation of scripture. Like most of his contemporaries Philippe does not love the Jews. He loses no opportunity of an unflattering example where they are concerned:

> E par l'asne entendum
> Judeus par grant raisun,
> Asne est fols par nature
> Si cum dit escripture . . . (ll. 79–83).

He is also somewhat anti-feminist (cf. ll. 2873–85) in spite of the fact that the work is dedicated to a queen. But dedications are somewhat unreliable and could at times be conveniently changed or ignored.

There is much that is silly and trite in this *Bestiaire* and even more so in the *Lapidaire* (in which stones are treated in the same manner) which accompanied it and which was probably only a foretaste of a longer one on which Philippe was engaged.[1] It is allegory run wild. But what a gift these stories were for subsequent writers of all descriptions. There is the author of *Le Roman d'Énéas* with his accounts of crocodiles and magnets. There is the 'exemplum' of the 'unco gude' young man who will probably be like the lioness which produces five cubs the first year, then by successive yearly diminution becomes barren in the end owing to the wear and tear of too great productiveness. There is the story of the whale on the back of which St. Brendan's crew land (thinking it an island), and which does not move until a fire is actually lighted on its body. There is even the troubadour (Richaut de Berbesiu) who, having offended his lady, is like the elephant (*autresi com l'olifanz*) which, when it falls, cannot get up until others with their trumpetings come to its aid; he is not like the bear (*de la maneira d'ors*) which the more it is beaten the fatter it gets; only when in despair does he turn towards his 'Mielhs de Domna' like the stag which turns to face its pursuers when it is about to die. This last example shows how easily the allegorical treatment of animals could be applied to love as they actually were in the *Panthère d'Amour* and the *Bestiaire d'Amour* of Richard de Fournival in the thirteenth century. But for the most part serious moralizations are inseparable from the bestiaries, both Latin and French. The *Bestiaire Divin* of the Norman Guillaume le Clerc contains elaborate symbolic details, beginning as usual with the lion:

> Signifiance i a mult clere
> Quant Deu nostre soverain pere
> Qui est esperital lion . . . (ll. 171 f.).

Not far removed in date (end of twelfth or beginning of thirteenth century), the same metaphor opens the *Bestiaire* of Gervaise:

> Ausi l'esperital lions
> Jesus Christ ou nos nos fions . . . (l. 70 f.).

Everything on earth must have its 'significance' and mean something other than what it actually is, as the German Freydank author of the *Bescheidenheit*[2] (= worldly-wisdom) tells us. What is true of plants, of stones, of colours and animals can be applied to anything—even

---

[1] See Studer and Evans. *Anglo-Norman Lapidaries.* Paris, 1924.
[2] 'Die erde keiner slahte treit / das gar si âne bezeichenheit.
    Nihein geschepfede ist so frî / si'n bezeichne anders den si sî.'

R

to human movements and postures. It is not till we come to the
more encyclopædic, semi-scientific works, such as the *Trésor* of
Brunetto Latini, that the animal characteristics become de-
symbolized again and we return to the equally fanciful, but less
moralizing descriptions which were to be found, for example, in
Pliny. Latini may follow the bestiaries in telling us that the whale's
belly was so vast that Jonah thought he was in hell (cf. Guillaume le
Clerc: l. 2503, 'en sa pance, qui est si lee / come serreit une valée'),
but otherwise his 'nature des animaux' is free from mystical interpretation and gains proportionately in interest. He grows eloquent,
moreover, on the subject of domestic animals, chiefly the horse,
which is capable of such devotion to its master that it will fight for
him and protect him and even weep for him after his death. He
enlarges on the faithfulness of dogs, for these, too, are ready to die
for their master. He describes the various kinds, even going into the
question of the breeding of ladies' pet dogs. These can be kept small
and ornamental by careful treatment: 'on les puet en lor jovente
norrir de molt petit de viande, ou en un petit pot, si que il seront
si petit et si brief que merveille'.[1] But not all dogs are lap-dogs.
There are many examples of faithful hounds in early French literature. There is the dog (*Husdent*) in Béroul's *Tristan* which followed
its master into the forest and had to be carefully trained not to bark.
In both the versions (Oxford and Berne) of the *Folie Tristan* it
recognized its master when he came disguised as a jongleur before
Iseult did—which made Tristan remark:

> Mult par at en chien grant franchise
> E a en femme grant feintise (Oxford *Folie*, 937–8).

There was another faithful dog (the *Chien de Montargis*) which
fought and won a duel for its master in the Franco-Italian poem
Macario—a duel which remained famous for many years in France.
In the poem *Garin le Lorrain* the fact that Bègue was mourned by
his dogs was a sure proof that he was a *gentil'home*.

Faithful steeds are almost too numerous to mention—they came
down from antiquity in a way dogs did not, although both were
used by the huntsman. It was the horses' role in warfare which
endeared him to the public. The active part they took in the combat,
their devotion and understanding made them almost human. 'Why
can you not talk?' says Renaud (in the *Quatre Fils Aymon*) when he
arrives home alone and dejected—'You would have comforted me

---

[1] See *Li Livre du Trésor*, Livre I, ch. clxxxvi. Des Chiens.

in my grief.' But perhaps the silent sympathy shown by the horse was more tactful than any words would have been. This was the famous horse Bayard that carried all the four brothers to safety on its back. It engaged in single combat with Ogier's steed *Brojefort* on one occasion. 'Autresi se combatent com dui chevalier', the author tells us. Bayard was the victor, but then Bayard was a *cheval faé*. The great lover of horses in the epic songs was Guillame d'Orange, who would do anything to get possession of a good steed. Once obtained, the horse became its master's friend and confidante, to be addressed as if it were a man, and it would reply in its own fashion for it understood what was said to it: 'Ausi l'entent com s'il fust hom senez.' (Aliscans, l. 526.)

II. *THE 'ROMAN DE RENARD'*

A different treatment of animal legend, though sometimes used like the bestiaries to inculcate certain moral maxims, also came down from antiquity and had notable exponents in France in the twelfth century and after. The 'fable' was always a favourite form of didactic literature which could be understood by all. The French versions of Æsop's fables, generally known as *Ysopets*, started, as far as we know, with Marie de France, who claimed to have translated them from the English of someone she calls 'Li reis Alvrez' (probably not the English King Alfred):[1]

> Esopë apel'um cest livre,
> Quil translata e fist escrire,
> Del griu en latin le turna;
> Li reis Alvrez, qui mut l'ama,
> Le translata puis en engleis,
> E jeo l'ai rimé en franceis.

(See Epilogue to the Fables, ll. 13-18.)

Marie gives them a pleasant turn and they give her an opportunity of airing her views on the injustice of the exploitation of the weak by the strong. In the fable of the lion and the fox (*Del leün et del gupil*) she takes the part of the small fox (unscrupulous though he is) against the powerful and ruthless provost impersonated by the wolf:

> Tel purchace le mal d'autrui
> Que cel meme revient sur lui,
> Si cum li lus fist del gupil
> Que il voleit mettre en eissil.

---

[1] See Introduction to edition of the *Fables* by A. Ewert.

R*

This fable of the lion being cured by the wolf's skin with its moral application, comes direct from Æsop. It was destined to become a central point round which many other stories gradually clustered, for the cunning fox made a special appeal to somewhat irresponsible authors who loved a racy story for its own sake. It is the implacable enmity between the wolf and the fox, already hinted at, but not explained in Æsop, that, with many accretions, constitutes the main theme of the well-known collection of stories known as the *Roman de Renard*, which, loosely co-ordinated by the jongleurs of the twelfth and thirteenth centuries, formed a more or less coherent epic poem.

As regards the origin of this epic of Renard there are rival theories as in the case of the other epic poems. These theories resolve themselves into two main groups—the upholders of the folk-lore origin and those of the clerical or book-epic. The folk-lore origin is lost in antiquity; the book origin dates from the Middle Ages and the collection of poems on Renard have been called 'une des productions les plus achevées et les plus originales de l'ancienne France'.[1] Whether we can subscribe unreservedly to this judgment or not, at any rate the Middle Ages introduced a new spirit and motivation into the stories which it will be the object of this chapter to indicate.

Naturally, an important part is played by the lion in this cycle of poems, although he is not one of the principal protagonists. He is the king, the symbol of majesty (as in the Bible), whose roar causes all the animals to quake—but whom the bestiaries (both heathen and Christian) describe as kindly and almost timid—afraid of a white cock or a creaking wheel, strong in front but insignificant behind and liable to almost human weaknesses. The fable of Æsop to which we have already referred tells how he fell sick and could only be cured by being wrapped in a wolf's skin which had just been taken from the live animal. This ancient story, though not in the Latin fables of Phaedrus, was probably repeated in many forms through the centuries. In a short poem that has often been attributed to Paulus Diaconus[2] and in any case may be considered as belonging to the eighth century, the wolf has been replaced by the bear and some rather amusing details have been added. The fox, who learns somehow that the bear has called the sick lion's attention to his inexcusable absence, enters the court with a string of old, torn shoes

---

[1] See Foulet: *Le Roman de Renard*. Concluding sentence.
[2] See Paulus Diaconus: *Gedichte*. Ed. Dr. Karl Neff. München 1908. The editor concludes: 'so haben wir in diesen Fabeln, Gedichte, die sicherlich nicht Paulus zum Verfasser haben'. Anfang, p. 193.

hanging round his neck as witness to his wanderings in search of a remedy and even the sick king is obliged to laugh at the sight. The fox's excuse for his absence, his sly manner of speaking, and the lion's unfeeling haste in falling in at once with the cruel suggestion of the bear's skin are completely in character and the whole fable is humorously and very effectively told. The animals are not named —but they are briefly described: the boar with its glistening teeth, the bear with its uncut claws, the hare and the wolf side by side (*hic lepus atque lupus*), and dogs and cats in happy fellowship: 'Iungunturque canes atque simul catuli' (l. 16). The king's mood, changing from moment to moment, from anger to laughter, from threats to gratitude; the cunning, hypocritical fox, pretending to try and spare the king's feelings and then gibing at the wretched bear as he lies naked on the ground—these character-sketches are vividly depicted in this short Latin poem of sixty-eight lines, which gives us a pleasant example of the secular Latin poetry of the time, besides being a somewhat original version of the fable of the sick lion.

By the time we come to the tenth century a considerable development has taken place. The story has been worked up into real epic form in a curious monkish effusion known as the *Ecbasis captivi*. Here we have a genuine forerunner of the epic of Renard wrapped up in an allegorical covering describing a monk's escape and eventual return to a strictly ruled monastery. In a sense it consists of two fables: (1) the wolf and the calf—partly biblical, partly monastic; (2) the lion cured by the skin of the wolf as in Æsop, enlivened by many details showing the implacable hatred of the wolf for the fox for which the author genuinely attempts to find the cause. The poem ends with the customary moral. The double form of the poem renders it rather difficult to follow. In Part I the wolf-monk who insists upon eating the young calf which has escaped from the stable is set upon by an army of animals led by the shepherd's dog. He retreats to his stronghold, which he considers impregnable, but admits that the only animal he fears is the fox, that stirrer-up of trouble, who is determined on his ruin and can achieve by cunning what he cannot by force: 'Si desunt vires, regnabunt undigne fraudes' (l. 374). Here the wolf confesses his fear, for he fully realizes the truth of the old proverb: 'engin vaut mieux que force'. But he gives no reason for the hostility already existing between himself and the fox and his obvious fear of the consequences. His friends are perplexed and ask for an explanation of this hidden sore: 'Discere percupimus, celatum quod latet ulcus' (l. 391). In answer

to this the wolf tells a long story of what happened to his ancestor
when he was 'camerarius' to the king, in which the author makes a
genuine attempt to motivate his epic story, although in effect he
only carries us a step further back. But he gives us a wonderful
picture of the 'dramatis personæ'. The wolf relates how, just at the
season when kings go forth to war, King Lion fell sick and sent
forth an edict that all the beasts of the forest were to assemble in
his cave and bring or suggest some remedy. All with one exception
hastened thither, each bringing his favourite specific. We are in a
feudal court and each animal has his allotted function. At that time
the wolf's father was 'camerarius' at the lion's court and as treasurer
was in a position of great power. He noticed that the only remedies
missing were those of the fox and, as the 'sedulus hostis' of the
absentee, he does not fail to bring this to the king's notice—hinting
at other more serious charges, so eager is he to bring about the fox's
downfall. The indignant monarch sent a faithful messenger to fetch
the delinquent, and meanwhile the wolf made preparations for his
immediate execution. The only animal who felt sorry for the fox
when he saw the tortures and the high gallows that awaited him
was the gentle panther (*pardus*), whose attractive qualities are known
to us from all the bestiaries. He set out straightway to warn the
fox who, on hearing what awaited him, uttered a prayer to God,
but did not forget to join his friend in a hearty meal, after which
they started out together singing 'davitica carmina'. On arrival at
the court the fox justifies himself to the sick lion by relating his
wanderings in search of a remedy with a pitiful reference to his age
and the hardships he has undergone: 'Proque salute tui peragravi
climata mundi' (l. 481). All are moved and there is a general shout
of applause. The king's wrath diminishes as the fox's popularity
increases: 'Principis ira perit, nam vulpis gloria crescit' (l. 489). In
hypocrital wise the fox prescribes the well-known remedy for the
patient: although the wolf is his 'patrinus' (*parrain*) let him be led
outside (to spare the king's feelings) and flayed alive by the bear
and two lynxes . . . and let the sick lion be wrapped in his skin.
No sooner said than done. The wretched wolf is skinned (except
for his paws and head) by the lynxes and the growling bear. The
patient is anointed by the fox's orders and wrapped in the warm
skin and immediately begins to recover. The fox bids the attendants
put the king to bed and give him a good meal. We need not follow
in detail the remaining scenes in which the various offices are
assigned to the different animals. The fox having reached the height

of his power, his word now becomes law. He appoints the leopard to be his steward and the faithful 'parder', the leader of the services, becomes heir to the throne. The thrush and the nightingale sing to quiet the convalescent king's nerves and there is much feasting and rejoicing in spite of the pathos of the nightingale's song. Finally all depart and the clever fox, glad to get away from the court, slips back to his lair in the hills after composing the customary epitaph[1] for the wolf, who has died miserably while the rejoicings were going on. Most of the details were more interesting and comprehensible to a contemporary monk than they are to us now. But it is the development of a fable into an epic poem of nearly 12,000 lines which is of importance in studying the growth of a literary 'genre'. The *Ecbasis* of the monk of Toul is not far removed in date from the *Waltarius* of Ekkehard, and it marks as important a stage in the growth of the animal epic as the *Waltarius* does in the growth of the heroic epic if we may compare small things with great. The author of the *Ecbasis* genuinely tries to give a reason for the actions of his heroes—he sets out to account for the animosity between the fox and the wolf, and he must be given credit for this even though he does not succeed. The wolf, when accusing the fox for his undutiful attitude towards the king, mentions other worse crimes of which he had been guilty (l. 404), but he does not tell us what they were. It was left for the poems of a later date to delve further into the matter and find, or invent, the cause of this deadly hatred.

When we come to the twelfth century the story of this long-standing feud has developed still further. A great innovation has been made by the introduction of names for the various animals. The Latin poem of *Ysengrimus* by the Flemish poet Nivard is epic in length and construction. It contains many details, some culled from former works, others doubtless drawn from animal tales and fables current in his time. The section devoted to the story of the sick lion has some interesting details. The lion's name is Rufanus but the other two principal beasts have the same names as we find in the later epics—viz. Ysengrimus and Reinardus, and it is the bear (Bruno) who performs the function of executioner as in most other versions of the story. As in the poem attributed to Paulus Diaconus, the fox brings worn-out sandals (*multas soleas nec hiantes vulnere pauco*) hanging round his neck as proofs of his wanderings on the

---

[1] 'Ve qui praedaris, quoniam praedaberis ipse' ... ll. 113 f. Or as Marie de France expresses it at the close of her fable on the subject: 'Tel purchace le mal d'autrui / Que cel meme revient sur lui'.

king's behalf, and there are other elaborations of the story which it is difficult to account for, though quite a few it has in common with the *Ecbasis*. But there is one point on which the poem of Nivard does enlighten us, on which, as we have seen above, the earlier poems leave us in the dark. It gives a reason for the enmity which existed between the fox and the wolf and one which is quite in keeping with the spirit of the time at which the *Ysengrim* was written—viz. about the middle of the twelfth century. The fox is not merely an artful deceiver, full of tricks to obtain by guile what he cannot by strength. In addition to this he is a traitor, a danger to domestic happiness. He has gone to the extreme of treachery: he has violated the wife of the wolf, his own relative. He has developed into a lady-killer for even the queen (in the French versions) has a soft spot for him and has given him her ring. Here we are in the genuine atmosphere of the second half of the twelfth century—when the 'fabliaux' were becoming popular with their gibes against women and when, in more romantic circles, even a queen was not safe. Thus there is no longer any mystery about the cause of the warfare between the wolf and the fox. Indeed, the author of one of the 'branches' of the *Roman de Renard* (at which we have now arrived) can say that a former versifier:

> laissa le mieux de sa matiere
> quant il entroblia les plaiz
> et le jugement qui fu faiz,
> en la cort Noble le lion,
> *de la grant fornication*
> *que Renart fist, qui toz maz cove,*
> *envers dame Hersent la love* (Branche I, ll. 4–10).

This was the root of the matter for the medieval poet—the 'clerc' who picked up his material wherever he found it, no matter whether oral or written, in French or in Latin, and adapted it to the taste of his time. This first 'branch', which is typical in many ways, has been dated 'aux envrions de 1180'.[1] The feminine element, lacking in the earlier Latin versions, is much in evidence. The queen (*Fiere*) may regret giving Renard her ring, but she saves his life and is distressed when he gets into trouble:

> 'Mes, porce qu'il est afaistiez,
> me poise qu'il est deshaitiez
> et que tel honte li voi faire
> que mout est frans et debonaire' (ll. 1993–6).

[1] L. Foulet: *Le Roman de Renard.*

The branch ends with a furious fight between the respective wives of the fox and the wolf. They are separated by a pilgrim who advises each of them to go back and eat humble pie to her husband. This they do and in the case of the fox we are told:

> Puis fu Renart mout liement
> O sa fame mout longement (ll. 3243-4).

This branch is in many ways typical. Amongst the scenes and jests reminiscent of the 'fabliau' at its worst, occur pathetic passages, wise reflections and amusing details. As in other branches, we may find, amongst passages poor in construction and expression, a piece of quite outstanding merit in description and imaginative force, such as that of the appearance at the king's court of the five plaintiffs 'Chantecler et Pinte / qui avenoit a cort soi quinte /' just as Renard was about to be acquitted by a weak king. The actual story of the 'viol de Hersente' is told in Branch II, the author of which claims in his prologue to be the first to relate the 'estoire'

> '... des deus barons' (Renart et Ysengrin):
> 'Seigneurs, oï avez maint conte
> Que maint conterre vous raconte
> Comment Paris ravi Elaine,
> Le mal qu'il en ot et la paine:
> De Tristan que La Chievre fist,
> ... Mais onques n'oïstes la guerre,
> Qui tant fu dure de grant fin,
> Entre Renart et Ysengrin
> Qui moult dura et moult fu dure'.

It is obvious from the context to what episode the author is referring here. Branch II can be dated roughly as having been composed in the last quarter of the twelfth century, not far removed, therefore, in date from another poem which gives us a hint of contemporary taste. The Norman Chardri in his *Vie des Set Dormanz* tells us he is treating more serious matters than the 'fables d'Ovide'—

> ne de Tristram ne de Galerun;
> ne de Renard ne de Hersente....

linking thus the episode of Renard and the wolf's wife with other famous love-stories.

The episodes of Renard and Chantecler, of Renard in the well, of Renard at the court are well known and need not detain us. The branches overlap, are in wrong order owing to different dates and authors, and are sometimes incoherent—King Noble's court and the summons to his subjects is described more than once—in Br. I where Renard narrowly escapes being hung for his many delin-quencies, in Br. X where it leads up to the well-known episode of the sick lion being wrapped in the wolf's skin and Renard reaching a position of high favour at the court. But the unity of the whole is not seriously impaired. Many contemporary traits may be found in the various branches. In this last quarter of the twelfth century feudal conditions under a weak king were still a popular theme; love-stories were in full vogue in the more refined social circles; but mistrust of women and a tendency to admire anyone who by his wits alone could take a rise out of those more fortunate than himself were both favourite themes. For the general tone is that of the 'fabliaux' and undoubtedly these poems set out to amuse rather than to edify. One of the authors themselves describes the stories which combine to form the animal epic as 'une risée et une gabée', a description which hits them off well, for, besides the effort to amuse, there is in many of the episodes more than a hint of parody which increased in the later versions when the simplicity of the earlier animal-characteristics had been abandoned. In Branch I we have the ridiculous scene of all the animals mounted on horseback giving chase to Renard. They are led by the snail carrying the battle-standard, and urged on by the king who promises the reward of freedom to anyone who catches the delinquent. This can only be meant as a parody on some of the popular knightly adventures described in second-rate romances of the period, just as the episode of the lion's wife (Queen *Fiere*), giving her ring to Renard and then sending him a secret note by his friend Grimbert is surely a skit on the courtly fashion of 'fin' amor'. It is pleasant to turn back to the less sophisticated descriptions in this same 'branch', such as Renard escaping capture owing to his accidentally jumping into a vat of dye out of which he emerges brilliant yellow. He returns home disguised as a jongleur from 'Bretaigne' who can only speak a few words of broken English. 'Godehelpe . . . bel sire', he says on meeting his old enemy: 'Ne sai rien de ton raison dir.' When asked what his job was, he replied that he was a good 'gieugloier' and knew many a 'bon lai breton', including those of Tristan, Chêvrefeuille and Saint Brendan. 'Do you know that of Iseut?' asks the wolf. 'Iai, iai', he replies: 'Je les savrai mout bien trestouz' (ll. 2440–41). It is an amusing scene and once again we get a glimpse of the wandering minstrel's repertory to which, perhaps, a touch of satire is added.

These animal stories enjoyed great popularity, whether moralized in the bestiaries or collected into a continuous narrative as in the animal-epic. In the earlier versions of the romance of Renard most of the animals were wild beasts of the forest. As time went on domestic animals made their appearance coinciding with a greater tendency to anthropormophize the characters. In other forms of literature the horse was looked upon as the ally of man who actually at times fought for his master, and on one occasion a dog fought a successful duel on behalf of a murdered knight, as we have seen. Captive bears and fighting leopards were probably an importation from the East. Hawks were accounted of such value that the most serious events of his kingdom could not turn away a king's interest in them,[1] and the emperor Frederick II wrote a treatise on them. In the case of a feud such as that between the fox and the wolf, perhaps their different evil qualities were felt to complement each other in such wise that rolled into one they would produce the perfection of evil—just as the characters of Roland and Oliver would produce in solution the perfect knight, or Sultan Saladin and Richard Cœur-de-Lion, if joined in harmony (as the cunning bishop suggested),[2] would produce the perfect gentleman.

BIBLIOGRAPHY

Physiologus: Rédaction latine. Französische Studien. tom VI. M. Mann. 1888.
Le Bestiaire de Philippe de Thaün, texte critique, par E. Walberg. Paris et Lund 1900.
Le Bestiaire de Gervaise. *Romania* t. I. Paul Meyer.
Der Bestiaire des Guillaume le Clerc. Herausg (1) Mann. Heilbronn 1888. (Fr. St. VI.)
    (2) Reinsch. Leipzig 1890.
Le Bestiaire d'Amour. Éd. A. Thordstein. Études romanes de Lund. 1941.
Le Trésor. Brunetto Latini. See Bibl. ch. ii.
Fables. See under Marie de France. Ch. v, Bibl.
Renaut de Montauban. Hgg. H. Michelant. Stuttgart 1862.
Paulus Diaconus. *Gedichte*. Ed. Dr. Karl Neff. München 1908.
Ecbasis Captivi, das älteste Tierepos des Mittelalters. Herausgeg. von E. Voigt. Quellen ü Forschungen, Heft 8.
Le Roman de Renart, publié par Ernest Martin, 3 vol. Strasbourg 1882–7.
Le Roman de Renart. Premiere branche. Par Mario Roques. Paris 1948. (CFMA).

[1] See 'Lettres du roi Edouard I sur des question de Venerie.' Ed. Tanqueray, *Bulletin of the John Rylands Library*. Col. 23, Oct. 1939.
[2] Cf. ch. viii, p. 212.

INDEX OF PROPER NAMES